SABINA SPIELREIN AND THE POETRY OF PSYCHOANALYSIS

Sabina Spielrein, who has been mostly known for her relation with her analyst Carl Jung, came to the attention of the wider public following the discovery and publication of some of her diaries and personal letters some 40 years ago. The focus on her relationship with Jung, and her personal story have consequently led to a neglect of her writings, with many of her crucial texts even remaining untranslated into English. *Sabina Spielrein and the Poetry of Psychoanalysis* seeks to re-address this distortion of her legacy by examining her original contribution to the field, such as her early analytical work with children.

Spielrein referred to moments of intimacy between herself and Jung as "poetry". Indeed, as a response to what can be considered the inevitable failure in her relationship to Jung, Spielrein wrote poetry and songs, notes, and theoretical papers. These writings are examined here as her means of finishing her own analysis. She was the first person to become an psychoanalyst through her own psychoanalysis, a path that would later be recognised as a necessary part of the training for any analyst.

The book traces the poetry of Sabina Spielrein's writing through both its content and style, examining the effect of these writings upon psychoanalysis and inserting them into a lineage of what Lacan would later call the *passe*: a device that is open for the analysand to finish his or her analysis and accede to the place of psychoanalyst. This book will be of interest to scholars and practitioners of psychoanalysis and other clinicians, including those who work with children, those interested in the early history of psychoanalysis, and those concerned with women's writing more generally.

Michael Gerard Plastow is a psychoanalyst (Analyst of the School, *The Freudian School of Melbourne, School of Lacanian Psychoanalysis*, and member of the *Association Lacanienne Internationale*) practising in Melbourne, Australia. He is also a child and adolescent psychiatrist based at *Alfred Child and Youth Mental Health Service*. Michael convenes a seminar on *The Child, the Adult, and the Subject of Psychoanalysis*. He is the author of innumerable psychoanalytic papers, as well as the book *What is a Child?: Childhood, Psychoanalysis, and Discourse*, published by Karnac, London, 2015. His translation of Lacan's seminar *The Knowledge of the Psychoanalyst* appeared in 2013 as a bilingual edition in a non-commercial publication of *Éditions de l'Association Lacanienne Internationale*, Paris.

"This is the first book to take stock of the fact that Sabina Spielrein was the first person to become an analyst as an outcome of her analysis. Drawing upon Spielrein's writings in German, including those not yet translated, Michael Gerard Plastow shows us the importance of her love for C.G. Jung, which here is interpreted as the truth of love in the transference. Spielrein's sensitivity to the resonances of language, to the equivocations of the signifiers, as well as to the division of the subject, are a constant in her writings. Jung, wanting to retain his place as analyst but embarrassed by his love for his patient, made the error of not recognising the subjective disparity that is characteristic of the transference, and of interpreting signifiers with meaning. On the other hand, the sublimation to which her writings bear witness, allowed Spielrein a *savoir faire* regarding the resistances of her analyst."

— **Erik Porge**, psychoanalyst practising in Paris,
co-founder of the Association de Psychanalyse
Encore and editor-in-chief of *Essaim*.

SABINA SPIELREIN AND THE POETRY OF PSYCHOANALYSIS

Writing and the End of Analysis

Michael Gerard Plastow

Routledge
Taylor & Francis Group

LONDON AND NEW YORK

First published 2019
by Routledge
2 Park Square, Milton Park, Abingdon, Oxon OX14 4RN

and by Routledge
52 Vanderbilt Avenue, New York, NY 10017

Routledge is an imprint of the Taylor & Francis Group, an informa business

British Library Cataloguing-in-Publication Data
A catalogue record for this book is available from the British Library

Library of Congress Cataloging-in-Publication Data
Names: Plastow, Michael Gerard, author.
Title: Sabina Spielrein and the poetry of psychoanalysis /
Michael Gerard Plastow.
Description: Abingdon, Oxon; New York, NY: Routledge, 2019. |
Includes bibliographical references.
Identifiers: LCCN 2018039394 (print) | LCCN 2018049143 (ebook) |
ISBN 9780429444302 (Master eBook) | ISBN 9780367001414 |
ISBN 9780367001414 (hardback) | ISBN 9780367001421 (paperback) |
ISBN 9780429444302 (ebk)
Subjects: LCSH: Spielrein, Sabina. | Psychoanalysis–History. |
Women psychoanalysts–Europe.
Classification: LCC RC440.82.S66 (ebook) | LCC RC440.82.S66 P37
2019 (print) | DDC 616.89/17–dc23
LC record available at https://lccn.loc.gov/2018039394

ISBN: 978-0-367-00141-4 (hbk)
ISBN: 978-0-367-00142-1 (pbk)
ISBN: 978-0-429-44430-2 (ebk)

Typeset in Bembo
by Deanta Global Publishing Services, Chennai, India

MIX
Paper from
responsible sources
FSC
www.fsc.org FSC® C013056

Printed and bound in Great Britain by
TJ International Ltd, Padstow, Cornwall

To part!
Never will I return,
Never will I return because one never returns.
The place to which one returns is always another,
The station to which one returns is another.
It's no longer the same people, nor the same light, nor the
same philosophy.
To part! My God, to part! I am afraid to part…!

Fernando Pessoa, from *Là-Bas, Je Ne Sais Où…*
(n. d., p. 1041, translated for this edition)

CONTENTS

PREFACE

This present work is the fruit of a number of years of reading, reflexion, discussion, and study of the questions that are bequeathed to us by the neglected work of Sabina Spielrein. What became clear very quickly is the manner in which Spielrein's writings have been overshadowed by the story that has been created out of her, especially through her having been turned into a fabricated two-dimensional figure by the cinema. Even though many new studies dedicated to Spielrein continue to appear with increasing regularity, for the most part their emphasis remains upon the *story* of her relationship with Jung and Freud, as well as her biographical story. And in these stories Spielrein is portrayed as a madwoman, an hysteric, a victim, a seductress, and so on, that is, anything but a writer.

And even though some of her personal and theoretical writings have been in circulation since they came to attention through the publication of her letters and diaries nearly 40 years ago, the writings themselves remain neglected and poorly studied. Moreover, many critical texts by Spielrein remain untranslated into English. This has made my work slower than it might have been. On the other hand, however, it has obliged me to study German in order to pursue these texts, which has directly confronted me with the principal language of her writing. My endeavour here is not to retrieve a lost history, but rather to endeavour to discover Spielrein's writings afresh in order to appreciate her contribution to psychoanalysis. The insistence here is first and foremost on the writing, or what we can call from this study *the poetry of psychoanalysis*, and second upon what permitted Sabina Spielrein to play her part in this.

Some of the themes that find a place in this work first emerged in the seminar *Psychoanalysis and the Child* that I conducted for a number of years with Tine Norregaard, and I wish to thank her for her insights regarding Spielrein's writings. I would also like to acknowledge the participants of the seminar for their contribution to our debates and discussions. I also wish to acknowledge the contribution of David Pereira who assisted me over the course of writing this book, in particular for his participation in its theoretical elaboration, as well as for his discerning second listening and reading, both of Sabina Spielrein's words, as well as my own in regard to this work. David was able to help keep me on track to be able to pursue my grasp of Spielrein's writings and to not get distracted along the many possible paths along which one can easily get lost. I would also like to express my great thanks to Christian Fierens who read the manuscript as a whole, and who was able to assist me to pursue, and to present more clearly, the theses that run throughout the book.

In addition, I want to acknowledge other colleagues who have supported me throughout the writing of the book. This includes Erik Porge for his encouragement, and for his kind invitation to submit a paper regarding my work on Spielrein to the journal of which he is the director of the editorial committee, *Essaim*. I have also published a chapter that is derived from some of this work in the book *Lacanian Psychoanalysis with Babies, Children and Adolescents*, edited by Carol Owens and Stephanie Farrelly Quinn (2017). Some of the work that gave rise to this work was also presented to *Freuds Agorá* in Copenhagen in 2014, and I wish to thank Osvaldo Cariola and other colleagues there who contributed to the discussion and elaboration of Spielrein's writings. Other developments of the work have been presented within *The Freudian School of Melbourne, School of Lacanian Psychoanalysis*; and the *Corpo Freudiano* in Brazil in 2016. I was kindly invited by Dr. Jean-Louis Chassaing to speak at the Colloquium on the Transmission of Psychoanalysis of the *Association Lacanienne Internationale* in May 2015. I also presented on this theme at the Summer Seminar of the same association in August 2016, and at the *Lacanoamerican Reunion of Rio de Janeiro* in October 2017.

I greatly value the support and encouragement of other colleagues who are studying the contribution of early psychoanalysts, such as Marcos Silva of Belo Horizonte in Brazil. I wish to especially thank Renata Cromberg of São Paulo in Brazil for her generous support. Renata is in the process of editing a commented three-volume complete works of Sabina Spielrein in Portuguese, the second of which is soon to appear. In addition to Renata's own invaluable writings, her effort to make all of the scientific writings of Sabina Spielrein available in her native tongue is something that we are far from having in English. In particular, Renata's first volume made Spielrein's thesis available to me in a readable form while the German remained elusive to my grasp. I would also like to thank Dr. Sarah Knaus for her excellent part-translation of Spielrein's thesis into English.

Freud of course reminded us that translation is ultimately an impossible task, and that the translator is inevitably a traitor of the original text: *traduttore-traditore*. For this reason alone we cannot remain satisfied with any translation and must pursue the original text in so far as we are able. Consequently, it is problematical to study Spielrein's work without submitting ourselves to the trace of the signifiers and letters of the language in which Spielrein wrote. For this reason, in part, my study of German not only enabled me to decipher Spielrein's texts that were written in that language, but more specifically to follow the particular signifiers that Spielrein drew upon. I would thus like to thank my German teacher Katharina Kleiminger for her patience, especially since I have not been able to make the study of German my only priority. I also wish to thank Tina Weller of *The Freudian School of Melbourne* and the German Department, Monash University, for checking and helping with all of my translations from German in this book (particularly from Spielrein's early diaries and her thesis). I have endeavoured to refer to Spielrein's German words or phrases in my text when there are particularly salient and significant words or signifiers for Sabina Spielrein, especially those that most insist in her writing. For this reason, I also wish to express my gratitude to Patricia Le Coat Kreissig of the *Association Lacanienne Internationale* for correcting the spelling and format of the German words and terms that I have drawn upon in the manuscript. I would also like to thank Tine Norregaard once again, this time for her assistance with the translation from Danish of a piece of writing by Osvaldo Cariola regarding Sabina Spielrein's work.

I wish to express my gratitude to Rachel Berthoff Douglas for graciously allowing me to use her translations of two poems by Alexander Pushkin, and for helping me to better appreciate the place of Pushkin's work within Russian culture and literature.

I would finally like to thank my family for their forbearance, and my wife Debbie Plastow for her support and encouragement, as well as her meticulous editing of my manuscripts.

INTRODUCTION

The work of Sabina Spielrein and her original contributions to psychoanalytic theory have been obscured by the emphasis that has been placed upon her personal story, and in particular upon the love affair that developed with her analyst, Carl Jung. Interest in the case was precipitated, in relatively recent times, by the publication in 1980 of some of her personal writings that had been discovered in Geneva. These writings, which she had left behind when she returned to Russia in 1923, included her intimate diaries, as well as letters to Freud, Jung, and family members. They were published by Italian Jungian analyst Aldo Carotenuto in his work *A Secret Symmetry: Sabina Spielrein between Jung and Freud* (1980a). Prior to this time, Spielrein's place in psychoanalysis had been reduced to little more than a footnote in Freud's "Beyond the Pleasure Principle" (1920g).

Carotenuto's own contribution to his volume reads like a hagiography of Carl Jung, one which produces a devaluation of Sabina Spielrein and her work. Carotenuto even revises Jung's original diagnosis of Spielrein of hysteria, to that of psychosis, a diagnosis that has since been echoed by others, such as Bruno Bettelheim. Spielrein's analysis was put into jeopardy by the love affair that arose between analysand and analyst. This relationship, if we are to call it that, occurred during the very time of Spielrein's training as a doctor and psychiatrist, and her formation as psychoanalyst. Much of what has been written about Sabina Spielrein, moreover, has been written by Jungian psychoanalysts. These factors raise many questions regarding the skewed manner in which Spielrein and her work have been reintroduced into psychoanalysis, thereby determining the manner in which they have been received. But the publication of these personal writings, and others that have been subsequently discovered, also raise questions regarding the manner in which Spielrein was able to terminate her analysis with Jung.

Carotenuto poses, and answers, a rhetorical question: "Can the whole episode be understood in the light of the transference? *Non liquet*" (1980a, p. 166, italics in the original). In other words, Carotenuto answers his own question by saying "It is not clear". But to propose "the episode" cannot be understood in the light of the transference is to cast it into a mystical realm in which the love—the transference-love—of an analysand for her analyst can no longer be understood from psychoanalysis. In this manner it would exclude Spielrein's transference-love from the ambit of our ability to theorise and elaborate upon it. This serves the purpose of protecting Jung by denying us a grasp upon what transpired in that analysis, and by extension what transpires in any psychoanalysis, since when there is analysis, there is always transference-love. What becomes evident as a consequence of the exclusion of this "episode" as transference-love is the neglect into which the richness of Spielrein's theoretical works from this early time have fallen, for the most part remaining either untranslated or poorly translated. And what remains, then, is what others have written about her or the films that have been made about her, with the focus of interest mainly upon the love affair, and upon the relationship between Jung and Freud. What specifically get excluded from this schema are Spielrein's own words, and indeed her own critical examination of her transference to Jung. In this Introduction we will thus necessarily make an appraisal of certain tendencies by which Spielrein and her story have been recounted within and outside psychoanalysis in order to begin to establish a different methodology: to give prominence to Sabina Spielrein through her own writings, both personal and theoretical.

A most dangerous method

The subtitle of Carotenuto's book is *Sabina Spielrein between Jung and Freud*. This exemplifies the emphasis that has been placed on a triangle in which Spielrein is always to be found between Jung and Freud, and never present in her own right. This triangle is repeated in the depiction on the cover of many of the books that have been published, most prominently John Kerr's book (1993) *A Most Dangerous Method*, whose subtitle is *The Story of Jung, Freud, & Sabina Spielrein*, and which carries the photograph of Spielrein literally between those of Jung and Freud. Other books that carry a similar montage include the 1984 edition of Carotenuto (1980b), the detailed biography by Sabine Richebächer (Richebächer 2005a) in its Portuguese translation, the recent biography by the English author John Launer *Sex vs. Survival* (2014), and the recent account by the French psychoanalyst Alain de Mijolla *Sabina, "La juive" de Carl Jung* [*Sabina, Carl Jung's "Jewess"*] (2014). The title of Richebächer's biography in the original German is *Eine fast grausame Liebe zur Wissenschaft*, which translates as *An Almost Cruel Love of Science* (2005b). This title does not come from Spielrein herself— not at all her own words—but her husband's comment about her in the form of a complaint (Launer 2014, p. 208). Spielrein is once again reduced to what is said about her by others.

The insistence that has been placed on the relationship between Spielrein and Jung—the *story* alluded to in Kerr's subtitle—has led to further speculation regarding details of what transpired between them. Kerr's *method* is specifically that of speculation: piling one layer of speculation upon another. He also supports his argument by referring to another speculative author of psychoanalytic history, Peter Swales, who had claimed that Sigmund Freud had a sexual relationship with Freud's sister-in-law Minna Bernays, and, according to Swales, later forced her to have an abortion. According to Roudinesco, "Carl Gustav Jung, who loved juicy stories and never hesitated, sometimes with great flair, to invent anecdotes regarding the private lives of his contemporaries, thus projecting onto others his longstanding practice of amorous adventures, was the first to give the impression that Freud had perhaps been the lover of his sister-in-law". Swales claimed that this story was based on an anecdote that Carl Jung recounted when he was already in his 80s, raising the question of why Jung withheld it for so long. It also raises the question of Jung's motivation in telling such a story, given that he was never free of his antagonism and rivalry towards Freud, even long after the latter's death (Roudinesco 2005, pp. 30–31). In any case, what is important here is this repetitive way in which such *stories* always tend towards promoting the idea of a relationship, and specifically that of a sexual relationship.

This conjecture regarding Sabina Spielrein takes on a sensationalistic turn, both in Kerr's account and the film that has been made partly based upon this so-called *story*. No doubt this insistence upon a relationship is also the product of certain editors, since it is well known that sex sells. The first phrase on the back cover of my edition of Kerr's book is from a review that remarks that Kerr's book has "all the elements of a juicy novel" (1993). This is a logical continuation of the Spielrein *story*. We might also say that the familiar manner in which Spielrein is referred to—as Mijolla does in his title—by her first name "Sabina" speaks of an over-familiarity, a presumption of intimacy, and a diminution to a given name. When one considers that Freud is rarely referred to by these authors as "Sigmund", nor Jung as "Carl", this is a manner in which Spielrein is reduced to the intimate, just like one might refer to a family member, friend, or lover. No doubt this also reinforces a reduction of Spielrein to her story, to something that is already known—in other words to the level of imaginary narcissism—and if not known, then presumed. In these familiar accounts there remains little room for what is unknown in Spielrein's writings, let alone for the innovations and elaborations that might be made from these.

In her personal writing Spielrein often discusses and writes poetry and songs, and in her scientific writings she often draws upon poetry and poets. But she also writes of *poetry*—the word often in inverted commas—developing between herself and Carl Jung. According to Van Waning (1992, p. 403), the word poetry as a private reference for love between Spielrein and Jung derives from the speech of a psychotic woman who was the patient of whom Spielrein wrote in her thesis, which will be discussed in Chapter 4. Whether or not this is so, this reference to the poetry between herself and Jung has been reduced, by many authors, to a metaphor for the development of a sexual relationship. Whether such a relationship occurred is not at all clear from Spielrein's diaries—and one might be inclined to draw the opposite conclusion—the emphasis is always on this supposed sexual relationship. This interpretation was put forward most prominently and explicitly in John Kerr's book. This book inspired a play by Christopher Hampton, *The Talking Cure* (2002), a fictionalised account with many historical and theoretical inaccuracies, which nonetheless puts the sexualised relation between Spielrein and Jung on the stage. The play in turn inspired the film by David Cronenberg that takes a number of scenes from Hampton's play. In the film, Kerr's title is reduced to *A Dangerous Method* (2011), but the film portrays a sadomasochistic account of this imagined sexual relationship between Jung and Spielrein, which undoubtedly reveals more to us about the filmmaker than his subject. What is most curious is that Cronenberg's film—a fictional account, based upon a fictionalised play, itself based upon a speculative history—is often the only account that many psychoanalysts have regarding Sabina Spielrein. Details from Cronenberg's film are, moreover, not uncommonly cited as if they were historical fact. In putting this very specific sexual interpretation upon Spielrein's "poetry", moreover, what is missed here is what we hold to be most important, that is, the poetry of Spielrein's writings. But such story-telling is undoubtedly a most dangerous method in psychoanalysis in which it is the fantasy of the Other regarding Spielrein (that of Kerr, as well as that of Cronenberg, for instance) that prevails, to the detriment of the subject in question. The psychoanalytic subject, however, can only emerge through his or her own speech, and also as we are putting forward here, through writing.

The lesser-known Italian film by Roberto Faenza, *The Soul Keeper* [*Prendimi l'anima*] (2002), whilst more attentive to details in Spielrein's history, nonetheless gives primary place to a sexual relationship between Jung and Spielrein. A very different account is given in Elisabeth Martón's film *My Name Was Sabina Spielrein* (2002), which endeavours to produce a dramatised historical reproduction, but drawn from Spielrein's diaries and letters, including the title that conveys Spielrein's own words. Though it is not as sexy or exciting as the aforementioned ones, this film conveys another version of Spielrein, one that derives principally from her writing. Unlike the other films that convey a story, *My Name Was Sabina Spielrein* does not attempt to produce a construct of a sexual relationship, nor does it endeavour to produce a conclusion or a fixed meaning from Spielrein's words. Like Spielrein's writings themselves it retains an openness that allows for many possibilities.

On the other hand, in John Launer's recent biography to which we have already referred, the first word in the title is *Sex*. Launer even devotes a section to a discussion of the erudite literature as to the form in which physical contact occurred, and specifically as to whether or not penetration actually took place (2015, p. 100). Why is there such fascination with the sexual relation, including what degree of penetration might, or might not, have occurred? We might go so far as to ask what importance we should place upon the question of whether

Spielrein's love for Jung was consummated. Surely the other side of the titillation that might be derived from such authors' imaginings of the supposed sexual contact between Spielrein and Jung is the very moralism that condemns it. Neither of these currents contributes to the elaboration of the foundational experience of, and for, psychoanalysis, which took place in Sabina Spielrein's transference-love with Carl Jung.

We are in no doubt that there was love, but our interest is in the manner in which this love derives from the transference, a transference-love that Jung was not able to handle. What we would like to put into question is the manner in which our voyeuristic interest in Spielrein is reduced to the speculative and prurient imagining of a sexual relationship. We can also discern this tendency—from psychoanalysis—in the slip of the pen in Carotenuto's book in which the place of Jung's residence after he left the Burghölzli is mostly spelled not as Küsnacht, but rather as *Küssnacht*. There is indeed a place in Switzerland called Küssnacht, but this is not the municipality on Lake Zürich where Jung lived and had his private practice, whose spelling is Küsnacht. Carotenuto's or his translator's slip of the pen turns the place of Spielrein's evening visits to Jung into an eroticised *Kiss-night*. The effect of this reduction to a sexual relationship, whether intentional or not, is always to produce a certain meaning. It allows us to draw conclusions, no matter how fanciful these might be, but the sense that is made of the story adds nothing to what we know of Spielrein and her work, and in fact serves to obscure it.

Such stories and films endeavour to fill in the gaps of what is not known, to not allow for anything to be able to remain unknown or enigmatic. But it seems that the gap is always filled in a monotonous and repetitive way in the form of an imagined relationship. These accounts end up with a *story*. And the story uses, for its own purposes, whatever details it can find. For instance, one of Spielrein's early papers to which we will give some prominence in this book, *Beiträge zur Kenntnis der kindlichen Seele* [Contributions to the Knowledge of the Child's Soul] (1913), is an account of the analyses of three children, the first of which is an account of Spielrein's own history through the retrospective prism of her own analysis. It is drawn upon, however, by her biographers and other writers as a source of supposed facts about her childhood. That is, her own account of her analysis, in the form of fantasies and elaborations, is reduced to a *history*. In this manner psychoanalysis itself is reduced to the reconstruction of a *story*. In this, the biographers follow Spielrein herself who writes in a footnote that she had cross-checked the details of which she had written with her parents, brother, and uncle, and even the diary that she kept from the age of ten. But what matters in analysis is not the veracity of historical details, but rather what Spielrein makes of the details that are remembered, or come to be recalled, during the course of the analysis and beyond. Many other details which are equally or more pertinent are doubtlessly left out or obscured, suppressed, and repressed. The fundamental notion in psychoanalysis is that the history itself is determined by the fantasy— or the *fantasm* to use Lacan's more specific term. This is a finding that emerges in each analysis, but is given short shrift even by many psychoanalytic writers.

To draw upon Spielrein's own work, we could add that history is the fantasy of the past that is created in the present, and one that participates in a certain timelessness.

The biographer's way of proceeding, by turning psychoanalysis into psychobiography, or by reducing the words of Spielrein—such as *poetry*—to a particular meaning according to the fantasy of the biographer or cinematographer is, as we have asserted, a very dangerous method. Dangerous, that is, for psychoanalysis, in that Freud's notion of the transference becomes lost in a very predictable interpretation that is placed upon the history, an interpretation that leads only in one direction. This produces an impoverishment of our ability to read the history, and more particularly to be able to grasp Spielrein's own work. In these stories she is turned into a type of *femme fatale* of the early history of psychoanalysis. The vicarious voyeurism by which we imagine a sexual relationship between Spielrein and Jung has promoted a myth that was begun by psychoanalysts—pre-eminently Carotenuto in his initial presentation of Spielrein's papers—and continued by other authors and filmmakers. Spielrein's case, then, has been taken up by the media and the word made flesh, or at least into images of the flesh. There are two important effects of this tendency: first Sabina Spielrein's history has become distorted, and second, through this very distortion, we are led away from her own writings through which she endeavoured to articulate something of her own position. These writings are for the most part forgotten, or rather, *repressed*—if we are to bring psychoanalysis to bear upon this.

This myth has served to distort Spielrein's relation to psychoanalysis, and what she refers to as *poetry* has become lost. This is the means by which the *poetic*, a vital element in her original contribution to psychoanalytic theorisation through her writing, is elided. The beauty of Spielrein's work is that there is a singular openness in her writing, a style that has been denoted as "tentative" (Launer 2015, p. 254), a tentativeness that resists the attribution of a definitive meaning to elements of her work. Spielrein's writing style, at least in her thesis, is qualified by Balsam as "baroque", thus anticipating the later Lacan (Balsam 2015, p. 173). Marcus Silva, in referring to the paper "Destruction as Cause of Becoming", remarks that "Sabina Spielrein's text ... is particularly rich, but also refractory to any sort of categorisation or framing" (Silva 2015, p. 26, translated for this edition). Such comments from disparate sources suggest that one of Spielrein's contributions to psychoanalysis is not just in the content of her work, but also in its style, a style of writing that we might qualify both as properly poetic and psychoanalytic. Her writing is a *work in progress*, to refer to James Joyce. And as with any creative work, Spielrein's oeuvre is an invitation for us to continue and to build upon it.

In this work we do not intend in any way to attempt to write another story about Sabina Spielrein, or a biography, but to proceed in a manner that puts into question the very notion of history that continues to perpetuate a now well-worn account of Sabina Spielrein. The work of the biographer is perhaps necessary, but it is certainly not sufficient—not sufficient, that is, to produce a psychoanalytic work. If anything, we wish here to follow Spielrein's leads, such as her references to Freud, Nietzsche, and other poets. So, if we endeavour here to give an account of Spielrein's trajectory, it is in the form of what Nietzsche referred to as a *Genealogy of Morality*, against the prejudice of "psychologists", that is, the preconceptions of the already-known. What deserve to be regarded as the origin of Spielrein's work are "the actual *active* emotions" (Nietzsche 1887, p. 48, italics in original), in other words, the passion of her transference that lies at the heart of her work.

The biography, or story, endeavours to explain by locating cause in the past, in the history. The most coarse example of this is Launer's proposition that Spielrein's struggles were a result of having been sexually abused by her father as a child, an attribution that is based on the author's speculation and preconceived ideas. Such a view of Sabina Spielrein reduces her interactions with others to an extremely overdetermined, passive notion of her mode of relations, and moreover pre-empting a fixed notion of cause, or causality. Freud, however, invented psychoanalysis precisely in the moment in which he abandoned his *"neurotica"* (Masson 1985, p. 264), that is, he literally abandoned his endeavours to explain his own suffering, and that of his patients, by virtue of the history. Launer, and others, effect a retrogressive movement in which there is a return to the nineteenth-century seduction hypothesis.

To take Freud to the letter, his *neurotica*, that is to say, his neurosis, is precisely this attribution of cause to a past event, to occurrences in one's history. That is, the biography retains the structure of neurosis, indeed a *story* is always structured by neurosis. And as we have seen, the effect of neurosis, in addressing the case of Sabina Spielrein—and in any other case—is to produce a sexual relationship. This is one way in which we can take Lacan's aphorism that *there is no sexual relation*: the sexual relation, this imagined blissful conjoining or union, is the fantasm of the neurotic: it does not exist. It is a fantasm that fills the gap; it smooths over the holes in the history through imagining this ecstatic union of bodies in which nothing lacks. Here we would prefer to take up Freud's position articulated in his correspondence with Jung: "I have suppressed my habit of conscious speculation as radically as possible and have absolutely foresworn the temptation to 'fill in the gaps in the universe' (McGuire 1974, p. 125)", the latter being Freud's reference to the poetry of Heinrich Heine, specifically his *Buch der Lieder* [*Songbook*].

We must propose, however, that if Spielrein wrote it is precisely because *there is no sexual relation*, because something fails in relation to the other, in the relation to Jung through the transference. It is literally the failure of the relation that causes her to continue to write in order to attempt to capture something that is always missing. Nonetheless, because of the inevitable failure of the sexual relation in everyday life, each of us is lured to the cinema by lurid films—such as

A Dangerous Method—that conjure up an imagined sexual relation, or we curl up in bed, not with a sexy lover, but with a "juicy novel".

An abuse of language

A biography endeavours to impute cause through recourse to chronology. However, by reference to Spielrein's own writings, we might come to see the way in which the chronological does not function, or functions only to produce an imaginary account. And Spielrein, like Freud, repeatedly emphasises that time functions differently for the unconscious, "which simultaneously lives in the present, past, and future, and therefore outside of time" (Spielrein 1912c). In this regard we can cite Mijolla's book, which begins with the words "I imagine". The story that is produced is that of the imagination or fantasy of the author. In this work there is from the beginning, furthermore, a presumption of intimacy: "I imagine your surprise, dear Sabina, in reading how I decided to begin this account in my own way, of your amorous adventure with Carl Jung" (2014, p. 7, translated for this edition). This is diametrically removed from anything that we could consider to be produced by Spielrein herself, and anything that merits the name of psychoanalysis.

The chronological has tended to function, like the accounts produced from Spielrein's life have shown, as a *chronique scandaleuse*, as Richebächer asserts (2005b, p. 10, italics in original). Against this tendency we might need to effect a *scandal of language* (Barthes 1973, p. 10), as Roland Barthes proposes in regard to the approach that he elaborates from Edgar Allan Poe's story *The Facts in the Case of M. Valdemar*. In this short story, M. Valdemar, on his deathbed, agrees to undergo *mesmerism*, or hypnosis, prior to the point of death, and still under hypnosis, but clinically dead, famously enunciates *"I am dead"* (Poe 1845, p. 271, italics in original). This *"impossible uttering [énonciation]"* of death (Barthes 1973, p. 10) is articulated through the very principle of life: the voice and the breath. For Barthes, this constitutes an *"encroachment* (of Life on Death)" (p. 9, italics in the original), something that overturns the natural order in which Life is supposed to be opposed to Death. And for Barthes this encroachment comes about through the very means of language, allowing us to glimpse a scene other than that of the enunciation: that of the transgression of the taboo of death and the resultant disturbance of classifications. For Barthes it is the *text* itself, literally a textile or weaving of different voices, which gives rise to a field of listening to the written account. The text then is a registration of a voice that is not heard. Similarly, in Kafka's version of Odysseus' encounter with the Sirens, he states that "the Sirens have a still more terrible weapon than their song, namely their silence" (Kafka 1931, p. 101). This silence is the other side of the voice: it is the voice in so far as it is unable to be heard. And we can add that this approach renders what Barthes refers to as *the text* as a poetic work, located somewhere between the written and the spoken, in so far as poetry has to be declaimed: it is to be re-cited.

It is the text then that allows a voice to be heard. And this voice is the same one that Barthes writes of in his paper of the previous year, "The Grain of the Voice", in which the voice is what conveys enjoyment, or jouissance, and which in the end pertains to writing: "The 'grain' is the body in the voice as it sings, the hand as it writes, the limb as it performs" (Barthes 1972, p. 188). This jouissance of the voice is something of the real of the body, an enjoyment that is far removed from the imaginary sexual relation. This is what we propose to effect with Sabina Spielrein: to traverse the barrier between life and death, not in order to produce another story or biography, but rather to effect a new listening to her words—to her voice—through her writings. It is this encroachment of life on death that is one instance of the disturbance of categories that constitutes the notion of incest that is of interest to us here, not the sexual relation that Launer fancies in the form of imagined incestuous sexual abuse. Nor is this incest the desexualised libido that Jung put forward in his struggle to differentiate himself from Freud. For Lévi-Strauss, all prohibitions that are at the origin of culture can be reduced to one fundamental abuse: "they all constitute a *misuse* [*abus*] *of language*" (1947, p. 495, italics in the original). Rather than re-erecting such divisions and classifications, as we will see, it is Spielrein's assertion that destruction and death, far from being opposed to life, are the very *cause* of life and its creativity. This modality of incest is fundamental to Spielrein's theorisation: through it arises the very creativity that is produced by the encroachment of death into life.

Barthes' paper, entitled "Textual Analysis of a Tale of Edgar Poe", begins by making a differentiation that elaborates upon what we are endeavouring to effect here. He notes that semiological research first establishes a *narrative model*, which is formalised into a structure or grammar of what he refers to as an Account [*Récit*]. To this is applied a *structural analysis*, an analysis Barthes notes is, properly speaking, applied especially to an oral account or to myth. An Account has a linear trajectory that leads ineluctably to a certain relation or conclusion. Much of what has been written so far regarding Spielrein could be subsumed into such a model that conforms to what we have referred to here, via John Kerr, as a *story* or biography.

The other approach that Barthes sets against this is that of a *textual analysis* in which one does not examine a finished or enclosed account, but rather a production that is being made in an ongoing manner, connected to other texts and other codes, not according to deterministic lines—such as the notion of the attribution of causes in the past—but rather to lines of citation. Such an approach, Barthes remarks, is applied exclusively to written accounts. Writing, Barthes notes, is precisely this loss of origin, the loss of motives, "to the profit of a number of indeterminations or overdeterminations" (1973, p. 12). Rather than a question of determinations or causes, it is a matter of what the text produces, how it "disperses itself" (p. 2), and to what it might lead. Naturally, this implies the foregoing of the usual *common sense*. For Barthes: "Writing arrives just exactly at the moment when speaking ceases, that is to say sets out from the instance when one can no longer point out *who speaks* and when one only asserts that [*it*] *begins to speak*" (p. 12, italics in the original). The writings that we will examine here are precisely those that emerge in the moment in which Spielrein took up writing due to the impossibility of speech to effect an end to her analysis with Jung. In this manner we will be able to open up a fertile field of endeavour in regard to the work of Sabina Spielrein, to discern what speaks through her, and which is intimately tied to what she is able to transmit, despite herself, through her writing and its style. It is this that we consider to be a properly psychoanalytic methodology.

The other difference that we are establishing, in parting ways from the manner in which there has been a reference to Spielrein's *story*, is that of an evolution from Freud to Lacan. As Erik Porge notes, "if the major reference for Freud is that of the novel, for Lacan it becomes that of poetry" (2005, p. 45, translated for this edition). Whilst Freud makes innumerable references to the poets, it is generally in the form of couplets, and in this way, he is not able to evade his binary methodology. He draws upon the poets for their content rather than their form. Freud's approach is fundamentally that of the case history: the story or narrative. His paper "Family Romances" (1909c), or more literally translated, the "Family Novel of the Neurotic" [*Der Familienroman der Neurotiker*], makes direct reference to the *Roman*, or "novel". Such a novel, or story, also leads to a reduction to the *relation*, the Oedipus relation in this case.

The title of Lacan's paper "The Neurotic's Individual Myth" (1953a) would be better rendered from the French—and without the possessive that the title of the French original does not carry—as "The Individual Myth of the Neurotic, or Poetry and Truth in Psychoanalysis" (1953b). The "poetry and truth" derive from the title of Goethe's autobiography (1833), although *Dichtung und Wahrheit* in Goethe's title could also be translated as *Fiction and Truth*. Lacan's title nonetheless makes clear that his reference is to poetry. Lacan's own poetic style, as well as his theoretical elaborations of psychoanalysis in reference to the poetic, continue throughout his work, including in his penultimate seminar in which he says that "this practice, is also that of poetry—I am speaking of the practice that is called analysis" (1977–1978, p. 10). That is, the practices of poetry and psychoanalysis are both coextensive and intertwined.

Spielrein, in putting a term to her own analysis, also eschews the chronological in favour of the *achronological*. Some writers have painted Spielrein as a forerunner of various modern preoccupations and contemporary fads—such as a pioneer of evolutionary theory or feminism, or someone who built bridges between different disciplines—and in this way they impose reductionist and schematic notions upon her and her history. Launer, in particular, attributes his own pet ideas onto Spielrein in making her, amongst other things, a forerunner of evolutionary biology and psychology, conveyed in the second signifier of his title: *Survival*. In doing so, he avoids any consideration of Spielrein's references to poetry, to literature, to the music of Wagner, and to the ideas that she evokes of the pre-Socratic thinkers and their revival through Friedrich Nietzsche. What such authors produce is an *anachronism* with recourse to contemporary mores and received ideas, effectively producing a moralistic account of her history and analysis through such comparisons and judgements. This form of psychobiography, we can propose, produces no more than a flawed type of *auto*biography, in so far as it says more about those authors' tastes and prejudices than their purported subject. In such telescoping of present fads upon past events, in the words of the historian Philippe Ariès, "the anachronism falsifies the comparison … We know all too well that we can only grasp the past, in the first instance, through the differences, and only then the similarities, with the times in which we live" (Ariès 1960, p. 11, translated for this edition). Our first task then is to establish the differences between Spielrein's notions and our own contemporary ones.

The type of approach that imposes contemporary fashions upon the past distorts our ability to read Spielrein and to make something new from her writings. In Spielrein's initial letters to Freud, for instance, there is a freedom of expression and an ability to submit herself to the play of the signifier. It is through this that we can discern the poetry of her writing. Launer—who takes an interest in the question of whether there was sexual penetration or not—speculates that Freud found these letters "well-nigh impenetrable" (2015, p. 96). Spielrein teaches us, however, what is at stake in a history, in so far as any history is a destruction and simultaneous re-creation of what has come before. The scope of Spielrein's proposition is lost on Launer, who bemoans that "she had still not let go of the mystical notion of the 'need to die and be reborn' in a romantic relationship" (p. 251).

While we will endeavour to open up Spielrein's proposition regarding destruction and becoming, we might consider that her conception of history is not so far from Roland Barthes' notion of the historian as a magician, but a particular sort of magician of words, through his or her writings: "The historian is thus the one who overturns Time, who turns backwards, back to the place of the dead, and recommences their life in a clear and useful sense" (Cited by: Comment 2015, p. 8, translated for this edition). If there is a certain mysticism or magic in Spielrein's approach, it is the enigma of what can be done with words, of what can be conjured up through writing.

To love the questions themselves

This book sets out to be a psychoanalytic text that will endeavour to discern what we can gain from Spielrein's work, in order to be able to utilise it, rather than to judge or categorise it. This is to follow Spielrein's lead, including taking up the thread of many of her citations and references. She herself says something quite close to this during her Geneva period, in which she uses a terminology of her own: "It is only the collaboration of subconscious thought with conscious thought that can engender a creative work in this world: conscious thought must grasp what subconscious thought offers us and put it to use"

(Spielrein 1923, p. 309, translated for this edition). In this she also anticipates something of Lacan, who later spoke of knowing-what-to-do [*savoir-y-faire*] with the symptom. It is our task here then, to rediscover Spielrein's work for ourselves, in order to put it to use.

Our scope is modest as it proposes to focus principally on how Spielrein was able to end her analysis, to separate from her parents, and to part ways with Jung, and with Zürich. Accordingly, it particularly takes up her writings from 1909 to 1912, both personal and theoretical. We do not consider one to be superior to the other, but like Cifali, we read her personal writings as "words that seek to continue the analysis, and the analysis of her relationship to Jung" (1988, p. 136). The theoretical writings, then, are the realisation of Spielrein's wish expressed as a question: "Is it possible that a tiny bit of truth can be discovered in my 'fantasies'?" (Carotenuto 1980a, p. 11).[1] Hence the novelty and originality of Spielrein's work springs from the fact that it was through her analysis that she was able to elaborate upon her own psychopathology, and from this produce a theoretical work. The logical conclusion of her personal writings was to be able to end her analysis and become an analyst, and her theoretical writings are a testimony to this. Many of Spielrein's writings remain in private hands, however, and are not accessible to the public. We have striven here to work with what is openly available to us and to the reader, rather than lament what we do not have to hand, or to seek to cite from private sources what is not available to others.

Here we will endeavour to read Spielrein with an eye, and an ear, to the poetry of her work. By these means, we intend to build upon it and on her transference, and certainly not to reduce them to a limited number of specific imagined meanings. We wish to give prominence to Spielrein's transference to Jung in so far as the transference is the driving force of any psychoanalysis, and, we can add, of any work that can be called psychoanalytic. If Spielrein's analysis with Jung did not follow a format that might earn such a description today, and if it did not endure beyond her time at the Burghölzli, her transference certainly did. We wish to primarily put into question how she put to use the poetry of her transference to Carl Jung. During the course of her analysis Sabina Spielrein once again began to write, and it was through her writing that she was able to end her analysis. To this end, Spielrein drew on the medium of poetry: of the poetic but also the *poietic* or creative, in her own coming into being as a psychoanalyst. Her use of poetry was not just in the content of her work, but also in the very style of her writing.

It is striking, despite the media phenomenon that has made a wider audience aware of Sabina Spielrein, that many of the important writings that Spielrein produced in these early years, written in her adopted language of German, have not even been translated into English—nor French—let alone studied with any seriousness. Rather, stress has been laid upon the sexier interpretation of the relationship between Spielrein and Jung and once again the relationship has been privileged over the writings. When Spielrein left Zürich to move to Vienna and closer—geographically and theoretically—to Sigmund Freud, she was admitted as a psychoanalyst to the Vienna Psychoanalytic Circle on the strength of what she had written, specifically by virtue of the publication of her psychiatry thesis. This was a psychoanalytic account of a psychotic woman who was a patient in the Burghölzli. Hence Spielrein's theoretical debut in psychoanalytic thought came through her work with psychosis—rather than through hysteria, and thus neurosis.

This effectively gave her a different psychoanalytic formation to Freud. It is a trajectory that is closer to that of Jacques Lacan, who, some 20 years later, arrived at psychoanalysis through his own psychiatry thesis, which was also an analysis of a psychotic woman (Lacan 1932). Freud initially rejected Spielrein's work, specifically her notion of the death instinct from her paper "Destruction as Cause of Becoming", as he heard Jung's theoretical tenets in it. Oscar Zentner noted that, in doing so, Freud also distanced himself from the study of the psychoses, with dire consequences for Freudian psychoanalysis. He states that consequently "In fact one would need to wait for Franz Alexander and Melanie Klein, and later still, Jacques Lacan, for the psychoses to be once more within legitimate reach and interest in psychoanalysis" (2012, p. 82). Here we intend to take up some of the implications of Spielrein's particular psychoanalytic formation.

Like Lacan's thesis, Spielrein's thesis has remained untranslated into English, even though it was published in German now over 100 years ago (Spielrein 1911). The second important paper of this early period, "Destruction as Cause of Becoming" (1912a), has only relatively recently been translated, in two versions. We consider the first of these (1912b) a poor translation in so far as it does not respect the literality of Spielrein's paper; the second (1912c) is far better translated, with reference to the original German, but is incomplete, missing the third section entitled "Life and Death in Mythology". It was from this section, the one most influenced by Jung, that Spielrein presented to the scientific meeting of the Vienna Psychoanalytic Society on 29 November 1911. This was what provoked the hostility and rejection of her work, due to the growing enmity towards the direction that Jung's work had taken. Furthermore, the paper which we have previously mentioned, "Contributions to the Knowledge of the Child's Soul" that she published in 1913, and which was one of the first publications to address the question of the psychoanalysis of children, has also remained untranslated. In addition to being an account of her own childhood through her analysis, it addresses the analyses of two boys. Therefore, two of the three papers that we consider necessary to produce any valid reading of Spielrein's analysis and its ending, as well as to begin to evaluate Spielrein's overall contribution to psychoanalysis during this early period of her psychoanalytic writings, remain entirely untranslated and thus inaccessible to English language readers. The third paper, as we have noted, is inadequately or incompletely translated.

Here we will endeavour to not close the many questions raised by Sabina Spielrein's work, as we proposed has been done in many ways up to this point. We will, as the poet Rainer Maria Rilke proposed, "Try to love the *questions themselves*" (Rilke 1929, p. 35, italics in the original), rather than to love illusory and precipitous answers, which are the cancers of psychoanalysis.

Note

1 Excerpts from *A Secret Symmetry* by Aldo Carotenuto, translated by Penguin Random House LLC, translation copyright © 1982 by Penguin Random House LLC. Used by permission of Pantheon Books, an imprint of the Knopf Doubleday Publishing Group, a division of Penguin Random House LLC. All rights reserved.

1

I WANT A GOOD FRIEND TO WHOM I COULD LAY OPEN EVERY TUG OF MY SOUL

This lameness I feign
Your bounty to gain,
And not that to limp is a pleasure:
Then acquit me from blame,
If I choose to be lame,
Nor censure me thus without measure;
For if people complain,
My excuse I maintain,
It is lawful to limp for a treasure.

From The Makamah of the Denar *(Al Hariri of Basra 1054–1155)*

What we cannot reach flying we must reach limping
The Book tells us it is no sin to limp.

Rückert's German paraphrase cited by Freud in
"Beyond the Pleasure Principle" (1920g, p. 64)

In endeavouring to write an account of Sabina Spielrein's suffering from her own writings, and the treatment that took place through her transference, we are immediately confronted with what is at first glance an insurmountable difficulty, but at the same time a crucial indicator: although she had kept a diary from the age of ten, this childhood writing seems to have failed her during the periods of greatest anguish. Consequently, she often wrote of incidents of great import only some time after they had occurred. In February 1900, at the age of 14, Spielrein retrospectively set down a number of events that had a critical impact upon her, including the birth of her sister Emilia, as well as the death of her grandmother. She wrote that this loss left her alone in her grief, unable to speak to anyone about it: "Without grandma it is very difficult for me to live in this world" (Spielrein 2006, p. 33, translated for this edition). Adding insult to this injury was the pain of her grandfather then taking another woman. Regarding the latter, whom she does not deign to name, she wrote that she was "a very good woman, but a great fool … How often am I overcome with anguish, and it seems to me that only grandma was able to protect me. Cannot write any more" (p. 33).

Spielrein's anguish is associated with a number of losses, and with the pain tied to certain arrivals and departures. And in endeavouring to write of these, she reaches the point where she is no longer able to write, even to the degree where the "I" falls out of her writing: there is no longer any subject who might be able to write, or rather the subject falls silent as she is overcome by her distress: "Cannot write any more".

Accordingly, there is no diary—at least one to which we have access—for the two years that preceded her admission to the Burghölzli asylum in Zürich in 1904, a period during which her difficulties rose to a crescendo. But then, some two months following her admission—and the beginning of her psychoanalysis with Carl Jung—she once again began to write and, notably, this writing initially took the form of poetry. From the outset then, Spielrein's periods of inability to write were coextensive with her anguish and suffering. The corollary of this assertion is that her writing, and in particular the poetics of her writing, not only enabled her to overcome her distress, but also allowed her to create something through it, in the form of writing. That is, our thesis is that it was both the act and the style of the writing itself—mediated through her transference—that served the function of writing, and righting herself, out of her difficulties. We will begin to pursue this proposal here in reference to the accounts of the circumstances of what she later describes as her "illness", in other words, her symptom and its vicissitudes. We shall then examine the form that this took through her experiences of love, and ultimately through her transference-love to Jung at the Burghölzli.

My pain of parting

Sabina Spielrein was born on 25 October 1885, the first child of Nikolai and Eva Spielrein. When she was taken from Rostov-on-Don in her native Russia to the Burghölzli asylum in Zürich on 17 August 1904 by her mother and maternal uncle, Dr. Lublinski, she was 19 years old. Her family brought her to Zürich, not just for the treatment of her mental troubles, but also with a view to her studying medicine there, something that was not possible for her in Russia by virtue both of being a woman, and because she was Jewish. She had spent a month prior to the admission to the Burghölzli at a private sanatorium in Interlaken under a Dr. Heller where she exasperated the staff through her quickly changing moods and her provocative conduct.

Nonetheless, this was not Spielrein's first voyage to the West. She had been on a previous trip—together with her mother and sister Emilia—during which she did give testimony to her difficulties and struggles in her diary. On that occasion, when Spielrein was 15, the party of three left Russia during the summer of 1901 to visit family in Warsaw and Berlin, as well as going to Karlsbad for the treatment of her mother's nervous condition, and lastly, they visited Vienna to consult a specialist for her mother. From Sabina Spielrein's account, the whole of the trip was heavily marked by anguish, her mother's as well as her own. She wrote of the difficulty of leaving her "fatherland". After the big farewell at the railway station with family and friends, and in particular leaving her father behind, she described in her diary the troubles that would later recur in very specific moments:

> Only when the train had left, and Daddy, with Jascha, Sanja and Petra, had waved their kerchiefs and hats for the last time, did I manage to overcome my pain of parting [*Abschiedsschmerz*], but only outwardly, and I sat at the window to see and describe everything: at least our voyage would not be in vain. But my plans would not be fulfilled. In the evening my feet hurt greatly, and were so swollen that mummy was forced to make the decision for us to get off the train in Krakow.
>
> *(Spielrein 2006, p. 34)*

The pains in her feet and her consequent difficulty walking were to be a symptom that would re-emerge, both in her transference to Carl Jung and in her efforts to free herself from him. It was precisely this symptom, preventing her from walking on her own two feet—that was much later the alibi that precluded her from attending the third Psychoanalytic Congress in Weimar in 1911. This was at the period of Spielrein's endeavour to finally separate herself from Jung. It is no coincidence that that Congress was attended by both Jung's wife Emma, and Antonia Wolff, both rivals for Jung's love. Wolff indeed became Jung's long-term mistress and collaborator, replacing Spielrein in Jung's work and affections. Spielrein's pain of parting is incorporated, literally, in this symptom of a difficulty walking on her own, in the singular gait that was to both limit her movements, as well as marking the hobbling style of her progression.

This pain of parting was also the pain of leaving behind all that was familiar to her, her fatherland and her father, other family members, and friends, as well as her hometown where she had grown up, in addition to her own language and culture. And once again, some ten years later, it was this same pain that she had to confront head-on in order to finish her analysis so that she might leave Jung, to finish her studies and leave Zürich, and to finally separate from her family and homeland. But to do this entailed not just completing her study of medicine and writing her thesis, but also having the thesis reviewed by Jung in order for it to be published in the *Jahrbuch*. At that time, she wrote, "my paper does contain some interesting and stimulating material, and for that reason it will be good if it is read" (Carotenuto 1980a, p. 10). For her thesis to be read implies that Spielrein would be able to move not only outside her family, but also beyond the relation of her personal analysis to her analyst, to a public beyond. This was the first of her writings to be published, a truly psychoanalytic writing in which she is deeply implicated, both in its content as well as its style.

This act of writing itself, and its effect of going beyond the intimate circle of family and acquaintances, denotes a movement that crosses over a certain border or boundary designated by the family, and later by going beyond the confines of her analysis. And during that first trip abroad, to the West, it was specifically on the border, going into Germany, that she felt herself subjected to a strange experience. While the carriages were locked and the immigration officials inspecting documents, her mother was frantically looking for their passports. It was of that moment, with her sister Emilia close to tears, that she wrote: "I myself didn't know why, and what was happening to me: for me it was either very funny or difficult: I was seized by some unusual boldness, and I wished for something frightfully big, and I laughed and prepared myself" (Spielrein 2006, p. 35). This was a singular moment of traversing the frontier between her homeland—Poland at that time being part of Greater Russia—and Germany, in which she was moving from her fatherland to the West: the "*Ausland*", or Outland. On this occasion she was subjected to something beyond herself, but it was nonetheless an experience through which she was able to summon an uncommon strength and boldness in the face of her mother's anxiety and distress. Through this occurrence, not only does she experience a type of transformation, but she is able to articulate something of this experience through her writing.

This voyage was also an eye-opener, not just to the architecture and cleanliness of Germany at the time, but also to different and more liberal relations between men and women, including a greater intellectual and sexual liberation. She describes, for example, how men and women worked side by side and how men might see women in their petticoats as they tried on dresses in clothing stores. She noted that people in Germany had the right to think and to say what they wanted, and hence they were generally free. Her impressions carry a certain ideal of a life that was not available to her in Russia, "What I liked best were the Germans. They are lively, helpful, funny, lovely people, and on no account stupid" (p. 36). These writings also prefigure her later diaries in which she frankly puts forward her independence of thought, and her disdain for the moralistic manner in which sexuality is perceived.

This first trip, though, was also marked by other anxious moments, strikingly at other moments of transition: those of crossing of borders and inspection of baggage. From Berlin, they travelled to Karlsbad for her mother's spa treatment, during which the mother felt very poorly. And in their hurry to leave Karlsbad for Vienna, they left a piece of baggage on the platform in Karlsbad, which contained, amongst their things, her mother's diamonds.

Spielrein's entry for their stay in Vienna was primarily filled with disquiet regarding the lost basket. She finishes her entry, the last for this trip, in the following way: "Finally the basket arrived, but the two days of the search and commotion went by, not without leaving a mark. If something like this were to happen to us at home, it would disappear without a trace" (p. 39). The trace, the mark that was left upon her from her trip abroad, fundamentally concerning the question of loss and anguish and the traversing of frontiers, was one that would not be erased.

After the death of my little sister, my illness began

It was after the return from this trip that her younger sister Emilia died of typhus, in October 1901, a period during which Spielrein writes nothing, at least in those writings to which we have access. It is only later, in 1910, that she refers to the death: "When I was in sixth [form], after the death of my little sister, my illness began. I took refuge in isolation" (Carotenuto 1980a, p. 24). Early in her admission to the Burghölzli, Jung recorded in his notes that "She loved her sister 'more than anything in the world'" (Covington & Wharton 2003a, p. 88). This event clearly left a heavy trace upon her, but not on the pages of her diary.

In her later diary, towards the end of her medical studies in Zürich, Sabina Spielrein traced the history of the manner in which her love was seeking out someone upon whom it could alight. The first in this series was her history teacher in fifth form. She singled out his high intelligence and the serious and sad expression in his eyes as factors that vanquished her. She writes that "My crush on the man who opened up to me previously unknown vistas grows by leaps and bounds. I want to make some sacrifice for him, I want to suffer for him" (Carotenuto 1980a, p. 25). Thus, she outlines a number of features that were to remain constant features of her recipe for love, that is, features of her fantasm. She extols the position of making a sacrifice for the other, submitting herself to being the object of the Other's desire.

She took the initiative of going to the teacher's home accompanied by her brother, under the pretext of asking him for some extra reading. He was not home but immediately afterwards came to her house. She continues, "I want a good friend to whom I could lay open every tug of my soul" (Spielrein 2006, p. 45). This designation of this person as a "friend" was a place that was prepared long before her encounter with Jung. The central feature of her love was that she could speak to her "friend" of her suffering. Such a friend needed to be one who could *bear* her soul, to bear to hear what she had to say. Her love sought out a man whom she supposed might be able to know something of her, of the vicissitudes of her soul. Hence her love went from one man to another until it was able to take the form of transference in her psychoanalysis. The teacher was not able to bear the tugs of her soul: he shared the psychological theories of her parents, and later used Spielrein's mother as a confidant, unburdening his own soul. He presently lost his appeal for Sabina Spielrein, becoming simply a bore.

The next in the series was her Uncle Adolf in Warsaw, who she later wrote was "an exquisite example of father-transference … He has my father's noble character and a decidedly artistic bent". On the other hand, she notes that her uncle loved music but "he has no ear" (Carotenuto 1980a, p. 26). We infer from this that her uncle was unable to hear her, to listen to her. Early in her admission to the Burghölzli, from the clinical history taken from the mother, Jung writes in the hospital notes, "Recently she fell in love with her old uncle who was a doctor. Mother listed all his faults for her, and as a result she was deeply disappointed and upset" (Covington & Wharton 2003a, p. 87). Curiously, both of these men, as Spielrein notes, shared a common fate. Each ended up not only failing her, but additionally falling in love with her mother, the teacher even attempting suicide when the mother departed on one occasion for Paris. But Spielrein did not enquire further into this fate common to each of the men with whom she was infatuated. She was not oblivious to her part to play in this sharing of her love interests with her mother. These beaux, however, did not serve the function of allowing her to depart from her mother, but, on the contrary, they provided her with another experience that was shared between mother and daughter. In a not dissimilar manner, her later infatuation with Jung is shared in juicy detail in letters to her mother, at least during her time in Zürich.

Moreover, these infatuations were not at all hidden from her mother, but on the contrary, the mother asked her, "Which of them do you really love? Your teacher or your uncle?" Spielrein recounts that she no longer remembered what her answer was, but, more importantly, she writes, "Later, when I went to Warsaw, my uncle won out, only to be replaced soon by my present friend" (Carotenuto 1980a, p. 26), that is, Carl Jung. Jung becomes the next in her series of "friends", but, in her characteristic mode of relation alighting upon him, her love was able to evolve into a transference-love in which it could be spoken of and expounded upon. One aspect of this love that is consistent in this series is an erotism that is attached to it, a sensuality that is evident in her writing.

There was one more man in this series, another doctor who was an assistant to Dr. Heller who treated her in Interlaken, prior to going to Zürich, possibly a Dr. Hisselbaum whose name is written by Spielrein upon the receipt from the Sanatorium. Notably, it is the disappointment—the loss and destruction of this love—that precipitated her admission to the Burghölzli. Jung writes in the clinical notes that "The most recent outburst in the hotel was the result of her feeling that a recently admired doctor had let her down … She left Interlaken because the assistant had left" (Covington & Wharton 2003a, p. 87). Moreover, the erotism attached to Spielrein's particular mode of loving is manifested through her writing about this series of men. Her particular mode of loving was sustained in each case, something of hers alighted upon each of these men in turn. This was precipitated in her transference to Jung from the beginning of her treatment with him, and evolved in different ways over time. Here we will first examine Jung's place in relation to Spielrein in his function as doctor and analyst.

Only the force of the spirit sustains the world and creates life

In the entrance of the Burghölzli, the visitor can observe a plaque inscribed with a poem by the Swiss poet and writer Gottfried Keller, whose title is *Zimmermannsspruch*, which might be translated as "The Carpenter's Motto". As the visitor can read at the bottom of the plaque, the poem was proclaimed personally from the top of the roof of the asylum on 6 October 1866 by Keller himself—whose own father had been a tradesman, a lathe-worker—on the occasion of the celebrations of the conclusion of the building of the Burghölzli:

> Workers! Come near!
> A pious work was carried out here.
> Erected there the building stands.
> Reaching over lake and lands!
> The noble art and science, and
> the active strength of our hands,
> built until the house was consummated,
> to the deepest unhappiness dedicated.
> As around errs the warning sign,
> of the soul so heavily consigned.
> And a right-minded folk recognises
> that which on high it rightly prizes,
> it knows that only the spirit's might
> sustains the world and creates life!
> In order to elevate measure and light,
> did this people fulfil its noble plight
> and build this house with rich hands
> through our courage to understand.
>
> *(translated for this edition from the plaque at the Burghölzli)*

Despite the spirit of the Enlightenment that is evoked in Keller's poem, the first directors of the Burghölzli were German psychiatrists who were reputed to be more interested in looking down their microscopes than listening to their patients. The first director was Dr. Bernhard von Gudden, who became the director of the asylum in Munich after his two years at the Burghölzli. He was later infamously involved in a decree that declared King Ludwig II of Bavaria mad and no longer able to rule for the rest of his life. Von Gudden established a commission—which included his psychiatrist son-in-law—that declared the King was suffering from paranoia. This decree was, however, written and signed without any of the psychiatrists actually meeting with the King, let alone hearing him speak or examining him. It was made in connivance with the Prime Minister and government of Bavaria with the specific aim of depriving Ludwig of his power. Von Gudden suffered the inglorious fate of being found drowned—together with the King—in Lake Starnberg near Munich (des Cars 1975).

Dr. Auguste Forel was fourth director of Burghölzli, but its first director who was both Swiss and French-speaking. He was an indefatigable fighter against alcoholism, as well as the prostitution that was rife in and around the Burghölzli. Forel was a leading thinker and researcher in biological psychiatry, having spent time under von Gudden at the Munich asylum. But he was also interested in psychological methods of treatment, particularly hypnosis, studying that method, like Freud himself, under Bernheim in Nancy. Accordingly, Forel became a proponent of dynamic psychiatry, which purported to describe the dynamics of the interaction between the brain and the soul of the patient. We can say that Forel re-introduced the Enlightenment into the Burghölzli, both in the understanding of the patients as well the introduction of new treatment methods based on moral and psychological principles. Consequently, during his directorship at the Burghölzli, hypnosis became the principal treatment for hysteria.

Forel's successor was Eugen Bleuler, who, up to that point, had been Forel's assistant. Amongst other things, Bleuler had studied with Charcot in Paris, and had read Freud's translation of Charcot, as well as Freud and Breuer's *Studies on Hysteria*, and Freud's early psychoanalytic works. Under Bleuler, psychoanalysis became both a means of understanding, as well as a possible treatment method, of the psychoses. In these early days of psychoanalysis, Eugen Bleuer was responsible for the introduction of psychoanalysis into institutional psychiatry, attracting many young psychiatrists who would later become early luminaries of psychoanalysis. Thus, at the time of Spielrein's admission, under Dr. Eugen Bleuler's directorship, the asylum had opened up its thinking and treatment to the new movement of psychoanalysis that was being disseminated from Vienna by Freud and others. Nonetheless, as is evident from the Freud-Jung correspondence, Bleuler, in regard to the new science of psychoanalysis, always retained a certain reserve and *ambivalence*, to coin one of the terms that he used as a pathognomonic of the illness that he named schizophrenia, a term that Freud referred to as "Bleuler's happily chosen term" (Freud 1905d, p. 199) to describe what Freud considered to be the opposing pairs of drives, an opposing pair of importance to Spielrein's developments.

As one of the few hysterical and private patients at the Burghölzli, Sabina Spielrein came to be treated by Jung with psychoanalysis, at least what he understood of it from what he had read and knew from other colleagues including Bleuler. Clearly, his treatment was not what might now be considered to be a stereotypical psychoanalytic treatment with armchair and couch. In fact, the use of the armchair and couch is attributed by Freud, first of all, to a personal motive: he wrote that he was not able to tolerate being stared at by other people for eight hours a day or more. Although Freud's publications up to that point had been few, what we can call the psychoanalytic *method* was clear: that of free association of the patient and the evenly-suspended attention of the analyst.

What was much less clear from Freud's publications up to that point was his *technique*, how he actually conducted the sessions. In fact, Freud was reluctant to prescribe any technique—fearing that others would copy what he considered to be a technique that was nothing more than a solution based on his own psychopathology—in a type of mimicry of psychoanalysis and a neglect of its *method*. He was for this reason initially reluctant to publish works on technique that could be construed in this way, and he did so only after being pushed by other analysts, particularly by Jung in their correspondence. In the first of the so-called *Papers on Technique*, "The Handling of Dream-Interpretation in Psycho-Analysis", Freud writes: "There are undoubtedly different ways of going to work in the matter, but then the answer to questions of technique in analysis is never a matter of course" (Freud 1911e, p. 91). This citation was given as an epigraph to a paper on technique by the early analyst of children, Hermine Hug-Hellmuth, demonstrating the commitment to a liberty in technique among early psychoanalysts, a freedom that seems to have become lost. Freud's fears were more than justified in the way in which various aspects of technique have been adopted, for instance a large portion of the psychoanalytic and psychotherapeutic world working to the 50-minute sessions that were determined by the practice that Freud established by virtue of his own particularities and circumstances. This, of course, is despite Freud's own lack of hesitation to break his own rules when the situation called for it.

Sabina Spielrein was the first patient that Jung treated with the new method of psychoanalysis, and of whom he later wrote to Freud that "She was, so to speak, my test case" (McGuire 1974, p. 228). If one of Freud's reasons for not wanting to publish his ideas on psychoanalytic technique was, as the editors of the *Standard Edition* assert, that he disliked the notion of future patients knowing too much about the details of his technique, this was not to be the case for Sabina Spielrein. During her admission Spielrein had access both to clinical texts including those of psychoanalysis, as well as to works of literature. In the hospital notes, Jung remarks that he had recommended that she read a story by Gottfried Keller, specifically one in which the protagonist is caned by other boys. She also had access to Forel's book *Hypnotism, or Suggestion and Psychotherapy* (1899) (cf. Covington & Wharton 2003a, p. 96). We note that, even if hypnotism has been mostly abandoned as a treatment method at the Burghölzli, there was certainly still a marked suggestion in the reading materials provided for Sabina Spielrein by her psychotherapist.

Bleuler clearly saw that Spielrein's psychopathology was too deeply implicated in that of her family to allow her to be easily able to separate from them. Her *Abschiedsschmerz* was also a wish to depart, a wish to establish a life separate from that of her family. Accordingly, at various times, both Bleuler as director of the asylum, and Jung as her treating doctor, forbade Spielrein's mother and father to write to her, and later for her to share an apartment with her brother who was sent to Zürich to study, or even to live close to him in which case she might happen upon him. Bleuler specifically wrote to Spielrein's father and told him that it was characteristic of his daughter's nervous disposition for her to link all kinds of pathological obsessional fantasies with his person, and that of her brother, and that this had the effect of making her worried and disturbed. Here the emphasis was not upon the supposed reality of the situation, but rather on Spielrein's fixation upon such fantasies—and ultimately upon the reality that she constructed around these—which was part and parcel of the difficulty she had in separating. Bleuler's emphasis was upon the need for Spielrein's independence, and he accordingly stressed that the decision needed to be in her hands.

On the other hand, even relatively early during the course of her admission, Spielrein was involved in the scientific pursuits of the asylum. She was also at times invited into Bleuler's family circle. Spielrein decided to commence studying medicine, as she had previously wished, at the beginning of the academic year in 1905. A few months after being admitted, Bleuler writes in her notes that Sabina Spielrein had "Made a correct diagnosis of epilepsy from a letter handed out at the clinic and correctly supported her diagnosis" (Covington & Wharton 2003a, p. 93). She also joined the dining table of the assistant doctors at lunch on a daily basis, which was considered a significant success. She later wrote, "It is also significant that right at the beginning of my therapy Dr. Jung let me read his dissertation" (Carotenuto 1980a, p. 105). Furthermore, she took part—both as an experimental subject as well as a researcher—in Jung's association experiments that had been begun by Bleuler and continued by Jung, initially as an endeavour to empirically prove the assertions of psychoanalysis. Hence during the course of her hospitalisation, Spielrein had a unique position not just as a patient, but effectively also part of the medical staff involved in case and theoretical discussions, a staff that was now taking on the new Freudian theories. Given the emphasis on psychoanalysis in the Burghölzli at that time, from the beginning Spielrein was effectively placed as patient as well as doctor, as analysand and as psychoanalyst.

I want you to do something really bad to me

In the first few months of Sabina Spielrein's admission she manifested intermittent periods of anguish, suicidal gestures, and so-called childish pranks. These troubles were much the same as they had been at the sanatorium at Interlaken where the staff had not been able to successfully manage them. At the Burghölzli, although Spielrein's psychiatric treatment was provided both by Jung and to some extent Bleuler who also supervised Jung's work, her transference was clearly to the former. A week after her admission Jung writes, "Every conversation with her, aimed at obtaining information, is as difficult as walking on eggshells" (Covington & Wharton 2003a, p. 88). She, and the more extreme manifestations of her behaviour, were consistently able to settle down in the physical presence of Carl Jung. She is quite specific regarding the position that she asks Jung to take up in her transference. Jung writes in her hospital notes, "She asks Ref. [i.e. Jung] never to display the slightest sense of being at a loss about her but only the utmost fortitude and a firm belief in her recovery" (p. 90). And on 10 October 1904, he notes, "She constantly demands that the writer inflict pain on her, do something to hurt her, treat her badly in some way" (p. 90). The transference to Jung had been established from the moment of her admission, articulating the place that she demanded he take up for her in the transference, and in addition the place that was established for him within that transference in respect of her wishes and fantasies.

A week or so later, Jung writes that on their first walk together, she suddenly started to limp and this quickly got worse. In response to this complaint, Jung gave her a physical examination of her feet, noting "exaggerated hyperaesthesia" in both feet, an increased sensitivity seemingly "exaggerated" or accentuated due to the examination. He continues, "With a sly look she urgently demands treatment. Meekly stays in bed for two days. On the second day there is a profound abreaction, and on the third day the pain has completely gone" (p. 90). Jung writes that in the analysis, Spielrein had used the walk with Jung as an external cause for the pain in her feet. Her association was that she had developed unbearable pain in her feet for the first time after a violent row between her parents. On that occasion, it was her father who spent the following two days in bed. The symptom thus ties her to her father, sustaining a particular mode of relation. She also tells Jung of the pain in her feet that occurred on the first trip abroad. It is the so-called "abreaction" of her limp and foot pain that gives the opportunity for her symptom to unfold. The function of the symptom is articulated by Jung: "Pat.[ient] knows now that she gradually has to get used to a freer way of life ... She is afraid of going out and of the future; so she tries to postpone going out as long as possible by means of the pain in her feet" (p. 92).

Sometime later, specifically on 23 October 1906, Jung wrote to Freud regarding a detail that is not to be found in the hospital notes. He does not name the patient to whom he is referring but describes her as a 20-year-old Russian female student, except that at that time she is no longer his patient. Jung remarks, "Saw her father spanking her older brother on the bare bottom. Powerful impression. Couldn't help thinking afterwards that she had defecated on her father's hand. From the 4th-7th year convulsive attempts to defecate on her own feet, in the following manner: she sat on the floor with one foot beneath her, pressed her heel against her anus and tried to defecate and at the same time to prevent defecation" (McGuire 1974, p. 7). Clearly, Spielrein's feet are an exceptionally eroticised part of her body. To be unable to walk then is a manner in which to stay detained in this "blissful" position, a position that keeps her fixed in a mode of sexual relation which Freud would come to call a *family romance*.

Spielrein's speech is already imbued with the method of psychoanalysis, as her writing comes to be as well. During some extended leave that Jung had taken in order to fulfil his military service, Bleuler attributed a deterioration in her clinical state to this absence. He remarks in another note that "She composes songs about the clinic doctors which she cannot recite for laughing. She breaks off writing a letter in order to write down with her eyes closed, all the fantasies that go through her mind." (Covington & Wharton 2003a, p. 93). Soon after this is the first diary entry for two years, in the form of an untitled poem:

> Empty, dark and cold.
> Empty and dark all around.
> I am alone in the world
> Completely alone.
> No dear father,
> No dear mother,
> No homely roof over me.
> To no one can I speak my thoughts.
> My head
> My head, little head.
> Nowhere can I let you calm down,
> Upon nothing can I rest you.
> My poor heart
> My shattered heart
> Why so disturbed and plaintive
> Why do you beat so painfully?
> Dark anticipation
> And unspeakable disquiet.
> Ah, my youth is lost.
> Ah, my life is ruined.
>   *(Spielrein 2006, p. 42)*

This dark poem has a raw truth about it, even if in its style it tends to limp along, dragging its signifiers of separation, damage, and destruction from one line to the next. There is a heavy insistence on abandonment by her parents, a negation that pervades all of her experiences, and of an absence or lack. It is also an articulation of an experience of loss and annihilation, leading to its final line regarding the destruction of a life lived hitherto. It contains, nonetheless, even in its dark anticipation, a foreboding of another life to come after the mourning over this shattered and lost youth: a transformation of her suffering into a form that would allow her to work. That is, we can say that there is contained within this poem, an expectancy of new coming into being that will arise from the ashes of this ruined life.

Although Jung's entries in the hospital notes are infrequent, they are none-theless evocative, both of the intermittent time that he spends with Spielrein, as well as her transference to him, viz.: "If the pat.[ient] is not given the usual close attention for a few days, she becomes increasingly shut in and it is more and more difficult to get through to her" (Covington & Wharton 2003a, p. 94). Jung's "analysis" consists of allowing her to speak, indeed he remarks, "with great effort", although we are left uncertain whether the effort is Spielrein's or Jung's or both. This effort results in Spielrein reporting to Jung accounts of scenes of herself or her brother being beaten on the bottom, or being threatened with such a beating. Jung notes that such scenes had been long associated with sexual arousal and masturbation through pressing and rubbing her legs together. Jung notes that when he had recently told her to agree to regulations, "'agree' was perceived as 'submit'; it triggered the complex and caused her to masturbate". The scenes then evoked become those of her fantasm: "She pictures these as vividly as possible, in particular being beaten on her bare bottom, and, in order to increase her arousal, she imagines that it is taking place in front of a large audience [*Publikum*]" (p. 95). In the analysis, we note a movement from a scene of seduction to the elucidation of her fantasm. Through her symptom—which is intimately associated with her body and its arousal—she limps from a family scenario or Oedipus complex, to move beyond it and to appeal to a public outside the family circle.

In his manner of writing of the sessions with Spielrein, Jung follows the Freudian method, that of Freud's abandoning of the seduction hypothesis. Freud destroyed the basis for his *neurotica*, his previous theory of the neuroses, by this abandonment of his prior theory, which was also the theory generated by his own neurosis. Thus, like Freud, Jung—as analyst—moves from Spielrein's seduction hypothesis towards its abandonment and emphasis on the fantasy, or rather *fantasm* that is produced by the subject, Spielrein in this instance. In particular, he notes that the signifier "to beat" [*schlagen*] is one that has a privileged pertinence for her: Jung calls it "her complex trigger word" (Covington & Wharton 2003a, p. 96). It is also a word that would have a prominent place in her first piece of published writing, her psychiatry thesis. At the beginning of 1905, the "abreactions" continue, and Jung once again notes what the direction of the analysis is:

> After the New Year the abasia had as its main reason the fact that she could not make up her mind to abreact this innermost and most important part of her complexes. The New Year only made the necessity of the decision clearer to her. At the same time the shifting of this complex would have meant the first step into the world which is always reacted to with abasia. After abreaction great relief, pains in her feet and headaches disappear.
>
> *(p. 95)*

Abasia is literally an inability to walk: to not have a *basis* or *step*, to not have a leg to stand on. In her first poem at the Burghölzli, Spielrein wrote of her lost youth and ruined life. Her previous life with her family, her former family romance came to an abrupt end through parting from her home country, her admission to hospital, and through speaking in the analysis. She was destroying the former basis to her existence, abandoning her own seduction hypothesis. Through the analysis, through her elaboration of her fundamental fantasm, Spielrein is able to find some new basis upon which she is able to walk on her own, even if it requires limping along. On the other hand, through the "abreaction" of the analysis, she uncovers and implants in Jung something of her own: a seed of destruction, a seed of something that goes beyond the family, beyond the Oedipus, and thus beyond the pleasure principle. And Jung was able to be her analyst so long as he was able to bear what was unbearable for others to hear, for others such as Bleuler and the doctors at Interlaken.

It is impossible to open up to these children

Spielrein wrote more poetry whilst in the Burghölzli, poetry that begins to take on a different tone. Here she writes of the itinerary of a creek—the itinerary, to be sure, of the subject—through its vicissitudes:

> Through the neat field
> Through the velvety-soft meadows
> A creek flows and runs
> To unknown shores.
> A storm comes, a storm goes by,
> It is always clear.
> Storms make it ripple
> Yet it knows no waves.
> No groves, no forests
> Grow upon the shore.
> Azure-blue flowering bushes
> Are mirrored in the stream.
> The creek meanders
> And glides between stones.
> It disappears into the small pit
> To emerge gleaming once again.
> It never dies out completely,
> But is always in the same finery.
> For its life-force [Lebenskraft]
> Only the sky is thankful.
> But for how much longer
> Will it glide between flowers?
> The sea's chasms await
> There in the hazy distance.
> *(Spielrein 2006, pp. 43–44)*

The stream—or the subject—is itself born of the water of snowstorms, like the great river Rhine or *Rhein*, homophonous with the latter part of her family name. Once created it makes its way, swollen by more storms that deform its surface but do not disrupt its splendour, the beauty of its soul only discerned by the heavens. It continues on its way, its course determined by the fortunes of the times: of weather and topography. However, it pursues its course, never knowing what awaits it. It anticipates what can only indistinctly be made out in the hazy, turbid, or troubled [*trüben*] distance. It anticipates great events to which it will be subjected, cataclysmic perhaps, but from which it may be able to survive, and contribute to the swelling of the waters. Finally, it must encounter the sea, a coming together and mixing of the fresh water with the salty, an inmixing born of difference rather than sameness.

Even though this excerpt shows Spielrein in a more lyrical mood, or style, there is a certain darkness that remains a threat, but here relegated more to the background. There the chasms that await in the troubled distance spell death itself, the final adventure of the subject towards which it inexorably hurtles. Death then is the final chasm, but one which is indubitably also present in every living moment in the guise of destruction, if one has the courage to recognise it. But against this backdrop something more is possible, both in the content and the style in which she writes. Already from the ruins of her life, she carefully selects some of the pieces, the words, through which she is able to create something new, something that did not have an existence prior to the writing of these lines.

And her writing maintains a connection to Jung. Following this poetry, she once again starts to record her thoughts in her diary, but just twice prior to her discharge from the Burghölzli. The day prior to the commencement of her medical studies, she writes of her dark foreboding: "I am anticipating this blissful moment, somehow in a deadly sinister way" (Spielrein 2006, p. 45). The *deadly* then is the precondition for the blissful, the moment which she has awaited for so long. A certain sinister death then is the precondition for acceding to a moment of aliveness. After expressing her doubts, she notes, "Jung is in the corridor. Shortly he will come in to see me: I must hide the diary so as not to show him what I am doing, but why not show it to him? The devil knows!" (p. 45). It is the devil—or the Other—to whom she attributes knowledge, but Jung also continues to be the one whom she supposes to know something about her.

This also evokes something she enters in her diary when she is 11 years old: "I will no longer give my diary to daddy to read because he said that if I have to be forced to do music practice, then he will burn it (i.e. the diary)" (p. 19). Here there is a limit imposed upon her, one in which her writing is interrupted. But this interchange modifies her relation to her father, or is at least the pretext for this, such that she vows to no longer share her writing with him. Similarly, even though her writing from this period is nominally addressed to Jung in this moment, it is nonetheless not for his eyes. The writing, both the act of writing as well as its content, become a means of effecting a separation from him, in so far as the writing henceforth becomes private. There is a question at the end of her time at the Burghölzli of whether it is possible to no longer share what she writes with Jung.

When she left the Burghölzli to attend Zürich University in June 1905, she incurred the consequences of her lost youth and ruined life: she is left permanently altered by this experience. In regard to the other students she writes, "Somehow it is impossible to open myself up to these children. I feel more thorough, more serious, developed in a more critical manner, more independent" (p. 45).

Referring to the other students as children is clearly not a question of age, but rather that she herself is no longer a child. She has been broken but has managed for the time being to recreate herself in another way: a mode which enables her to make something of her life through study. She gives voice to her doubts once again and expresses the wish to dedicate herself to science. To marry, for her, is an awful thought: even though she yearns for love and affection, the thought of marrying is one that is covered in "the poorest prose" (p. 45). Spielrein aspires to poetry, not to the prose of a mundane and domesticated subsistence.

The path to a different life is dictated by her transference: "I want a good friend to whom I could lay open every tug of my soul. I would like the love of an older person who loves and understands me (inner-similarity), like parents love their children. … If only I were as clever as my *Jung*[a]! Devil! I want to know if something can become of me. It is so stupid that I am not a man: everything is easier for them" (p. 46). Her "I would like the love of an older person" has notably been translated as "I want the love of an older man" (Lothane 2003, p. 194), inexorably tending to sexualise what is not explicitly sexual from the outset. But this "good friend" is, as we have noted, the term that is provisionally reserved for Jung, for he who takes up this position for her in the transference. This place is one also defined by what Richebächer calls the "ambiguous term" (2005b, p. 101) of *Junga* [*юнга*], which she tells us is on the one hand a term of endearment, but which in Russian also means cabin boy, or deck hand, in other words someone whom one can boss about. As Lacan said, the hysteric "wants a master she can reign over" (1969–1970, p. 129). If there is masochism as is suggested by her fantasies, it is inevitability accompanied by its companion in arms, sadism. But rather than being a sexualised scene imagined by authors, playwrights, and filmmakers, it is something that, in her analysis, contributes to the further elucidation of her fantasy, of her fundamental fantasm.

Language is there to bewilder itself and others

We have noted that Jung described Spielrein as his test case. A more literal translation of what Jung wrote is the following: "It was, so to speak, my psychoanalytic training case" (McGuire & Sauerländer 1974, p. 110). So, we can put the shoe on the other foot and say that it was Spielrein who taught *him*, that she made Jung an analyst in not allowing her suffering to be reduced to a family romance or Oedipus complex. She came to the Burghölzli by virtue of her symptom, one form of which was her *Abschiedsschmerz*, her pain of parting through her experience of loss and separation. Through her analysis she found a place upon which her transference could alight, at least provisionally. But when she parted from the Burghölzli and separated from Jung at the end of her admission, she was able to partly direct her transference towards her studies, and to her personal reading and writing, as a means of making something more of herself beyond the personal or individual. Her suffering, however, was also a seed of destruction, a destruction of her youth and life, out of which a new life was to germinate.

This seed that she implanted in him is that of the ability for psychoanalysis to go beyond the individual and the Oedipus, towards the *dividual*. This is something Spielrein later develops in her "Destruction as Cause of Becoming" paper, but we discern the early threads already in these personal writings. Through Spielrein's hysterical symptom, the physical complaint was able to become a creative act through the "abreaction"—through the speech that elicits her associations to her complaint. In her theoretical writings, she refers to the "the desire for self-damage, the joy [*Freude*] in pain", as something incomprehensible for the "I-life" or ego, given that it is the ego that is subject to the pleasure principle. Here we also discern the "Freud" by which her writing is already impregnated. She reaches the conclusion that there is no individual, but rather a *dividual* [*dividuum*] (Spielrein 1912c, p. 94). That is, the subject is divided on the one hand between an "I" or ego that is a subject of the pleasure principle, and on the other to a subjection to a "type", or "we", manifested by an incomprehensible suffering and joy, or jouissance. But out of the damage of this pain, there is some play to be had through the joy of speech and writing in the transference.

Spielrein describes this differentiation in the following way: "a tree, growing up out of a seed, is certainly the same with reference to the type, but not the same with reference to the individual" (p. 99). Here, borrowing from Jung's terminology, Spielrein is able to differentiate the *I* from the *type*, the type for her being a transcendent Otherness, not reducible to the family members: to the little others. She goes on to say that:

> words are certainly symbols, which virtually serve to make the personal [*persönliche*] generally human and understandable, i.e. to rob [*berauben*] it of a personal character. The purely personal can never be understood by others, and it does not surprise us when Nietzsche, a man with a powerful I-consciousness, comes to the conclusion: Language is there to bewilder [*verwirren*] itself and others. And yet we feel a relief with expression [*aussprechen*], when we form a type-image at the expense of our I-image, just as the artist enjoys his "sublimation-products" when he creates the typical instead of the individual.
>
> (p. 100)

Spielrein speaks of the structure of analysis, of her own analysis, as submitting oneself to an Otherness beyond the homely roof, beyond the purely personal. Through this, the words no longer succumb to the common meaning of a family story. The words also have a signifying side in which they become bewildering and lose their previous sense, their previous basis. Through such an experience in her analysis she encounters the necessity of enunciation, or speaking out [*aussprechen*]. The expression of the abreaction produces in turn a creativity. Here the creative seed that Spielrein plants is also that of Nietzsche's work that she took up particularly in her "Destruction as Cause of Becoming" paper. She goes on to say that the "most dangerous phase of the reproduction-drive, however, is accompanied by feelings of rapture, since the dissolution [*Auflösung*] takes place within the similar beloved (= in love)" (p. 101). What is dissolved is the imagined inner-similarity that she discerns—the identification—in her transference-love to Jung. This dissolution, or destruction, of the similar that is experienced through the relation to the beloved, and the jouissance that corresponds to this moment of destruction, is precisely what in the next moment allows something new, something different, to be produced out of it: an instant, or instance, of pure becoming.

2

WHAT REALLY IS THIS ABOMINABLE THING CALLED LOVE?

I sit behind bars in the dankest of blocks.
A captive young eagle, the king of the hawks,
My sorry companion here, lifting his wings,
Pecks bloody food by the sill, pecks and flings,

And looks out the window, away, away off,
As if he, with me, fell to thinking one thought.
He summons me now with his look and his cry,
And wants to speak plainly, aloud: "Let us fly!

We're free birds in truth; it is time, brother, time!
To go, where o'er clouds, the high mountains are white,
To go, where the sea realm's as blue as the sky,
To go, where the wind alone wanders … and I!"

Pushkin, The Prisoner *(Douglas 1999, p. 67)*

Spielrein's interest in the literature and the poetry to which she refers is palpable throughout her writing. She remarks that her reading of literature makes her want to be able to write well herself. For instance, in her diary of 1909, she speaks of the expression "jumping into" [*hereinfallen*], literally allowing herself *to fall for/into* situations. She utilises this to write specifically about her own difficulty of acting upon her wishes. On the other hand, this inhibition is also perceived by her as an admirable quality: "Do not act in the first flush of excitement: this principle of mine is a good one" (Spielrein 1983, p. 28). She even begins the next diary entry, that of 21 September 1909, with the following words, "Always later … everything later, and now, too, I say—later" (Carotenuto 1980a, p. 5). In regard to falling into situations, she further writes: "I found the best description of this in Peter Nansen's *The Diary of Julia*. The book gave me great pleasure. What tormented me as I read it was that I cannot write so beautifully myself (I mean in terms of language). My heart is still youthfully fresh, my intellect already very old, and the constant examining, weighing, caution, mistrust" (p. 6). If Spielrein's intellect is old, it is through the lost youth and a life destroyed of which she wrote in her poem of the Burghölzli, and from which she is becoming something else. Though she states modestly that she herself cannot write so beautifully, she nonetheless articulates the aspiration to write well, even to write poetically.

Sabina Spielrein's writings, however, are only now being discovered, and many are only just beginning to be translated, whilst Nansen's *Julie's Diary* (1893) remains all but forgotten. The latter is a fictional work regarding a young woman, one who also aspires to poetry rather than the prosaic life of a married middle-class woman. Like Spielrein she keeps a diary in which she composes some of her own lines of poetry, whilst also citing those of others. The novel recounts how she resists the inevitability of being married to her foster-brother, initiating a covert relation to a man reputed to be a great seducer. Julie first saw this man on the stage playing a sheik who abducts a young woman, and she perceives him as conveying, "so much passion and poetry" (p. 15). On the stage her lover also aspires to "the mysterious and fascinating element which we call poetry" (p. 100). Poetry is also what endeavours to compensate for what falls short—or what cannot be realised—in the sexual relation. Julie's lover is, thus, also driven to write poems, confessing to her that: "You have even made me attempt poetry" (p. 115).

The fictional Julie, and Sabina Spielrein, are "modest girls, to which category I also belong" (Carotenuto 1980a, p. 4). This modesty is also a veil that is drawn over what is immodest, like the veil that Julie wears when meeting clandestinely with her lover. In other words, the veil reveals as much as it conceals: it is the sign of her involvement in this illicit relation. This modesty is, at the same time, a false modesty since the language in which Nansen and Spielrein write is also a veil: the veil of *language* which conceals as much as it reveals. But nowhere in Nansen's novel, in this aspiration to poetry, is there any suggestion that the word *poetry* is a metaphor for sexual relations. Indeed, it is quite the opposite: *poetry* here is the endeavour to make up for the lack of sexual relations, for the failure of the sexual relation. What distinguishes Spielrein from the fictional Julie is precisely Spielrein's difficulty of allowing herself to fall into situations, that is, of permitting herself to act upon what she already knows. Allowing herself to jump into situations is of course not without consequences: there might remain a lovely memory, but there is a drawback, such as the ensuing "disappointment" (p. 6). At this stage, in 1909, Spielrein already knows what must be done, but must come to the point of being able to enact it. What this chapter will address is precisely the question of a disappointment: the dis-appointing of Carl Jung as her analyst, in order to be able to put a term to her analysis through her writing.

In this section of Spielrein's 1909 diary entry, after referring to Nansen's novel, she immediately goes on to write about Jung, noting that her mother says that it is impossible for her and Jung, "my friend", to remain friends once they have given each other their love. Spielrein goes on to articulate her solution, repeated in a number of places during the rest of her time in Zürich, to leave him and love him *à distance*: from a distance. In this chapter we will examine the progression of Spielrein's transference to Jung through her writing, following her discharge from the Burghölzli, up to the time of her ultimate departure both from Jung and Zürich. We propose that there is an equivalence between the style of her loving—her transference-love—and the style of her writing through which she also addresses Jung. Stemming from her analysis, through which we have witnessed the renewal of her writing which had previously ceased, we note that Spielrein's writing becomes marked by her transference. The transference at this stage remains firmly fixed upon her analyst Carl Jung, and it continues to be played out through the analysis, albeit in a written form.

I don't want to write, or rather I do but that it would all be written by itself

Even from her early years, Sabina Spielrein expressed an awareness and a concern, not just for the content of her writing, but also for its style. In February 1900 at the age of 14, upon re-reading an entry that she had made some time previously that described a wedding that she had played out with her brother Jasha, she asks herself, "Did I really think that I could have children from this comedy? No, I had rather only expressed the wish, although I knew that it could not be fulfilled" (Spielrein 2006, p. 32). She then writes of having other "fantasies" at that time, fantasies of herself and her imagined husband having a lovely, easy, and cosy relationship, and of entertaining her parents in their apartment, serving them tea, and giving them their favourite meal for dinner. Children remain part of these fantasies in this family romance in which she locates herself in a limbo, somewhere between her family of origin, and an imagined family of her own. Whether it is the earlier fantasies that are enacted with her siblings, or the later ones that become private and only articulated in her diaries, we discern here some of the same elements of the fantasies that she later articulated and elaborated at the Burghölzli.

Beyond this content, however, she goes on to say, "Even the whole style of that earlier time and all of the comments seem awfully stupid for my age" (Spielrein 2006, p. 32). She remarks upon the style of her writing, in a manner, to be sure, that is modest and even self-critical, but the question regarding the style remains central. Strikingly though, she begins this diary entry of 14 April 1898 by stating, "I don't want to write, or rather I do but that it would all be written by itself" (p. 25). In this entry that contains the first poem that we have from her hand, she expresses a wish for the writing *to write itself*, in which her place as author would thus be veiled. Such a writing would allow something to be transmitted through her, via the writing that writes itself from her. This evokes the position that Lacan attributed to himself in reference to his place as subject: "I am not a poet, but a poem. A poem that is being written, even if it *looks like* a subject" (Lacan 1964, p. viii, my italics). There is an illusion of a subject that writes, but Spielrein articulates the possibility of a writing that writes itself through her.

In this entry she writes of her album, an album like other girls at school had, and in which they wrote love poems. She describes the book that she made into her album as having a coloured pattern on the cover, colours later evoked in a conversation with her brother. Here are the four lines of what she says is such a love poem, a poem that she began, but did not finish, at least at the time of writing in her diary:

> It is getting dark, the stars are shining,
> in the house all is quiet.
> Only a curly haired boy [Junge]
> is crying at the window.
> > *(Spielrein 2006, p. 26)*

This self-styled love poem contains her formula for love, we could say, although the place in which she can be located in the poem remains veiled. It is a poem that pertains to a broken or unrequited love whose object is lost or missing, and which must be mourned.

She writes that she had given as a title of the poem "Wokra", as if this were the boy's name, but then thought about it differently. When her brother Jasha asked her what Wokra meant, she replied that she didn't know what the poem's title was, but that Wokra was the name of a colour. But then this would be the name of a mysterious and unknown colour. Here we can say that through her poem and its enigmatic title, she endeavours to give a name to that which has no name. There is even a slippage in what it is she is naming with this term "Wokra": in one moment it is the title of the poem, in another the boy, and in a third moment it is the name of a colour. We could say that she submits herself to the slippage of the signifier: the name Wokra is not definitively tied to any fixed object or referent and has no inherent meaning. Even in this first poem, there is an endeavour to name something that has no name.

Otherwise it comes from a "poetry"

Spielrein was discharged from the Burghölzli when she was ready to be able to live independently and study. It is not clear what form Spielrein's contact with Jung took following her discharge. Jung was no longer formally her doctor, nor were there any outpatient appointments at that time as the cinema might lead us to believe. Spielrein's diary of the time, moreover, does not suggest that there were any regular meetings between them of any sort, quite the opposite. Nonetheless, she attended his lectures, and she continued to write in transference to him in her journal, a one-sided address that, perhaps even because of this, Spielrein was able to continue to elaborate. Hence her transference and her analysis continued unabated in Jung's physical absence, even if the manner in which it manifested evolved over time. Jung's place as analyst for Spielrein, thus, did not cease with her discharge from the Burghölzli.

What did alter, however, was the position that Jung took up in regard to this transference, as we will examine here. Even whilst still at the Burghölzli, in an often-cited passage, Jung writes in his clinical notes: "Yesterday at my evening visit, pat. was reclining on the sofa in her usual oriental, voluptuous manner, with a sensuous, dreaming expression on her face" (Covington & Wharton 2003a, p. 96). The sensuousness and voluptuousness are surely also in the eye of the beholder, the one who wrote the notes that are not so clinical but infused with a certain erotism of their own. Jung's own desire was something that made Spielrein's analysis and her ability to end it problematical. Spielrein herself later comments upon this, reflecting upon her time at the Burghölzli, "At that period I told him once I had dreamed about his wife, who complained to me about him, saying he was so terribly dictatorial and that life with him was difficult. Even then he did not respond to this like a doctor, but sighed and said he had realized earlier that living together was difficult." (Carotenuto 1980a, p. 101). Right from that early stage, Spielrein was conscious that Jung was not able to remain in the place of the analyst.

What Spielrein wrote in was referred to as a diary, however the entries that are available to us, particularly between the years 1905 and 1908, are not addressed to the diary as a *dear diary*. For the most part they are specifically addressed to Jung: the writing both addresses him, and is dedicated to him, even if he never reads it. She continued, in this manner, to write, we must conclude, in transference to Jung. The transference was manifested in her mode of address to Jung, a mode of address that is marked by the passion of her transference-love. The analysis had not ceased, but, on the contrary, it continued in her articulation of it in her diary and in the direct encounters that did occur with him. The fascination of many biographers and commentators upon Spielrein has been in regard to what we could call the imagined *undressing* of Spielrein with Jung. To follow the line of her transference, however, leads us, on the contrary, to the manner in which she was *addressing* Jung. That is to say that her libidinisation leads along the lines of her transference, not in its short-circuiting into conceptualising this as a love affair.

From 1906, a change took place: from having written her diaries up to that point in Russian, she now wrote in her newly espoused language of German. This represents a departure in her writing: a departure from the language of her fatherland and an adoption of a new language. Whilst still in the Burghölzli, she had told Jung that when she prayed to God as a child, she was answered in the form of an inner voice and it had seemed to her that this voice was speaking to her in German. Gradually the idea had come to her that this voice was that of an angel sent to her because she was an extraordinary person. The latter idea coincided with the content of childhood dreams in which her maternal grandfather blessed her and said, "A great destiny awaits you, my child" (Carotenuto 1980a, p. 80). Curiously this angel returned in her writing since, in the later parts of her diary from Zürich, those contained in Carotenuto's book from 1910 and

1911, she no longer addressed Jung, but rather her "Guardian Spirit" (Carotenuto 1980a, p. 11). She writes that "Relinquishing God proved very difficult for me. What resulted was a void. I kept my 'guardian spirit'" (p. 23). If relinquishing God proved difficult, relinquishing her analyst was no less so. The guardian spirit, though, stands in for the place of the void for Spielrein, a transferential place that becomes vacated through the eventual deposing of Jung from the place of analyst.

She writes, in 1909, of her motivation for using German, at least in her writing: "The German language, which I have adopted for my journal, clearly shows that I want to stay as far away from Russia as possible. Yes, I want to be free! Where shall I go? What shall I do with my life?" (Carotenuto 1980a, p. 35). The freedom of which she writes also involved the departure she found so difficult: a separation, a departure from the language and homeland of her family. To be capable of doing this, however, she had to first finish her analysis and separate from Jung. "Should I see you once more, or was it the last time? Should I speak with you once again or not?" (Spielrein 2006, p. 56), she asks the Jung of her diary in 1906.

In the same era, once again addressing Jung, she writes that she has not yet met any people in whom such moral strength, strength of character, and idealism were united as in him. She writes in a manner that is hyperbolical in her idealisation of Jung, an idealisation that inexorably carries in a veiled form a corresponding denigration of the other, Jung in this instance. The latter is articulated when she thinks, for instance, of her acquaintances, and it consequently puts her into a colossal rage: "It is too much, it is impossible to describe. Good; let's leave that—if one speaks virtually no words, often for days on end, one can go mad" (Spielrein 2006, p. 56). Her proposed solution is to feel useful through physical labour, which is something she had wanted to do in the summer just past, "Through practical physical work in the open air, among capable healthy people, I would be sure of being useful" (p. 57). To be capable and useful is something that she desires for her whole being. She writes in her diary, addressing Jung: "I want to be a capable combination (in your language—'useful' [*nützlich*])" (p. 57). Not only is this period a continuation of her analysis, it is a critical phase of the analysis in which she endeavours to give her symptom a use value. This development then, is coextensive with the period of her adoption of the German language as her language of study, work, and of writing.

There is a question for her of what to do with her life, a life that so far has been determined by her parents and by her symptoms, the vicissitudes of which, under the influence of Carl Jung, led her towards psychiatry and psychoanalysis via her previously chosen field of medicine. Her way of being such a "capable combination", at this stage, passes through her transference to Jung, as well as through reading his works. She wishes to overcome what she perceives as her "weaknesses" in order to be "useful": literally to make something useful out of her symptom. Here in 1906, even though she writes in German, she refers to this tongue—in addressing Jung—as "your language". She has not yet appropriated her language of work, a task that lies ahead of her. This is a task by which she can be useful: an undertaking to be achieved through her studies, through her work and through her writings.

In 1909, Spielrein wrote to Freud, "Four and a half years ago Dr. Jung was my doctor, then he became my friend and finally my 'poet,' i.e., my beloved" (Carotenuto 1980a, p. 93). In other words, over these four and a half years, Jung took up various positions, or roles, for her, but what is striking is the way in which there is a continuity over this time. We perceive that her relation to Jung becomes manifest in these three distinct modalities: my doctor, my friend, and poet. These positions are described by Sabina Spielrein as following on from one to the other. We have already examined in the last chapter how Jung came to be referred to as "my friend", a place prepared by Spielrein long before she met him. But here we examine the evolution that takes place in what we can call three positions in respect of her transference.

The first, that of *my doctor*: that in which the transference was first established in the Burghölzli, in which Jung takes up the authority of the physician for her, a preliminary to his being located in the position of analyst. It is in this position that Jung is able to assume, for Spielrein, the place of the one who knows something about her and her suffering. In other words, Jung in the position of *my doctor* takes up the place of what Lacan called the subject supposed of knowledge. And it is through Spielrein's supposing or attributing a knowledge to him that her transference-love towards him is determined. What is problematical for her is that Jung is not able to sustain the place of analyst. He himself recognises this, writing rhetorically, "Will you forgive me for being as I am? For offending you like this and forgetting my duty as a doctor towards you?" (Covington & Wharton 2003b, p. 37).

As *my friend*, Jung is now placed within the lineage of those whom she loves beyond her parents; he is the one to whom she might be able to lay open her soul, now through the adopted language of German. To open her soul to those outside the family is the first movement from endogamy to exogamy. One medium through which analysis occurs is speech and language, first through speech, or then following her discharge from the Burghölzli by addressing him through writing. In her conception of the unconscious, Spielrein draws upon Jung's notion of the *complex*, but puts forward rather that "symbols" are what allow the complex to come to light. She writes in 1906/1907, "A symbol is nothing else but a lateral association which has only a little of the feeling of the main association" (Spielrein 1983, p. 26). It is by pursuing these lateral associations towards the main association—from the S2 towards the S1 in Lacan's algebra—that the analysis is able to proceed. And even amnesia cannot make disappear, "the whole chain of associations … for symbols remain" (p. 26). These "symbols" are what are able to be used, and to be useful, in the progression of the analysis. The symbol—or signifier—leaves a trace that can be followed through its chains of associations, through the chains of the signifier.

Finally, as *poet*, Jung would no longer personify the position of Otherness; rather the poetry might be able to stand in for what does not function in the sexual relation. It is the very apprehension of this failure that would mark the end of the analysis. Here the poetry no longer has a use value as such, the *person* of the analyst is now contingent and may now be allowed to fall. The poetry has the value of an enjoyment: it allows for a means by which she can continue to live her life beyond the analysis. Spielrein writes: "You see: I do not love you now, that is, not in the ideal sense—no, and this state is much more dreadful than death. Nothing matters to me … Why don't you want to kill me, if you love me even though you know that I am a degenerate? But that does matter to me—and when I can explain that, I shall be free!" (p. 24). Her analysis, then, also works towards such a freedom, but freedom here already becomes connected to death, and later to the destruction or death instinct. It is also in this context that she writes, "In poetry too, we see objects expressed differently and one can say again that one is expressing oneself" (p. 25). Through her writing, she comes to be able to express a differentiation, a singular difference that might allow her to terminate her analysis.

Carotenuto's book contains a section entitled "Letters from Sabina Spielrein to Sigmund Freud". These "letters", though, are described by Carotenuto himself in his Introduction as "written on small folding cards and may actually be rough drafts, since there are a number of crossed-out words and corrections" (1980a, p. xvii). Spielrein also addresses Freud in the third person in some of these "letters". Thus, such a description is hardly consistent with actual letters that were posted and received; indeed, we have no idea regarding exactly what Freud received from Spielrein. The "letters" moreover, like the rest of Carotenuto's excerpts of Spielrein's writings, are highly abridged. Nonetheless, Spielrein writes, "I possess a letter written on 25 November 1905 to Prof. Freud in which Dr. Jung describes me as 'highly intelligent and gifted person of greatest sensitivity'" (p. 101). In the later German edition this date is amended to 25 September 1905, which is still several months following Spielrein's discharge from the Burghölzli. A duplicate of a letter of this latter date—on Burghölzli letterhead—was more recently found in the records of the Burghölzli. The letter was given the following heading: "Report on Miss Spielrein to Professor Freud in Vienna, delivered to Mrs Spielrein for use if the occasion arises" (Minder 2003, p. 138). There is no indication that Freud, however, ever received this letter, which was written a year prior to the beginning of the correspondence between Jung and Freud. Jung mentioned the case to Freud for the first time on 23 October 1906.

Although we are primarily working from Spielrein's writings, it is worthwhile nonetheless to pause upon a remark that Jung makes in his account. In beginning the last paragraph of his Report to Sigmund Freud, Jung declares, "During treatment the patient had the misfortune to fall in love with me" (p. 139). It is extraordinary that Jung, who had read what Freud had written on the topic of the transference, should make such a declaration in this letter nominally addressed to

Freud himself, through Jung's own transference-love towards Freud. For Freud, however, there was ultimately no distinction between love and transference-love. Freud eloquently clarified that the transference, experienced as real, is elicited in the contrived situation of analysis. He wrote that the analyst must recognise that the patient's falling in love is induced by the analytic situation, "and is not to be attributed to the charms of his own person; so that he has no grounds whatever for being proud of such a 'conquest', as it would be called outside analysis" (Freud 1915a, p. 161). Jung, on the contrary, saw himself as a young and handsome man, one who made the mistake of taking Spielrein's love personally.

Freud tries to warn Jung about this in their correspondence on 7 June 1909, following Spielrein's first letter to Freud. In doing so, for the first time he uses the term that has been translated as *countertransference*, but which we can render more immediately and more usefully as *against-transference* [*Gegenübertragung*]. In other words, Freud designates Jung's reaction to Spielrein's transference as something that could be called the transference of the analyst towards the patient, and something that Lacan later designated as the "resistance of the analyst" (1954–1955, p. 228). This transference of the analyst goes against the patient's transference, particularly when acted upon. Freud writes to Jung that he himself had "*a narrow escape*" (McGuire 1974, p. 230, italics in the original). It is by virtue of his *against-transference*, and his propensity to act upon it in response to his own libidinal desires, that Jung places himself as a resistance to Spielrein's transference and thus to her analysis.

Spielrein wrote in her first diary entry following her discharge: "The only thing I have is my freedom and I take care of this last treasure with all my powers. I cannot even bear the smallest criticism of my personality, even if it is in the form of a simple instruction … Only from Jung[a] can I bear everything" (Spielrein 2006, p. 46–47). This last precious possession of hers is also her freedom to love. After she first wrote to Freud in 1909 when her relation to Jung was at an impasse, Freud replied by asking her whether the feelings that had "outlived this close relationship are not best suppressed [*unterdrückt*] and eradicated" (Carotenuto 1980a, p. 114). But Spielrein, perceiving that Freud had thought she was asking him to mediate between herself and Jung, rightly rejects this suggestion. She replies that "*My dearest wish is that I may part from him in love*", and that "for me an infatuation *à distance* would be best. Supressing an emotion will not work for me", she continues, "for if I do it with Dr. Jung, I will never be able to love anyone else" (p. 92, italics in the original). Freud here considered that the transference could be liquidated. For Spielrein, however, the transference is not a misfortune, but rather her last fortune—or treasure—that she does not wish to relinquish, a renunciation that would be equivalent to giving up on her last chance.

Spielrein feared losing her freedom through acceding to the slightest influence from others. She writes of her wish to dedicate herself to others, to the Other: "I am so happy if I manage to help someone or at least give them some pleasure. For me it is so nice to offer something to the children, to bring the patients some delicacies!" (Spielrein 2006, p. 46). For this reason, she feels vulnerable to the effect of others upon her: "The more someone has an influence upon me, the more it puts me into a rage" (p. 47). As we have noted, the exception to this is Jung, but even this has its limits. She is aware, nonetheless, that there are other sides to her complaint: not only can she in fact *not* bear Jung's judgement, but there is also a certain joy in the pain she experiences from it: "This hopeless unbearable pain that he gives me (the Professor as well), is also often pleasant and I am happy, if he gets annoyed I get joy in the pain [*Schadenfreude*] of my humili-ation. If only someone knew how much it hurts me to write these lines!" (p. 47). These themes are tightly woven, that of her resistance to being influenced, her wish to influence the other's opinion of her, the joy in pain, as well as her pains to put her experience into writing: "Always being duty-bound to sympathise and commiserate, and forever doing what I am told … Damn it! Perhaps I express myself too harshly, I cannot put my feelings down in writing" (p. 49). The effort to write of her experiences, nonetheless, continues unabated.

As we have noted, Spielrein maintained a correspondence to Jung and attended his lectures. On 29 August 1906 she refers to a letter that Jung had sent her, as well as a lecture of his that she had just attended. It is in this diary entry that there is the first reference to poetry in relation to Jung. Here she is referring to the effect of Jung's lecture upon her, an effect that seems to over-come her usual discomfort of being with others: "I was completely transfigured, soft and warm towards people. Even when I went home in the most miserable state, I was calm and firm in my decision. … one needs nothing more than this, otherwise it comes from a 'poetry'" (p. 55). Here *poetry* is in inverted commas and is preceded with the indefinite article. We can infer—whether intended or not—that this *poetry* refers literally, in part, to the writing which takes place here in her diary, and in her letters, and which is exactly what we are able to read. The "otherwise" belies the assertion that "one needs nothing more than this": the little that she receives from attending Jung's lectures or whatever other casual contact she has with him at this stage. It is precisely because she wished for and experienced something more than this that she wrote at all. On the contrary, the *poetry* endeavours to make up for what lacks in her relation to Jung: it gives her something more, something that is in excess of the relation to Jung.

This "decision" to which Spielrein refers is one that involved how to deal with the fact that for her Jung was at once not enough, but at the same time too much: too much to bear. Her solution was to leave Zürich: "For these reasons I wanted to leave Zürich for at least three years, only there is no other suitable university. … Should I try to leave you in peace completely for three years?" (p. 55). This is a question that continued to trouble her for her remaining time in Zürich, when, finally, in 1911 she left that town definitively. But analysis cannot be terminated by geographical means: neither just by being discharged from the Burghölzli, nor by leaving Zürich, could she effect a conclusion to the analysis she had begun.

In addressing Jung in her diary once again, Spielrein writes of Fräulein Berg, a young Russian woman who had worked as an assistant doctor at the Burghölzli during Spielrein's admission there, and whom she had befriended. Spielrein questions her own wish to speak with Berg regarding Jung, putting forward definitively—still addressing Jung in her writing—that:

> The less I want to speak about you with her, the more I do so, and then Truth and Poetry [*Dichtung*] get mixed up (pertaining to me rather than you). Regarding what pertains to you—it is only in so far as it becomes written as poetry [*gedichtet*] that it becomes clear, as your actions arise in one moment from your most noble motives, in the next from your most abominable ones, and with this you present yourself on the one hand as a miracle, and on the other as a scoundrel.
>
> *(Spielrein 2006, pp. 57–58)*

For Spielrein, it is only in so far as it becomes written as poetry that the motives behind Jung's actions become clear. But what muddies the water for Spielrein's analysis is precisely her effort to discern Jung's motives in regard to her, what it is that he wants of her: literally his against-transference.

In this passage we also find a reference to Goethe's work *Autobiography: Truth and Fiction [Dichtung]] Relating to My Life* (Goethe 1833). The *Dichtung*, or "Fiction", as we have already noted, in the title may also be translated as *poetry*, the rendering that was favoured by Lacan in his paper "The Individual Myth of the Neurotic, or Poetry and Truth in Neurosis" (Lacan 1953b), but published in English with the reference to Goethe's work in the title suppressed, or rather repressed, as "The Individual's Neurotic Myth" (Lacan 1953a).

Jung, in contrast to Spielrein, suppresses the poetic. On 6 July 1907 he wrote to Freud:

> An hysterical patient told me that a verse from a poem by Lermontov was continually going round in her head. The poem is about a prisoner whose sole companion is a bird in a cage. The prisoner is animated by only *one* wish: sometime in his life, as his noblest deed, to give some creature its freedom. He opens the cage and lets his beloved bird fly out. What is this patient's greatest wish? "Once in my life I would like to help someone to perfect freedom through psychoanalytical treatment." In her dreams she is condensed with me. She admits that actually her greatest wish is to have a child by me who would fulfil all her unfulfillable wishes. For that purpose I would naturally have to let "the bird out" first. (In Swiss-German we say: "has your birdie whistled?")
>
> A pretty little chain, isn't it? Do you know Kaulbach's pornographic picture: Who Buys Love-gods?
>
> *(McGuire 1974, p. 72, italics in the original)*

There is little question that this clinical scenario recounted anecdotally by Jung refers to Sabina Spielrein, to whom he refers as a patient, leaving Freud to falsely infer that she is still in treatment with him. Since the question of her freedom is still very acute in her diaries of the time immediately following her discharge from the Burghölzli, it is likely that this episode occurred during her treatment with Jung during the admission. It is noteworthy that part of her psychoanalysis with Jung consists in the citation of poetry. In other words, poetry is part of the medium by which her analysis unfolds: it is an aspect of her adoption of the psychoanalytic method of free association that for her includes the citation of, and associations to, poetry. As we have noted, Spielrein was still in analysis with Jung, but in the sense that her transference continued to be addressed to him.

In a footnote to this passage in the Freud-Jung letters, Vladimir Nabokov claims that there are two mistakes in Jung's reference to the liberated bird, first that the poem is not by Lermontov but rather by Pushkin, and second that it is absurdly paraphrased. There is indeed no Lermontov poem that corresponds to such a theme. Pushkin's poem was composed in 1822, 2 years after Pushkin was expulsed from St Petersburg:

> *Ptichka* [The Little Bird]
> Away from home, I reverently observe
> The age-old custom of my native land:
> At Eastertide, the bright feast of rebirth,
> I set a little bird free, by my hand.
>
> And thus I have access to consolation;
> For why 'gainst God should I e'er grumble so,
> If on one little being of His creation
> I was allowed its freedom to bestow!
> *(Douglas 1999, p. 67)*

However, what Jung recounts may well be a conflation of *Ptichka* and another poem *The Prisoner* which we have utilised for the epigraph to this chapter and which is concerned with a prisoner behind bars described as a bird. In Jung's recounting of the incident of the poem to Freud, nonetheless, he takes away its poetry, turning it into a type of pornography, in so far as his rendering would allow him to "naturally" realise his own carnal desires for Spielrein. If we accept that one of the poems referred to is *Ptichka*, then in that poem there is no prisoner apart from the bird itself. In any case, what matter here are Jung's comments. It is Jung who is imprisoned by his neurotic inhibitions on the one side, and on the other by his wish to maintain the appearance of a virtuous middle-class married man. In this sense we can also say that in Jung's account, regardless of which poem Spielrein actually referred to in analysis, he makes Spielrein the prisoner of his imagination. Spielrein's stated wish, to which Jung claims she "admits", is to help someone to perfect freedom through psychoanalytic treatment. It is Jung's condensation that perverts this liberty into her freedom to have a sexual relation with her now ex-analyst. We have noted that for Spielrein at the time, the question of freedom is that of an ability to depart from her homeland, her parents, but in the first instance to depart from her analysis. It also encompasses an ability to love, but no particular indication at this point in her analysis of a wish to have sexual relations with Jung. In fact, as we will remark as we proceed, Spielrein's wish to have a child by Jung is something quite separate to her wish for freedom through psychoanalytic treatment.

For Jung, "to let the bird out" would imply that he could have her as his mistress, as if the transference would disappear in the moment of the physical or geographical conclusion of her psychoanalysis. That is to say, Jung's reception of the poem cited by his patient is taken by him personally as the possibility of his own liberation. The prisoner that Jung has added into the anecdote then is none other than himself. Jung treats the poetry that Spielrein cites in a manner that distorts it into his own wish fulfilment. In doing this, he betrays the poietic possibilities of his patient, and thus the promotion of Spielrein's coming into being through her analysis. On the contrary, he appropriates it for himself, reducing it however into something banal: the imagined freedom to be able to realise a sexual encounter with his patient.

The picture by Kaulbach referred to by Jung was inspired by a poem of the same name by Goethe, also on the theme of birds. Despite the fact that in Jung's personal family mythology, Goethe is Carl Jung's great-grandfather (McGuire 1974, p. 211), Jung does not refer at all to the poem, but only to the "pornographic picture" that he describes as "Winged phalli looking like cocks, getting up to all sorts of monkey-tricks with the girls" (p. 73). Goethe's poem describes a foreign salesman of birds, hawking his wares at a market. Here is the first stanza:

> Of all the beauteous wares
> Exposed for sale at fairs,
> None will give more delight
> Than those that to your sight
> From distant lands we bring.
> Oh, hark to what we sing!
> These beauteous birds behold,
> They're brought here to be sold.
> *(Goethe 1795)*

Like the character in *Ptichka* by Pushkin, the bird hawker comes from a distant land. He has something of beauty on offer, something that offers the promise of love. Jung favours the sexualised interpretation of the poem by Kaulbach, the image of the phalli getting up to monkey tricks with all the girls, the image of his wished-for sexual freedom. For Spielrein—at least as recounted by Jung—it is something different. As we have seen, she places herself both as the bird still in analysis who seeks her freedom to depart, but also as analyst: as vendor of the possibility of freedom for another through psychoanalytic treatment.

The desolation is once again limitless

The notebook of Spielrein that was first published as *Unedited Extracts from a Diary* (1906/1907?) in 1983 is described by its editors as a diary written in three parts, probably at different times. Once again, however, it addresses itself to Jung even though he is not named in it as such. It starts out as a postulated dialectic between two speakers, but then continues as a nascent theoretical discourse upon psychoanalysis based upon the experience of her own analysis, but also foreshadowing her paper "Destruction as Cause of Becoming" (1912a). Finally, it ends on a note of despair, or "desolation": that of not being able to realise the love for her analyst, nor the fruits of this love.

The most striking aspect of this diary is its elaboration of the notion of difference: the different positions of a lover and the beloved, the various means by which difference can be produced by the effect of analysis, and ultimately the irreconcilable difference, or subjective disparity, between analysand and analyst, between herself and Jung. Through this piece of writing, she also differentiates herself from him theoretically. Furthermore, she gives voice to the enigma that she discerns in the analysis, as well as concluding with the impasse that will lead her to end the analysis.

Spielrein begins though, by differentiating between the two speakers. The first of these is no doubt herself, as she says that this speaker "reaches the summit of his art only when he gives himself up to passion". The second speaker, on the other hand, is clearly Jung, who "is at the peak of his power when he resists the impetuosity of his emotions and, as it were, makes fun of them: it is only then that his spirit comes right out of its hiding place, a logical spirit, derisive, playful but nonetheless terrible" (Spielrein 1983, p. 16). It is in this diary that Spielrein for the first time refers to Nietzsche, and we perceive immediately, in these two positions, those that Nietzsche attributes to Dionysus and to Apollo. Spielrein—and this is sustained through the thrust of this diary—places herself alongside the former, and her theoretical direction is also determined by this position. Jung, on the other hand in his terrifying logic, stands in for the implacable Apollo. Let us allow Nietzsche to elaborate upon these positions: "the name 'Apollonian' designates the enraptured lingering before the world of *beautiful illusion* as a redemption from *becoming*. Dionysos, on the other hand, stands namesake for a becoming which is actively grasped, subjectively experienced, as a raging voluptuousness of the creative man who also knows the wrath of the destroyer" (Nietzsche 1885–1886, pp. 80–81, italics in the original). We hear in the latter the direction that Spielrein's theoretical elaboration will assume in its ability to encompass and theorise the jouissance that lies beyond the pleasure principle.

It is towards the beginning of this diary that Spielrein poses the fundamental question concerning the transference: "What really is this abominable thing called love?" (Spielrein 1983, p. 17), a love that she differentiates out from sexual attraction. She notes, once again addressing her analyst, "Two years ago you yourself asked me a question that you considered essential for determining my love for you: you asked me, 'Do you have many points in common with me?' My answer was an angry 'no'" (p. 17). For Spielrein, love is determined through difference, not superficial commonalities or affinities. Or, if it is a question of similarities, it is because "one loves one's ideal in the other" (p. 22). This is true, she puts forward, in the sexual affection between a patient and doctor who are in a psychic relationship. However, it is not the sexual affection that is primary: "One goes to the doctor because one needs to be free of a complex, one confides in a doctor because one knows, or notices, his interest and sympathy; the interest corresponds to understanding, that is, to possession of the same complex. Hence the sexual feeling" (p. 23). At this time, for Spielrein, the transference-love is determined by the supposition that the analyst understands by virtue of having the same complex. Although she speaks theoretically, she also makes it clear that she is referring to herself, which she posits was also the case for Galileo, "Galileo, whose words 'And yet, it turns', are believed to express the individual's life" (pp. 19–20), that is they pertain to Galileo himself. For Spielrein, life is something that is in movement: "it turns", it is not limited to the stasis of a "complex".

But the difficulty for Spielrein is that Jung is not able to sustain the place as analyst, giving her cause to believe that it is not just an analysis that is in question. At the end of the second section of this notebook, she lucidly outlines two separate things that she says must be taken into consideration during the treatment of hysteria—here surely the treatment of herself as hysteric by her analyst Carl Jung:

> *N. 1* Make it possible for the psycho-sexual component of the ego to transform itself (most of the time or always?) (whether this be by means of art or a simple reaction—as you wish); in this way that component is constantly weakened like a phonograph record going round and round. What's more, the feeling brings about corresponding innervations and the psyche does not exhaust itself by resisting them.

> *N. 2* Might it not be necessary perhaps, more often than it seems, to prevent as much as possible the excitement of a psycho-sexual expression by deflecting the feeling towards other components of the ego? It is dangerous to attach too much importance to the complex, to feed it with new representations; only an artist can live in this way, and even for him there are certain limits which are beyond his strength: in other words the rest of the psyche ends up being hostile to the complex.

> *(pp. 27–28)*

Due to Jung not being able to remain in the position of analyst, Spielrein was being taxed beyond her limits. Indeed, she concludes this section by writing, "The desolation is once again limitless. Will I be able to come out of it safe and sound?" (p. 28).

Spielrein's perception of Jung is confirmed by his letters from around this time. While we do not have letters from this exact period, he writes the following to her on 30 June 1908:

> I must tell you briefly what a lovely impression I received of you today. Your image has changed completely, and I want to tell you how very, very happy it makes me to be able to hope that there are people who are like me, people in whom living and thinking are one; ... You can't believe how much it means to me to hope I can love someone whom I do not have to condemn, and who does not condemn herself either, to suffocate in the banality of habit.
>
> *(Covington & Wharton 2003b, p. 33)*

But Jung's position is one that insists upon sameness; once again it makes the analysis untenable. The brief third part of Spielrein's diaries of 1906/1907 seems to follow a discussion with Jung in which the question of a child has arisen. She writes:

> I am so tired of turning things over and over in my mind continuously! *Should I write this or should I not, as I do not want to read this letter again? And yet, I had to write it! For I cannot bear you to speak to me in this way: either we decide that we no longer discuss such areas, or if we do discuss them, I must respond to your remarks as I see fit.* My wishes cannot of course change as a result of one conversation, because there needs to be a long period of conscious reflection for it to be effective. But my wish has never been formulated thus: 'I want to bear you a child'; for this means first of all: 'I agree to give you up for good'... I have never believed that my son was destined for me; I know too well that he will have his own life to live and that he belongs to me as little as I do to my parents. It is then that I realize how alone I am. But one must not think of oneself; the dark powers of destiny use us as they see fit, without worrying the least about the person's own wishes.
>
> *(Spielrein 1983, p. 30, italics in the original)*

For Spielrein, writing becomes an imperative for what is unable to be spoken to her analyst: for her there needs to be *Wahrheit und Dichtung*, truth and poetry. Her truth can only be written in the poetry of difference, not the sameness of an agreement or an identification with the other. The question or idea of bearing Jung a child is far more complex than Jung had put forward to Freud. As she puts forward, the very idea of having a child is already that of the separation from that child, for the child, like the bird, to attain its own freedom. Such a freedom can only come at the cost of loss and loneliness. In her later diaries she writes of seeking some respite for the *Weltschmerz*, the world weariness or literally the world pain. But the *Weltschmerz* is at the same time the *Abschiedsschmerz*, the pain of parting which she has to realise in her analysis in order to put an end to it.

Abschied

At the end of her very last diary entry in Zürich just prior to her parting from Jung, a dream returns Sabina Spielrein to typhus, the illness responsible for her sister's death. We recall that she had attributed the death of Emilia to the beginning of her "illness". In this dream, now a doctor, Spielrein effectively makes a diagnosis of typhus in a young child, a little boy whom she describes as a child analogous to her little brother. The now long-departed Emilia returns in Sabina Spielrein's sleep, through the signifier *typhus* in the current context of another *Abschiedsschmerz*, the pain of departing from her analyst and her analysis:

> The action takes place in the mental hospital. The building has three (instead of two) floors. The people involved are: Father, Mother, my older brother (who, as has been mentioned, always represents my friend [i.e. Jung] in my dreams), my little brother, and another, analogous child. The little brother comes down with spotted fever. ... You become terrified of contagion and of death and can simply not understand why your parents, who are always so kind, are unwilling to make sacrifices themselves in this case, instead exposing their children to this risk. When the little one needs help, you go in with your brother. You reproach the brother with being very superficial in his diagnosis: why in the world should the little one have spotted fever when he has neither a fever nor a rash? Thereupon your brother shows you that the little boy has a swollen abdomen, as in *Typhus abdominalis*, and also several blue spots on his back. You are still a little suspicious.
>
> (Carotenuto 1980a, p. 40)

This dream marks Spielrein's coming out of isolation, out of the quarantine imposed by what we are proposing was her analysis: that is, through all that transpired in her transference-love towards her analyst and her efforts to deal with this, addressed both directly to Jung, as well as through the medium of her writing: there remains the excess, or the surplus, of the analysis. In what we can then describe as the final dream of her psychoanalysis, the action takes place in the very location in which her transference began: the Burghölzli. Although she begins her account in the first person, she is soon addressed in the second person by the dream: "You become terrified", etc. Her reference to Jung and his central place for her in the dream indicate that this dream carries the mark of the transference. It also involves the family, and in particular, a distancing from them. In the dream, she takes up a different place to them, one in which their knowledge, wisdom, and sacrifice for their children is put into question. Now as a qualified doctor within the dream and without, Spielrein takes up the place of parent in their stead, in the place where the Other no longer has all the answers.

   On another level, the knowledge of her analyst is also questioned and designated as superficial. He no longer has the knowledge that she is seeking. She is now on her own, able to let go of Jung and of Zürich. The knowledge that

Spielrein supposed Jung to have is discredited. The account of the dream, however, terminates with her suspicions: not all is able to be understood, an enigma remains, the diagnosis is not clear. There are questions that have to be pursued, but henceforth on her own. The analysis must be pursued in Jung's absence—literally *ab-sense*, away from sense—that is, through her writing beyond Jung's physical presence.

She is now parting from her analyst, not without the *Abschiedsschmerz*, or pain of parting, and entering the world as a doctor herself, a psychiatrist, and towards becoming a psychoanalyst. Her departure from her analyst was made possible through the means of her writing, a writing she pursued by virtue of the failure of her analyst to function in that place for her. She is now also a published author, a poet of sorts through the very style of her writing, and it is through her writing that she will be recognised by others as an analyst. Indeed, in her next diary entry, in Vienna, she writes, "Now I have actually become a member of the Psychoanalytic Society, on the strength of my dissertation" (Carotenuto 1980a, p. 41).

3

I WROTE A POEM TO YOU

> You, ancient tools, I've never used
> You're here because my father used you,
> Ancient scroll, you've darkened too,
> From smoking candles burned above you.
> Better the little I had was squandered,
> Than sweat here under its puny weight!
> What from your father you've inherited,
> You must earn again, to own it straight.
> What's never used, leaves us overburdened,
> But we can use what the Moment may create!
>
> *Goethe,* Faust Part I *(1808)*

Through her writings, Sabina Spielrein was able to effect an ending—not a definitive *end*, but nonetheless an *ending*: a gerund rather than a noun—to her analysis with Carl Jung. In the first instance this took the form of the writing of her diary entries directed, through her transference, to Jung. Given Jung's inability to bear her transference and remain in the place of analyst, Spielrein wrote to Freud in 1909 requesting to speak with him, for him to listen to her. This was also the moment of her movement towards the place of psychoanalyst. This moment that we are here elaborating as the ending of her analysis also corresponded with other major changes in her life. It ultimately allowed her to physically move away from Jung and Zürich to begin her own independent professional life, to decide to not accede to her parents' request to return to Russia, to distance herself from the religion of her parents, and to continue to move closer—geographically, theoretically, and personally—to Sigmund Freud.

Spielrein had met an impasse not just within her analysis, but also in her love relationship with Jung. From psychoanalysis, however, we must construe both situations in terms of her transference-love to Carl Jung: to differentiate *love* from *transference* would be artificial. Her effort to extract herself from the impasse in her analysis—an impasse that was enacted transferentially with Jung and which was coextensive with the other impasses in her life—led to her writing to Freud. The impasse was also exacerbated by Jung's enactment of his own transference. When Freud received Spielrein's first letter, he immediately wrote to Jung about it. In reply, Jung made a partial admission to Freud of what had transpired, namely that he had prolonged a supportive "relationship" with her, and devoted "a large measure of friendship to her". However, he claimed in his own defence that Spielrein was "of course, systematically planning my seduction" (McGuire 1974, p. 228). Freud responded in a consolatory manner, more indulgent than with other colleagues, since Jung was still his Crown Prince, the Christian who was to take psychoanalysis out of the Jewish ghetto into which Freud felt it had become lodged. As we have noted, it is in this context that Freud first used the term *Gegenübertragung*, remarking that Jung was acting in response to his own transference to Spielrein, his *against-transference*, stepping out of his place as analyst.

In this and the following chapter we will endeavour to discern how Spielrein was able to put a term to her analysis through her writings. We will examine her letters to Freud and her diaries from this period onwards. In the following chapter we will also consider her medical thesis in the field of psychiatry. In her letters to Freud and her diaries of this era, as well as in her thesis, the effects of her analysis and her newfound ability to submit herself to the play of language, as well as her burgeoning theorisation in psychoanalysis, became evident.

In examining her personal writings, particularly her diaries, from the time that followed the beginning of her analysis, we note that they are imbued with the method of psychoanalysis. It is notable that she commenced this mode of writing during her time at the Burghölzli. Her singular style became even more apparent in her letters to Freud and the diaries from this period onwards. In these writings, she allows herself to be subject to the play of the words she employs. This method is indeed derived from the Freudian method of free association, explicitly detailed in Freud's early works on the unconscious. Spielrein also used associations through the assonance of the signifier, including that of her own name, which she also recounts in her writings. It is what Lacan later called "the play of the signifier", a theorisation stemming from de Saussure's structural linguistics. Curiously, Spielrein would later be exposed to this theoretical development in Geneva—albeit in distorted form—through de Saussure's colleague and one of the editors of the *Course in General Linguistics* that is attributed to Ferdinand de Saussure (1916), Charles Bally.

We have already denoted the place that poetry had in the writings of Sabina Spielrein. There are a small number of poems, fragments of poems, and songs from Spielrein's own hand that are to be found in her personal writings. In her diaries she also refers to writing other poems and songs, to which we do not have access. In addition, these diaries contain brief fragments of poetry from other authors, corresponding to the content of her life, analysis, and work. Here we will further elaborate upon the way in which, through her personal writing, Sabina Spielrein was able to take the first steps towards finishing her analysis.

He has ceased to figure as a doctor in my life

Spielrein first wrote to Freud on 30 May 1909, asking him "to grant me a brief audience" (Carotenuto 1980a, p. 91), in other words for Freud to listen to her, to hear her out. Freud, perhaps in part to gain some time, replied to Spielrein suggesting that she, "let me know in writing what it is all about" (p. 113). Spielrein took this invitation seriously, and write she did. In Carotenuto, however, only the first two letters to Freud are actually written in the form of letters. What are accessible to us of the rest of her "letters" are abridged notes that resemble, in their style, her diary entries. Nonetheless, we will refer to them here, as Carotenuto does, as letters.

Her diary entries though, following her discharge from the Burghölzli, were addressed to Carl Jung, even if they were not intended for him to read. At the time the only direct contact that Sabina Spielrein had with him was in attending his lectures. Here in these letters, however, there is a change of address: it is no longer Jung who is addressed. Her writings are directed in the first instance towards Freud whom she repeatedly mentions: "I wanted to write to Prof. Freud again" (p.102). Her letter of 4 June 1909 seems to differentiate the place Freud takes up from that of Jung, with whom she repeatedly says she wants to have a friendship *à distance*, differentiating her new contact with Freud as that of a discourse, "a conversation: "'All's well that ends well.' A conversation *à distance* is difficult, and since I am dealing with 'Freud' …" (p. 103, italics in the original). Through her letters she addresses Freud. In her writing, moreover, she addresses the writings of Shakespeare, Nietzsche, Goethe, and other *belles lettres*.

She refers specifically to her writing, and the mode in which she writes to Freud, as a means through which she might be able to separate from Jung:

> For two days I raged and wept; in between I wrote a letter to Dr. Jung, which he has not yet received, in which I described my state to him. I also realized that we must separate, and could not bear the thought that this had to happen after such a horrible scene. At that time Prof. Freud first appeared to me as an angel of deliverance. I wrote a poem to you.
>
> *(p. 97)*

And in her entry of the following day she notes her difficulty in writing of this: "I cannot get a single word out, but from all sides all sorts of poems thrust themselves upon me" (p. 99). Spielrein's accession to the possibility of separation appears through the means of writing, and specifically through her recourse to poetry.

She refers to the means by which Freud manifests himself to her in her transference: as an "angel of deliverance", literally an angel who, like a midwife, delivers her from her analysis. We have already seen how this angel had a childhood antecedent connected with dreams of her grandfather. And as we shall see, this position of Guardian Angel, assumed transiently by Freud, manifests itself in the writing as a more impersonal Guardian Angel and Guardian Spirit in the diary entries that follow this redirection of her transference. This angel of deliverance, this new addressee stripped of a reference to a particular person or deity, will give rise to yet others. She begins her second note in the following way: "I knew I would be unable to sleep. Now, Wanderer, the moment comes, 'you must stay cool and clear'" (p. 93). Here she addresses an instance that she nominates as "Wanderer", a figure from Germanic mythology, and which is of course a preoccupation of German writers and scholars. The Wanderer is also manifested by the character of Wotan from *das Rheingold* and the other operas of Wagner's *Ring Cycle*, the love of which Sabina Spielrein shared with Carl Jung.

She also begins a diary entry from a few months later with this same reference (p. 11), but here adding another line in rhyming verse, the source of which is not given in Carotenuto. In fact, she is citing Friedrich Nietzsche's poem *The Wanderer* from his *Prelude in German Rhymes* to *The Gay Science*:

> "No more path! Abyss all around and deathly chill!"
> That's what you wanted! To leave the path was your will!
> Now, Wanderer, it's time! Eyes cool and clear!
> You will be lost, if you believe—in fear.
>
> *(Nietzsche 1882, translated for this edition)*

In his poem, the Wanderer is the one who strays beyond the end of the path; he goes out into the wilds beyond the beaten track. In order to pursue his will, he must confront the abyss, or the chasms, and the silence of death—the danger of the *unbeknownst*: the unconscious or *Unbewusst*—to continue to seek out the object of his desire.

In the diary entry of 28 August 1909, Spielrein gives an indication of the significance of this Wanderer to her. At this stage she is reassessing her ideals, and writes the following:

> And what about my old ideal of wandering through the world like the ancient Greek philosophers, surrounded by a crowd of disciples, teaching them outdoors, in harmony with nature? I would want to teach them genuine love for everything in nature, not forced sentimentality. My imagination painted pictures for me of how we would sit at sunset among the rustling golden ears of grain and after our day's labors enjoy a modest supper of bread and cucumbers. "No pomp ... no divine splendor, let love alone remain blissful in joy and sorrow," I would say

now, be it tumultuous, be it tender, be it calm and broad, but true, great love is what I would wish to teach my disciples. Is there Someone who knows this?

(Carotenuto 1980a, p. 5)

This true great love is her transference-love, the love that was awakened with Carl Jung in her analysis. Jung, however, made the mistake of responding to it, of thinking that he could take his own person as the object of that love, to be that *Someone*. In other words, Jung was unable to sustain the place of recognising that the object of that transference is a wandering or errant object, one that wanders through the world but cannot be pinned down to a particular place or a particular person. The question here for Spielrein is that of where to place her love, what to do with her love, given that this transference-love reaches a dead end in the romantic relationship with Jung. The "true great love" of her transference was one that she had to come to direct elsewhere, to be able to "teach" and elaborate it through her theoretical writings.

In the Athens of Ancient Greece, Socrates was the one who was referred to as *atopía* or atopic, that is, literally of not having a fixed place, or being unable to be placed anywhere, in any pre-existing philosophical doctrine. It is also a reference, as Spielrein makes, of Socrates being a wanderer, being errant, and not sleeping in any fixed place. This is also what Lacan refers to as the *atopia* of desire: something that always lies outside, unable to be situated or classified. It lies beyond the end of the path, to refer back to Nietzsche's poem. In her question, "Is there Someone who knows this?", a personification that is not in the original German which is, "is there One [*Einen*] that knows this", she prefigures the question of knowledge that is fundamental in the transference, and which was later elaborated by Jacques Lacan. For Lacan the transference is established by the analysand placing the analyst in the position of Subject Supposed of Knowledge, that is, in attributing to the analyst a knowledge regarding the analysand, literally as *one that knows*. In other words, this position is only supposed, it cannot be embodied by one person, or a "Someone" as substantialised by the translation in Carotenuto, but rather only provisionally by One [*Einen*].

But the fact that this is articulated as a question foreshadows the fact that such a One is missing: it is absent or faulty. The construction of the Subject Supposed of Knowledge is one that the analysand must allow to fall at the end of the analysis. This is surely the point that Spielrein came to in her analysis in confronting the failing of her analyst, and his inability to occupy this place of analyst for her. The One that occupies the place of analyst is also the object of the analysand's love—transference-love for Freud: it is the name of the place in which she invests her love. The analyst occupies the place of the semblance of the object, given that he or she cannot be the object of desire for the analysand, but only provisionally a semblant in that place. This was precisely one of Spielrein's difficulties, since Jung did not take Spielrein's love as transference-love but imagined that he occupied the place of the object of her love. It is in this way that Jung abandoned the place of analyst and made himself Spielrein's lover. Nonetheless, we can propose that it was in Jung's vacating the place of analyst that Spielrein was ultimately able to recognise that what she had erected in that place was something that was not substantial, it was not a place of flesh and blood.

In the aforementioned diary entry, Spielrein gives another citation, but again one not referenced in Carotenuto: "No pomp ... no divine splendor, let love alone remain blissful in joy and sorrow". It derives from the fourth of Wagner's operas in the *Ring Cycle, Die Götterdämmerung*. This is a passage that Spielrein would cite more fully in the third part of her paper "Destruction as Cause of Becoming" but the passage that she refers to here is missing from modern versions of the opera. It is its penultimate passage, just before Brünhilde throws herself on Siegfried's funeral pyre to join him in death. For Spielrein, this final song is a victorious song to love, as Brünhilde merges into Siegfried. She writes, in accordance with her thesis of that paper, that: "For Wagner, death is often nothing other than the destroying components of the instinct of coming into being" (Spielrein 1912b, p. 178). The ultimate bliss of the merging of the two lovers, Brünhilde and Siegfried, is the radical eradication of the sorrow of their separateness, in order to accede to the joy of creating something new. We must stress of course that this eradication of separation is both logically and practicably impossible, given that the lovers are separated by death.

The "joy and sorrow" here are two dimensions of bliss: the two dimensions of jouissance or enjoyment that she would come to elaborate in her paper of 1912 "Destruction as Cause of Becoming". There we can read the way in which the prevalence of sorrow and pain of destruction can tip over towards the joy of becoming through the means of the transference. Destruction here must be read broadly as the violence by which a certain image—or beautiful illusion—such as the preeminence of the ego, is destroyed. This destruction is then able to give rise to other possibilities, such as the coming into being of the work of the unconscious in the production of a creative act, one that produces a new act of speech, a poem, or a work of art.

The themes developed in that later theoretical paper are presaged already in Spielrein's letters to Freud. She writes, in particular, of her struggle to preserve the ideal that Jung represents for her, and her perception of Jung's failure to do so for her. This ideal personage that she had constructed in this way was based on the ideal in which she had endeavoured to locate him, through an imaginary identification. She can only maintain him as her "beloved" in so far as she can find affinities or "similarities" (p. 92). She notes, for instance, how she speaks to Jung about how "Wagner's music is 'plastic music'. I liked *Das Rheingold* best, I say. Dr Jung's eyes fill with tears. 'I will show you, I am just writing the very same thing'" (p. 100). Jung also says to her after their work together, "Minds such as yours help science. You must become a psychiatrist" (p. 101).

In other words, for Jung, she must become like him. But effectively what she writes about to Freud is the impossibility of sustaining these identifications, thus underlining the difference that she encounters.

She acknowledges, moreover, that the account of Jung that she is present-ing to Freud is a partial one in which she keeps Jung's words from his letters to herself, words in which he calls her "anything but a friend or says anything sentimental to me" (p. 102). Here again we hear this division of friend, doctor, and beloved: she endeavours to keep the beloved alive, but her complaint is still that he does not sustain the place as doctor. This ideal of Jung as lover is some-thing she holds onto by citing some lines that Carotenuto tells us come from a German folk song:

> No ashes, no coals
> can have such a glow
> As a secretive love
> of which no one must know.
> *(p. 102)*

This is a secret whose function is to preserve her ideal. And yet the letters to Freud are at the same time the breaking of this secret, the breaking or destruction of the ideal in which she remains trapped.

Jung, however, does not sustain the place of the "doctor", that is, that of the analyst: "At that time Dr. Jung also failed to understand a number of things". Furthermore, "he did not respond … like a doctor" (p. 101). Following one of the letters to Jung by Sabina Spielrein's mother, Jung wrote back to her and jus-tified, in an officious manner, his abandoning of the place of analyst: "I moved from being her doctor to being her friend when I ceased to push my own feel-ings into the background. I could drop my role as doctor the more easily because I did not feel professionally obligated, for I never charged a fee". This was a cynical response from Jung who, besides his failure to sustain the ethics of psy-choanalysis, was in any case not entitled to receive fees while a psychiatrist at the Burghölzli. Subsequently, in his private practice at his new home in Küsnacht since May 1909, Jung proposed that Spielrein's mother pay a fee in order for him to resume his place as analyst, "My fee is 10 francs per consultation" (p. 94). In response to Jung's correspondence with her mother, Spielrein concludes that "He has ceased to figure as a doctor in my life" (p. 95). It was only at this later stage, and again contrary to what is portrayed in the cinema, that Spielrein had regular weekly sessions with him, sessions which nonetheless were utilised for editing her thesis, and later her "Destruction as Cause of Becoming" paper, as well as for further moments of intimacy, in which Jung dropped his "role as doctor" despite receiving a fee.

A little later on when Spielrein had moved to Vienna, she was offended when Jung acknowledged, officiously once again having received the documents she had sent him—both the revised thesis for publication, as well as the new "Destruction as Cause of Becoming" paper—with the briefest of notes:

> Küssnacht [*sic*] 5 February 1912
>
> Dear Colleague:
>
> I hereby confirm the receipt of both of your manuscripts. With best wishes, Yours sincerely, Dr. Jung.
>
> *(p. 42)*

Jung signed off with his letters "Dr.", but it is precisely because, in the transference, Spielrein had been able to address herself to this place of the doctor that she had been able to sustain a transference. Through the means of addressing Jung as doctor, she addressed the place of love itself, a love directed beyond the immediacy of a particular object. That is, despite her protest, the letters "Dr." had been necessary for her to be able to sustain a transference that did not simply become reduced to a love affair. Effectively, she had called Jung back to his place as psychoanalyst, a place that following Spielrein we can locate somewhere between "Dr.", lover, and poet. That is, when Spielrein writes Dr. Jung was my doctor, then my friend, and finally my poet, there is something artificial and schematic about these categories. We might say that it is precisely when the categories become disturbed in the analysis—which is quite the opposite of an acting out of the analyst's *against-transference* since it requires the analyst remaining in his place—that Jung might have been able to accede to the place of analyst for Spielrein. This is what we have referred to as a modality of incest that comes into play in the encroachment and blurring of the places of analyst, lover, and poet.

In her letters to Freud she referred to Jung, as he now referred to himself, no longer as "my friend" but as "Dr. Jung". In her diary she reacted to Jung's curt note by reference to a poem: "'Just another …'—'No, let's wait a bit,' just as it says in my poem" (p. 42), her fallback position of deferring or suppressing her impulses to finally break from him. On her side, she was moving on the one hand towards finishing her studies of medicine, and on the other towards being recognised as an analyst, that is, being able to accept the transference of others without reducing the analytic relation to just a twosome. That is, she was earning her own letters through the poetry of her writing that permitted her to address her love to a name and a place beyond those situated in the immediacy of the transference-love.

Following her first letter in which she made the request for an audience with Freud, she wrote in regard to Jung: "One sentence rings constantly in my ears: 'Judith loved Holofernes and had to murder him'" (p. 92). In her transference, she loved Jung to death. Her only way out of the dilemma that her analysis had become was to kill Jung, a symbolic death by which she could be free of the collapsed ideal that Jung represented for her. Here she writes to Freud of herself in the third person as Jung's beloved who had been self-respecting in her love, "until the last three weeks, when she suddenly lost her belief in everything noble in the world" (p. 106). She no longer respects her "self", or ego, she has once again lost the first-person pronoun by which she might denote herself as individual. That is, the loss of the ideal in Jung is coextensive with the loss of this part of her "self". We see the two sides of this destruction in her comment to Freud: "My ideal personage was completely destroyed; I was done for" (p. 97). The destruction of the ideal is coextensive with the destruction of the ego or I. It is exactly at the point of writing in her letters to Freud that she recounts how she loses her bearings, and that her symbolic murder of Jung emerges from the real:

> I stood there with a knife in my left hand and do not know what I intended to do with it; he grabbed my hand, I resisted; I have no idea what happened then. Suddenly he went very pale and clapped his hand to his left temple: "You struck me!" … And sure enough … my left hand and forearm were covered with blood. "That's not my blood, that's his: I murdered him!"

She had, at least in her account, murdered her Holofernes. As a consequence of this she drew the following conclusion: "I also realized that we must separate [*trennen*]" (p. 97). But the work of separation was yet to be done.

For you I did battle with the raging waves

The usual interpretation of what Spielrein refers to as "poetry" as sexual relations between herself and Jung, not only reduces the transference to a love affair, but it also insists upon the materialisation of Spielrein's transference as being addressed to a particular person. The transference, however, can only be transiently referred to the person of the analyst. This person of the analyst is only contingent to the transference, not necessary. And ultimately the transference, for the analysis to be able to end, must be referred to something outside the person of the analyst, something that has no name. The transference then is a letter—a love letter—written to an *atopia* beyond the place where "the path ends", to refer back to Spielrein's invocation of Nietzsche, to a place of "Abyss all around and deathly chill". A story or a history carries a predetermined meaning, but with Spielrein we can propose that poetry is the creation of a mode of address that carries no fixed meaning, directed to no specified addressee. In accordance with Spielrein's developing thesis of her "Destruction as Cause of Becoming" paper, love then is the means by which destruction, and hence becoming, is able to be effected.

But for this to occur, she had to first be in analysis, to allow herself to be subjected to the play of the signifier. But this analysis does not just take place in her sessions with Jung at the Burghölzli: it continues in her writing of her diaries and her letters, through her transference-love to Jung. We hear this in her letters to Freud, through the play on the signifier rob [*rauben*], robber [*Räuber*], and Rauber, the author of her anatomy textbook:

> One time I go to bed with Rauber's *Anatomy* and first quickly write a let-ter to Dr. Jung; I do not want anything that might deprive [*rauben*] me of him as my deeply respected friend, doctor, beloved; I want to be his abso-lutely unselfish friend, etc. Now I place the letter in Rauber's book and tell myself indignantly, "I don't want to be the robber [*Räuber*]!" "No," my other component replies, "you won't be the robber, he will!"
>
> *(pp. 108–109)*

But it is not just a question of a robbery that is in play in her writing. She also notes how she encounters her given name in Jung's speech:

> He told me he was going to the theatre, and once more something made me ask what play was being performed. He laughed: "A silly story: *The Rape of the Sabine Women*" [*Raub der Sabinerinen*] (My name is Sabina). Naturally I was taken aback, and he continued, "The director did not realize there was a people by that name, and in order to make the play sound more appealing, he called it *The Rape of the Sabinettes.*" [*Raub der Sabincherinen*]'.
>
> *(p. 109)*

We hear once again the robbery or *Raub* repeated in what she writes, a signifier that insists in her writing. This is a robbery literally effected in that moment by Jung, in so far as he robs her of the weight of her name, since he is not able to hear the name Sabina in what he says to her, let alone the impact of the title of the play: *The Rape of the Sabines.*

This name also evokes for us the reference that Lacan makes, in his Overture to his *Écrits*, to Pope's satirical poem *The Rape of the Lock*, the title of which Lacan writes that "thanks to parody [it] ravishes—from the epic, in his case—the secret feature of its derisory stakes" (Lacan 1966a, p. 4). This secret feature is Lacan's object *a*, an atopic object that is the motor of the poem, even if in itself it is insub-stantial, or derisory: Belinda's lock of hair, of which she has been ravished in Pope's poem. Jung's deafness ravishes, or robs, Spielrein of "a secret love of which no one must know". But this secret love has as its provisional object Carl Jung, an object that is in the process of failing—and falling—for Spielrein, a "rape of a lock" that might allow her to terminate her analysis.

Spielrein is alone in dealing with these words as signifiers, beyond the level of their meaning: a level at which Jung remains stuck. That is, it is Spielrein who must continue the work of analysis alone. In the same letter to Freud, she writes in a playful manner the way in which her surname also enters into play:

Today I had to have my card checked by Dr. Lutz. I was the last one of a small group. He reads off my name, which is written clearly enough as Spielrein, and he asks me twice, "Are you called Spieleréin [play straight/ clean] or Spieleréi [play around/game/gimmick]?" With the straightest face in the world I replied, "Spieleréin," and truly I said it without the slightest evil intent, but quite involuntarily, because my attention was blurred by the colossal effort I had to make to keep from bursting out laughing.

(Carotenuto 1980a, p. 111–112 & Carotenuto 1980c, p. 112)

Here her name is in play, and indeed *Spiel*, or, in the infinitive form, the verb *Spielen*, is quite literally *to play*. And here she enters into the game by putting forward that she is "Spielerein", that is, playing clean, or straight, and thus serious, while at the same time suppressing her laughter, implying that she is quite the opposite. *Rein* can have a number of meanings that pertain to Sabina Spielrein (*vide* Guibal & Nobécourt 2004, pp. 345–346), but here we might retain the signifier *r(h)ein* already used by Spielrein in referring to the opera *Das Rheingold*, which of course refers both to the gold from the river Rhine, but also to the "pure" gold, the purity of the gold that was robbed from the Rhine maidens at the beginning of that opera. Through her ability to play with the signifiers, and to be played by them—an ability that Jung does not possess as he remains firmly within the field of meaning—she is able to examine the manner by which she is determined by the names that she inherited. We might attribute her ability to utilise the signifier as something she derives from a reading of Freud's early works on dreams, jokes, and the psychopathology of every life, as well as her own intuitive grasp and ability in psychoanalysis.

It is in part her ability to utilise the signifier that allows her to accede to poetry, both in her recourse to reading, by citing it, as well as writing it at times. In her letters, *poetry* is, at least in one moment, defined by what Jung demands of her, but through a certain excess: "My love for him transcended our affinity, until he could stand it no longer and wanted 'poetry'" (Carotenuto 1980a, p. 96). Her love transcends the affinity, it goes beyond the similarities, it cannot be confined by their correspondences. Jung, on the other hand, wants to consummate the affinity. Here once again the word poetry is in inverted commas, something by which it transcends the usual meanings of words. The *poetry*, nonetheless, is something that becomes written in the attempt to harness the excess that transcends that affinity.

Her recourse to poetry is something of which she writes in her diaries—at least the excerpts of the diaries that we have from Carotenuto—that chronologically follow her notes for her letters to Freud. She writes, "I wrote poems for him, composed songs about him" (p. 12). Here the question of a child with Jung is also articulated, a child here of writing who is given the name Siegfried, born of their joint love of Wagner's poem. In this moment Siegfried is also the name of a separation from Jung that she imagined would follow the birth of such a child, "I dread the pain of parting [*Schmerz der Trennung*], dread the loneliness that would follow, perhaps for my entire life" (p. 13).

The poetry and songs of which she writes are intimately associated with the idea of Siegfried. She notes, "At the time our poetry began, he had two girls, and the potentiality for a boy within him". She continues, "I just played the piano. There is so much fire and so much love in me! *I feel the unshakeable conviction: Siegfried lives, lives, lives!* No one can rob me of that certainty but my own death" (p. 30, italics in the original). Here Siegfried becomes a conviction, or rather a signifier, rather than a child of flesh and blood. We are once again struck by this other signifier *rob*, a robbery of what is now her most precious possession: the mythical object Siegfried. What she fears is that the conviction that is Siegfried, and the function that it serves for her, would be taken away from her, a robbery of a signifier that she has constructed through her transference-love. Siegfried is the form that her symptom, her *Weltschmerz* (p. 31), takes in that moment.

Even in this period in which she was utilising her sessions with Jung, in part, to revise her psychiatry thesis for publication, she equates the "Destruction as Cause of Becoming" paper, which she was already formulating, with her child Siegfried. She records part of a poem that she says, "I composed with my friend after our first poetry". The poem recounts what the brave hero, "this esteemed and beloved man [who] will then become the father of my Siegfried" will say to her. We note here that the father comes after Siegfried.

> For you I did battle with the raging waves;
> now I come, brandishing my oars, as victor.
> You shall be my prize!
>
> *(p. 32)*

She falls pregnant with the signifier, the signifier Siegfried. Much later she writes to Jung: "I violently resisted the interpretation of Siegfried as a real child" (p. 80). This Siegfried, therefore, is a signifier unlike any other, a signifier that is not substitutable, not able to be replaced by a common name or object, such as a child. Siegfried is literally rendered as poetry in so far as it cannot be reduced to a fixed or common meaning.

Rather than being a real child that ties Spielrein to Jung, Siegfried is a signifier of her invention that allows her the possibility of parting. In the diary entry that follows this fragment of her poetry she writes, "Let me record my firm decision: I want to be free of him!" This resolution is followed by gathering her strength to write her new study that she names, at this stage, "On the Death Instinct". She follows this resolution by the statement, "Oh, Guardian Spirit, let me not come to harm in these storms of emotion. I am absolutely determined now that I want to be free" (p. 33). Not only is Sabina Spielrein the first psychoanalyst to articulate a death instinct, or destruction drive, but moreover it is specifically through her experience of producing an ending to her analysis that she is able to elaborate such a theorisation. She discovers its potential of giving the concept of freedom itself a new value. For Sabina Spielrein, it is precisely through the destruction of prior presentations, images, and illusions that one is able to accede to the freedom of coming into being in a novel manner. The freedom of which she writes is specifically that of a new becoming. This is the emphasis she comes to give to it through its ultimate title, "Destruction as Cause of Becoming".

Let me know in writing what it is all about

If we do not reduce the so-called "poetry" with Carl Jung to sexual intercourse or a romantic dalliance, then we can give this poetry a different and broader scope. First it signifies an ideal that Jung represented for Sabina Spielrein in her transference: that of doctor, friend, and poet. Furthermore, she did in fact write poems and songs in order to attempt to remedy the failure of this very ideal, as well as the ideal of the romantic relation. For Spielrein, poetry also refers to literature and the creative arts more generally. For a number of years Spielrein was divided between whether she would have a career as a composer of music, or whether she would have a "scientific" career as a psychoanalyst. We can take the term poetry, moreover, in its etymology as an "'art of literary fiction', from the Latin *poesis*, itself from the Greek *poiesis* or 'creation', especially as it applies to creation through language" (Rey 2013). As we will see, this notion of psychoanalysis as a creation through an act of language—via a corresponding destruction—was to be a central theme in Spielrein's early scientific writings. This theme was first developed, as we have affirmed here, through her more personal writings, well before it was more explicitly articulated in the writings that she had published.

Spielrein, in regard to her transference, underlined, in her letters to Freud, that it was not simply a question of the person of Jung, but of the struggle with her own demons that he represented for her:

> After all, my friend has told you a number of things in a distorted light! It was Wagner who planted the demon in my soul with such terrifying clarity. I shall omit the metaphors, since you might laugh at the extravagance of my emotion. The whole world became a melody for me: the earth sang, the lake sang, the trees sang, and every twig on every tree.
>
> *(Carotenuto 1980a, p. 106–107)*

Here Spielrein becomes lyrical in her dance with the devil in so far as she allows herself to be moved by the song of Wagner, by the Dionysian dithyramb. But the devil here is desire itself, and for Sabina Spielrein to finish her analysis, she must confront her own desires, which also requires a destruction of her pre-existing ideals. She must become a lost soul, a soul that is to be sold to the devil of desire and not receding from this.

In her letter to Freud that Carotenuto dates from around 1909, she cites Goethe's Faust, although without indicating where this "immortal saying" derives from:

> Part of a power that would
> Alone work evil, but engenders good.
> *(p. 107)*

She states that the demonic force, whose essence is destruction—or evil—is at the same time a creative force, and that a new being arises out of the destruction of two individuals. This she states clearly is a sexual drive which is by nature a destructive drive, an exterminating drive for the individual. The passage she cites from *Faust Part I* is the retort of the devil—in the form of Mephistopheles—who is responding to Faust's question as to who he is. Here we cite Faust's preceding question:

> We usually gather from your names
> The nature of you gentlemen: it's plain
> What you are, we all too clearly recognise
> One who's called Liar, Ruin, Lord of the Flies.
> Well, what are you then?
> *(Goethe 1808)*

In this passage, Mephistopheles is already referred to as *Ruin* or *Destroyer* [*Verderber*] by Faust, which is confirmed by his subsequent retort, in conformity with Spielrein's thesis from her "Destruction as Cause of Becoming" which she has already outlined here. In this it is the preliminary destruction, or "evil", that is required to engender "good", or becoming. But the devil's work, in its embodiment of desire, in stripping the subject of its ideals, is a necessary step in the path of coming into being. Faust, we recall, is endeavouring to extricate himself from the weight of his father's legacy, an ideal impossible to sustain. Here, in a not dissimilar way, Spielrein is also attempting to extricate herself, or at least establish a place for herself, from the fantasm of her parents, and other fantasms in which she finds herself caught. Again, we cite Faust, this time from the excerpt that we have used as an epigraph:

> What's never used, leaves us overburdened,
> But we can use what the Moment may create!

As we have read, when Spielrein wrote to Freud requesting an audience with him, Freud asked her to let him know in writing what it was all about. In that moment Freud did not offer Spielrein another analysis, but rather invited her to write something of her situation, of the sticky predicament of her transference-love with Jung. Sabina Spielrein replied in turn that she was not asking Freud to mediate between herself and Jung, but rather to be able to part from Jung in love, and to "go my own way" (Carotenuto 1980a, p. 92). To follow her own way, though, requires forging or creating that path, that is, to write her own map, to plot her own course. This is precisely what we have elaborated from Nietzsche's poem cited by Spielrein, to stray beyond the point at which the path ends.

Freud had thus encouraged Spielrein to deal with her confrontation with the ending of her analysis, and also to manage this without external intervention and the involvement of third persons [*dritte Personen*]. Yves Lugrin proposes that Freud's intervention directs Spielrein away from an intervention by a third party in the form of another person including himself—which would be another imaginary second position, or opinion—but rather to seek the third person in the form of a symbolic instance within herself. Prompted by his response, Spielrein wrote the beautiful and poignant letters to Freud articulating her situation, and the stalemate in her analysis. Yves Lugrin writes something that is quite striking in the elaboration of the topographical theme of Spielrein mapping her own way beyond the end of the beaten path by means of her writing:

> By refusing to be directly in the front line, and in contenting himself with being the potential place of address for a novel testimony of an unprecedented experience, Freud leaves it solely to Sabina Spielrein to construct an emergent knowledge regarding the transferential foundations of her analytic trajectory. To mark out this experience of the extreme end of the transference that overwhelmed her and led her astray, Sabina Spielrein was to plough and map the wild part of this transference-love.
>
> *(Lugrin 2009, p. 197, translated for this edition)*

By doing this, according to Lugrin, Freud avoided the necessity for Spielrein to undertake a second period of analysis, which would have only unnecessarily deferred the question of the ending of her analysis. Furthermore, Freud's intervention prompted Spielrein not simply to write about the difficulties that assailed her, which she did in her letters to Freud, but beyond this to theorise the conditions of her analysis and her transference. This she did, first in her thesis, and then more explicitly in her "Destruction as Cause of Becoming" paper, as well as in her following clinical and theoretical paper "Contributions to the Knowledge of the Child's Soul".

We can propose that, prompted by Freud, Sabina Spielrein begins to write herself out of her analysis by first articulating her singular position in the analysis, and her place in reference to the transference. This is her first step in being able to end her analysis; to be able to articulate "in writing what it is all about" is the means by which she comes into true possession of her inheritance. The next step that she performs is to be able to utilise the account of her singular trajectory, and clinical experience, to produce original theoretical writings by which she is able to transmit a new psychoanalytic knowledge.

4

OVER A BEAUTIFUL PICTURE, ONE CAN BECOME POETRY

Who has turned us around, so that we,
whatever we do, remain in the stance
of someone who's parting? Like he upon
the last hill, from which his whole valley
can once more be seen, turns, stops, tarries—,
and so we live, always taking leave.

Rilke 1923, translated for this edition

During early 1909 when Spielrein was writing her letters to Freud, she was also in the midst of the examination period, towards the end of her medical studies. Her thesis, which we presume was written in the meantime, is referred to in her diary entry of 23 September 1909. At that time, she was waiting to hear back from Eugen Bleuler, evidently her supervisor, fearing the worst. She spoke about the situation to Jung who "laughed at *Prof. Bleuler* as an analyst" (Carotenuto 1980a, p. 8, italics in the original). There followed from this a conspiracy of Spielrein with Jung in which she was to ask for the dissertation back from Bleuler and "send it to my friend", presumably to have it marked by Jung instead of Bleuler. She remarks that, "This perfidy toward my old professor tormented me constantly". She consoled herself by writing that she would later confess this betrayal to Bleuler, but noting that this would "not make him feel any less wronged by his triumphant rival, who only ten years ago was his humble student and now … derides his old teacher" (p. 8). What she calls her "traitorous role" in this conspiracy was, however, obviated when she went to see Bleuler who told her that he had only been able to look over one-tenth of the dissertation, "but this tenth was fine, and for the rest he would rely on me" (pp. 9–10). Bleuler furthermore asked her whether she would speak to Jung about having it published in a Freudian journal. In the diary she expresses her wish to have it published and thus widely read, stating modestly, as we have already read, "My paper does contain some interesting and stimulating material, and for that reason it will be good if it is read" (p. 10). Spielrein wished for her writing to be disseminated beyond her supervisor and her analyst to a public in the world beyond.

Sistine poetry is Catholic poetry

Spielrein's thesis concerned her analysis of a psychotic woman at the Burghölzli, the first published psychoanalytic account of a clinical case of psychosis. Spielrein's psychiatry thesis was her first published paper, in fact the first thesis of any kind to utilise psychoanalysis as its object of study as well as its methodology. We can read in Spielrein's account that she puts her emphasis upon a number of points of affinity with her own account, including the signifiers that insist in the report that she gives of herself in her diary entries and her letters to Freud, as well as the signifiers of her own name. From the beginning of the thesis, she describes the patient as being intelligent, having literary interests, even commenting on her "poetic expression" (Spielrein 1911, p. 337). She also refers to the form of her patient's suffering, like her own, as "*Weltschmerz*" (p. 398). Freud had recommended that Spielrein let him know in writing what it was all about. Here, through a type of fiction—via the means of another's case history—she was able to write of the place of the transference in her own psychoanalytic treatment. By this means, she was also able to redirect her transference from the person of Jung to the place of writing. It was by means of writing her thesis that Sabina Spielrein was able to work through the remnants of her analysis in order to put this to use in becoming a psychoanalyst.

If the thesis is her means of termination of the analysis, Jung as editor of the *Jahrbuch* could not be bypassed in taking her writing from the privacy of the consulting room out to the "public" whom she now addressed through her writing. But when Jung read it, Spielrein reports that, "He is miffed that everywhere I omit his name, as if intentionally, do not cite his works, and in the end even make fun of him a bit" (Carotenuto 1980a, p. 14). Subsequently, due to the ensuing emendations, the published thesis reads like there have been references to Jung and his mythology inserted into it afterwards, with constant footnotes referring to his work with his interpretations and suggestions of the content of the thesis. What we take to be Jung's additions and suggestions often seem to go against the grain of what Spielrein is endeavouring to produce through her own writing.

While the thesis is at once an account of a psychotic patient, it is also an account of Spielrein herself, articulated through the patient. In this sense also, it is a truly psychoanalytic text in which Spielrein makes herself the instrument of her patient's analysis. Through the patient's utterances, it also anticipates some of the same themes that had already developed in her diaries, which would be further elaborated in her paper that was to follow, "Destruction as Cause of Becoming". Guibal and Nobécourt locate Spielrein's self-authorisation as analyst in her thesis: "She authorises herself to hear, as analyst, a love story that turned out very badly" (2004, p. 185). Sabina Spielrein's patient, like Spielrein herself, is captivated by her love for Carl Jung. This is an account of her patient's, and her own, transference-love to Carl Jung. The patient also took part in Jung's association experiment, and, as Spielrein remarks in a footnote, transference can even arise through this experiment. In other words, the patient, like Spielrein herself, has a transference to Jung, a transference that comes to be articulated through the thesis.

One of the points of originality of Spielrein's thesis is also to be found in its close examination of the speech of a psychotic patient, not just through the analysis of a memoir like Freud effected with Schreber, but rather in clinical practice with the patient. What she discovers, through the literal meanings that her patient attributed to her words, are the laws of language that govern thought and speech, or what she calls the patient's "symbol formation" (1911, p. 333). She gives emphasis to the homophony of words that the patient utilises, such as Sistine and sexual [*Sixtinisch und sexuel*], thus stressing the function of these terms as signifiers. Spielrein also notes in her examination of the patient, the latter's tendency towards the play of the signifier, or "wordplay" [*Wortspielereien*] (p. 332). In this term we recognise the playful form of her surname that she had suppressed in responding to Dr. Lutz that she was "Spielereien", playing around, or games or playthings, as opposed to "Spielerein", playing straight, or being serious. She gives emphasis to Freud's notion of the antithetical signification of certain words, first articulated in *The Interpretation of Dreams*, and more specifically elaborated in his text "The Antithetical Meaning of Primal Words" (Freud 1910e) which she does cite. In deference to Jung, she remarks that psychotic thought follows the same laws as that of the dream. She discovers that the speech of her patient reveals the mechanism of dreams, and thus the unconscious, remarking that "This impression positively imposed itself upon me during the study of this patient" (Spielrein 1911, p. 396).

In the medical history of the patient given by Spielrein, she notes that this Protestant woman was married to a Catholic man who was a teacher by profession. She remarks early in the history that the patient had always had religious inclinations, and was cold in sexual relations, emphasising that sexual relations with the husband were repugnant to her. She had presented during this first episode in an acutely disturbed state with religious delusions. At the heart of these delusions was a belief that she had been seduced, or in her words, "catholicised". This unusual word is curiously one that had been used by Daniel Paul Schreber in his *Memoirs* (e.g. Schreber 1903, p. 57), which Freud drew upon to write his case history of paranoia. Schreber's *Memoirs* were published only a few years prior to Spielrein's patient being admitted to the Burghölzli and were widely read. It would not be surprising then if Spielrein's patient—who we know was an intelligent, literate, and well-read woman—had read them.

Accordingly, besides accusing her husband of having little religion and other reproaches of a religious nature, she also stated that he had been seduced by two of his students. One of these in particular, according to the patient's account, was a rich and beautiful young woman to whom she gave the name "*Frauenzimmer*" (Spielrein 1911, p. 331). This derogatory term for a woman, which might be translated as "wench" or "strumpet", literally signifies "lady's chamber", and thus designates a space. Freud refers to this term in *The Interpretation of Dreams* and elsewhere, and puts forward that in the language of dreams and of the unconscious, a woman, or her uterus, is often represented as a room. In this case the *Frauenzimmer*, as indicated by the patient, was both the one who implies that the patient has sexual relations with her own brother (in the place of the fantasy of having sexual relations with the father, as interpreted by Spielrein), as well as being the patient herself. When asked by Spielrein, "What is the *Frauenzimmer's* name?", the patient replies, "She took my name". Spielrein goes on to comment that "With *Frauenzimmer* the patient expresses not just the identification with the [*Frauenzimmer*] herself in the sexual relation, but also through the same name" (p. 350).

Immediately following the introduction, history, and examination that she gives, Spielrein introduces, from the delusions of her patient, the theme of poetry. This takes a number of forms that the patient initially calls "Catholic poetry", then "tropical poetry", and "the way to school poetry". We will examine the first of these here. The patient often tells Spielrein that she was "catholicised". Spielrein asks her what she understands by "catholicise". The patient responds:

> Michelangelo, Sistine art, and the Madonna were in contact with the history of art [*Kunstgeschichte*]. The latter came in contact with Lao art; that is associated with Laocoön. Sistine art is sexual art. The branch of Sistine art is Lao art, or generation art. Sistine art can evoke sexual art: Over a beautiful picture, one can become poetry [*über einem schönen Bilde kann man zur Poesie werden*], perhaps forget one's duty. Sistine poetry is Catholic poetry; it must be associated with Madonna, with Raphael, with all Catholic poetry.
>
> *(p. 333)*

Sistine art, and by implication all Catholic art, is the sexual art by which the patient's husband was seduced by the *Frauenzimmer*, according to the patient's delusions. It is also a sexual art to which the patient attributes the power of generation or procreation. For Spielrein's patient, what fails in the sexual relation is redeemed in the real of her delusion, the real by which the sexual is actualised for her. It is striking that Spielrein cites her patient as saying that "over a beautiful painting, one can become poetry". For Spielrein it is through the very act of writing—a *poetic* act, which is moreover a *poietic* act—that both her patient, as well as she herself, are able to come into being in their own right.

The patient states that her lack takes the forms of "lack of money" and "lack of love" (p. 356), perceived by the patient to be the basis of her embroidery [*sticken*] and suffocation [*ersticken*], two terms that, as Spielrein notes, she does not differentiate. Her suffocation, according to the patient, is a consequence of her masturbation and subsequent displacement of her larynx, oesophagus, and intestines. At the end of the thesis we see the way in which the patient literally produces a sexual relation in the account that she gives, whether it is a sexual relation between the patient and her brother, between her and her father, or the affirmation that she can be cured by coitus, etc. Furthermore, through her transference to both Jung and Spielrein, the patient recounts a dream in which Dr. J. realised the sexual function upon her. This delusional relation, which is always at risk of being destroyed or "dissolved" [*lösen*] for the patient, is also at the heart of her belief in "generation", that is, it is a sexual act of creation. What inevitably fails in the sexual relation of the patient and her husband is redeemed by her emphasis on a sexual relation in the world outside. Spielrein remarks that "the Turks impress the patient by their exuberance in the sexual relation" (p. 393). If her patient responds to the failure of the sexual relation in a psychotic register by producing a delusional sexual relation, Spielrein's response to what lacks is to write, the writing of poetry, as well as the writing of a thesis.

The limits of painting and poetry

In a footnote, Spielrein remarks upon the emphasis that Jung places upon the mythology of Laocoön, a Trojan priest who was killed, together with his two sons, by giant serpents sent by Apollo, whom Laocoön had offended by des-ecrating his temple. Jung's interpretation, as always in regard to mythology, remains limited to the level of meaning as Claude Lévi-Strauss has pointed out (1955). Laocoön, however, also lent his name to the classical statue represent-ing this myth which is now in the Vatican Museum in Rome, and thus can also be included, we might say, in "Catholic art", or the visual arts to which it pertains. Jung's preoccupation with mythology and consequent influence upon Spielrein, however, might draw our attention—as well as Spielrein's—away from the written work of the same name, *Laocoön: An Essay on the Limits of Painting and Poetry*, first published in 1766 by the Enlightenment poet, philosopher, and critic Gotthold Ephraim Lessing, a work that was very influential, particularly upon German thought and literature. Both Jung and Freud were, moreover, familiar with Lessing's work.

Sabina Spielrein first wrote to Freud in response to accusations by Carl Jung that it was she who had spread rumours regarding Jung having an affair with one of his students. At that time Jung wrote the following to Freud:

> A woman patient, whom years ago I pulled out of a very sticky neurosis with the greatest devotion, has violated my confidence and my friendship in the most mortifying way imaginable. She has kicked up a vile scandal solely because I denied myself the pleasure of giving her a child. I have always acted the gentleman towards her, but before the bar of my rather too

sensitive conscience I nevertheless don't feel clean, and that is what hurts the most because my intentions were always honourable.

(McGuire 1974, 207)

When, shortly afterwards however, Freud received Spielrein's letter, which put Jung's face-saving account into question, he asked Jung to send him a telegram clarifying the situation. In his subsequent letter, Jung endeavoured to exonerate himself, and so in reply Freud reassured Jung that "To be slandered and scorched by the love with which we operate—such are the perils of our trade" (p. 210). To emphasise how he himself had been vilified, Freud cites Lessing from his dramatic poem *Nathan the Wise*: "One way or another, the Jew will be burned" (p. 211).

The subtitle to Lessing's work *Laocoön*, "An Essay on the Limits of Painting and Poetry", is hence very pertinent to this patient's utterances, and was surely also known by Spielrein's patient who was an educated and literary woman with an interest both in visual arts as well as poetry. The *Laocoön*'s masterstroke, according to Michael Fried in his Foreword to this work (Fried 1984), was the distinction between language as a medium of communication and language as a medium of poetry. That is, language as poetry cannot be reduced to the communication of meaning or information, as is commonly put forward to the present day. Rather, Lessing asserted that not only were the symbols of poetry successive, and thus able to express time, but that they are also arbitrary. This, he wrote, "is a peculiarity of speech and its signs in general and not as they serve the aims of poetry" (Lessing 1766, p. 85), thus articulating an aspect of the theory of speech and language that was much later taken up by Ferdinand de Saussure in his structural linguistics, and indeed by Spielrein herself in her apprehension of her patient's speech.

From classical times and through the Middle Ages, there was a belief that poetry was no more than a speaking picture. This is attributed to Horace's aphorism, *Ut pictura poesis*, or "Poetry is like painting". Lessing has been considered the first modern aesthetician, since he took this notion to task, underscoring the difference of poetry from painting, and thus also of the differentiation of the word from the image. Lessing's aim was to re-establish poetry in its proper place amongst the arts, which he did with considerable success given his subsequent influence upon subsequent German poetry and writing more generally, including upon Goethe. Lessing stressed that painting and sculpture, as well as being confined to the depiction of a single moment in time, were also restricted by having to resort to allegory or description, as well as devices that Lessing calls "instruments". These include, by way of example, the lyre or flute in the hand of a muse that for Lessing are not symbols at all.

The poets have no use for these "instruments", but Lessing affirms that the ancient poets were able to articulate attributes beyond such crude devices. He refers to the "attributes which the ancient poets sometimes put into their descriptions and which I might for that reason term poetic, in contradistinction to allegorical. The former signify the thing itself, the latter only something resembling it" (p. 61). For Lessing, "the poet causes us to linger over a single object without entering into a tiring description of its parts" (p. 82). Hence he asserts that in contrast to the visual artist, the poet is able to brush closer to "the thing itself" and consequently make us "feel the real impressions which the objects of these ideas would produce on us" (p. 85). Spielrein's privileging of poetry and writing more generally, as an effort to apprehend the vicissitudes of her life and her analysis through her study and work, indicates a tendency of the same order. It is an endeavour to grasp something that goes beyond mere description and simile.

Spielrein's patient speaks of a certain Herr Lauers who is said to be from Basel, like Jung himself, as the patient knows very well. In this name, Spielrein recognises the assonance with the initial sound of Laocoön. She states that Laocoön is a symbol of genesis for the patient and notes that the patient had referred to Laocoön as "Doctor" (1911, p. 341). Spielrein notes that despite the fact that this presentation [*Vorstellung*] of Lauers as Dr. J. occurs to the patient, she does not want to accept it: "I wouldn't know if Dr. J. has any connection to this". For Spielrein, this "symbolic substitution" serves the function of a "symbolic covering" (p. 341). She later cites the treating doctor who says of the patient, "She tries to bewilder [*verwirren*] one" (p. 356). This comment evokes her later citation of Nietzsche's comment regarding language in the paper "Destruction as Cause of Becoming": "Language is there to bewilder [*verwirren*] itself and others" (Spielrein 1912c, p. 99). This is something she has herself encountered in clinical practice in this case. That is, it is not the patient who tries to bewilder, it is language itself. Such a function of language, which Sabina Spielrein is able to derive from the speech of the psychotic, undermines the notion of language solely as a means of communication.

Spielrein adds that the patient "makes any suitable things into symbols of the same thought, exactly like in the dream" (1911, p. 356). While Spielrein is elaborating something of her own transference to Jung, she is also developing a theory of language in psychoanalytic treatment and elaborating the very structure of psychosis. She draws upon the term "complex" that Carl Jung introduced into psychoanalysis to further elaborate her theorisation. She cites her patient as saying:

> Dreams signify symbolism that must be interpreted. But what if we cannot grasp the symbolism, or if we do not want to grasp it? What if we have to give ourselves over to dreams? If I had to speak about dreams I would have to experience it all over again. Dreams are experiences.
>
> *(p. 342)*

That is, for her patient as Spielrein articulates it, there is no difference between speaking of dreams and having the dream once again. That is, to speak of the dream is to evoke the reality of the dream experience, even to brush against the real. She begins from the patient's statement that a "supposition could become reality" (p. 342). We are reminded of her earlier statement that "Over a beautiful picture, one can become poetry", such that the terms poetry and reality are interchangeable. Thus, the poetry of speech is a means of acceding to a reality, or rather a means of allowing one to touch upon the real. Spielrein theorises this position of the psychotic, first proposing that "such suppositions … are not just arbitrary possibilities, but make the complexes 'objectively' conscious, or rather psychically great, and in any case strive to form reality in accordance with their images [*Bild*]" (p. 343). Spielrein goes on to say that in this way, under favourable conditions, the psychotic creates reality from such "assumptions".

A man can be dissolved [lösen] in water or in spirits in order to result in new life

Spielrein's endeavour is to follow her patient and to articulate the logic that is contained in her speech, not the neurotic logic that is attached to meaning, but the logic of the succession of associations, or the chain of signifiers as we would call it with Lacan. Spielrein, like Lacan, began her theoretical investigations with a psychotic patient. With Spielrein's reading, the psychotic reveals something of the logic of the unconscious—the discourse of the Other—that is obscured in the neurotic: obscured by layers of confounding meaning. With the neurotic we have to wait until this meaning is disrupted by what Freud calls *the return of the repressed*, or with Lacan *the formations of the unconscious*. The difference is that in the psychotic the functions of the ego have effectively been disrupted or destroyed. It is this place of the subject in respect of language that we endeavour to hear through psychoanalysis.

Sabina Spielrein continues to develop her thesis of "Destruction as Cause of Becoming" through her patient's utterances. While for the patient a woman can be equated to earth on the one hand, on the other a man can be dissolved [*lösen*] in water or in spirits in order to result in a "novozoon" or new life. We might also note the assonance of the last part of novozoon with Laocoön as a thesis of creativity. At the same time Spielrein points out that "For the creation of the new generation, a negation [*Verneinung*] that is concomitant with the affirmation [*Bejahung*] is thus necessary" (p. 344). Here Spielrein articulates her thesis, but in relation to a fundamental logic that concerns signifiers and statements: those of negation and affirmation. She posits that a negation is necessary for the production of an affirmation. Spielrein continues, "I would like to draw special attention to this representation, as well as a notion of the novozoon, which plays [*spielt*] the role of life-giving sperm, as a '*dead substance*'" (p. 344, italics in the original). We note that it is through death, in the form of a dead substance, that life can be produced or given.

The dissolution, or solution, according to Spielrein's patient, takes place in the amniotic fluid, or *Fruchtwasser*, literally fruit-water. The patient asserts that this water—the Italian lakes—emerges from a split [*Spaltung*] in the sexual parts in the woman's body (=earth). Spielrein notes that the word "Italian" is used by the patient as an expression of beauty, poetry, art, and love; an Italian lake would then be a beautiful lake, or a lake full of love. The patient goes on to expound that "The new animal comes forth from dead bones (dead matter = sperm), it comes from evaporation of its watery solution [*Lösung*] … in the world". For Spielrein's patient, it is specifically through the dead matter that the amniotic fluid is fertilised to produce new life. Thus, the negation connected with death that is concomitant with the affirmation of the amniotic fluid is necessary to produce a new generation. The fruit-water, which is then saturated with animal elements (the dead bones), evaporates "and the animal elements crystallize out in the air, as it were, into the new animal" (p. 391). Spielrein perceives in this description of a chemical, or physical process, a transition from the physical to the psychological: from the head of the animal to the soul of her patient.

But for the patient the head is the seat of the soul, the symbol of the spiritual, while the promotion of the spiritual is also a denial of the sexual. Spielrein reports: "The fertilizing [*befruchtende*] spiritual love came into the patient's mind. For this, her head had to be 'split' [*gespalten*], as if something physical, which has extension in space, had got into her. I will note here that the patient calls this cleavage 'phrenology'" (pp. 391–392). Phrenology had already been referred to by the patient as "Soul-section [*Seelensektion*]". The sexual, for Spielrein's patient, retains the extended quality of the outside world, causing a split to occur. For Spielrein, the "spermatic development" of her patient is a "direct affirmation" (p. 344), while the patient's promotion of the spiritual is a denial of sexuality. And in this very refusal of sexuality, the patient takes sexuality as arising from the outside geographical and animal world. That is, the psychotic patient responds to what fails in the sexual relation by effectively perceiving, or producing, a sexual relation in the world outside, in the real.

From this we can see how intertwined are the emerging notions of the death and destructive drive (negation) on the one side, as well as the creativity of the drive of becoming or creating (affirmation) on the other. Again, that is, a negation [*Verneinung*] that is concomitant with the affirmation [*Bejahung*] is necessary for the creation of a new generation. Although the emphasis that Spielrein gives to the signifier is something she had discovered through her writing regarding the remnants of her own analysis, here in her clinical and theoretical work with this psychotic patient she gives it a different value. In the analysis of the psychotic patient, she discerns how the determining signifiers function, but in a manner that is different to the logic of the neurotic: rather than being repressed, they are cast out by the patient onto the world outside. Then, rather than emerging in a return of the repressed as a dream, slip of the tongue, joke, etc., as in neurosis, they return to the patient from the outside world. In other words, as Freud put it in his account of the Schreber case, "what was abolished internally returns from without" (1911c, p. 71).

The psychotic patient no longer can sustain the illusion that he or she is able to play with language, but rather he or she is now overtly the plaything of language.

We are also able to discern Spielrein's psychoanalytic method in this, that is, the way in which she is able to follow the words and signifiers of her patient, e.g. *Wasser, lösen, Frucht, -oon, See/le, Spalt-ung, Poesie*, etc., without endeavouring to reduce these to meanings or sense. What emerges from her analysis is not the production of a narrative, or the reduction to psychiatric signs and symptoms, but rather the writing of the psychical structure of her patient, and the outlining of the structure of psychosis itself.

We also hear in Spielrein's singular account in the thesis the insistence of the signifiers of her own name. There is reference for instance to *Karnevalspiele*, or carnival games (p. 390), as well as to use of the verb *spielen*, to play: "The brother-type plays [*spielt*] an important role for the patient" (p. 395). There are also constant references by the patient—commented upon by Spielrein—to the question of being unclean or impure [*unrein*] and purity [*Reinheit*], both in regard to the body and to the spirit, crucial elements for Spielrein herself. Through the thesis, Spielrein also breaks down—or destroys—the signifiers of her name into its component parts. The functioning of the signifier in psychosis effectively then allows Spielrein to apprehend the way in which her own name is broken down into its constituent letters. This destruction is a cause of the coming-into-being of poetry, since it allows something new to be created. This creation is not of a new identity, that of herself as a poet for instance, but very precisely the creation that occurs through the patient's speech: "Over a beautiful picture, one can become poetry". That is to say that the undivided picture that forms the basis of the subject's image of him or herself, the ego in other words, is ruptured by the emergence of the words or signifiers from the unconscious. By virtue of her grasping of the signifiers of the patient's speech—as well as her own speech and writing—in its radical destruction of common meaning and communication, Spielrein is able to accede to the position of becoming a psychoanalyst, not through taking on another identity and becoming a "doctor" or a "poet", but rather by literally becoming poetry.

In closing this thesis, Spielrein draws remarkable conclusions regarding time in reference to the patient's psychopathology, including regarding the future. These inferences are not just of concern for the psychotic patient, but are important elaborations of psychoanalytic theory. She states, "It seems to me that a symbol actually owes its origin to the effort of a complex towards its reproduction, through the dilution in the general totality of thought". She goes on to say that "The complex becomes robbed [*beraubt*] of the personal" (p. 399). Here once again we understand, through Spielrein, the way in which the personality—the ego or self—is robbed or destroyed through the emergence of the unconscious in an act of becoming.

The unconscious, she remarks, dissolves [*auflösen*] (p. 399) the present in the past. She notes that the dream, while being a wish-fulfilment, is concerned with the future which is itself transformed or represented as the past. Spielrein proposes that "in the unconscious we see that there is something that is outside of time or which is at once present, past and future". The unconscious potentially tells us about the future development of things in so far as the subject is drawn towards his or her object through a movement into the future, since "the dream is a wish-fulfilment and thus is concerned with the future" (p. 399). This forward-moving nature of Spielrein's conclusions—in contrast to the prevailing retrogressive view of psychoanalysis as a return to infantile complexes—contributes to the creative aspect of her theorisation, with its emphasis on becoming, or coming-into-being.

Towards the end of the thesis, in regard to the theme of dissolution, Spielrein recounts an exchange where she asks the patient what she means by the expression "to lay on the body" (p. 382). In response, the patient states that it is like a sheet being bleached. She then speaks of a sheet being bleached with *Scheidewasser*, aqua fortis or nitric acid in English. Spielrein herself evokes the different significations of *Scheide*, first that of "vagina or sheath", and then that of "separation", from the verb *Scheiden* "to part or separate". This of course conjures up Spielrein's particular form of *Weltschmerz*, that is, her *Abschiedschmerz*, or pain of parting or separation. In the very next paragraph, Spielrein clarifies that "*Wasser*" or water, is always understood by the patient to be "spermatic water", or men's water. This water, in which the man's semen or procreative essence is dissolved, then fertilises the earth which is the woman. She notes that the patient is separated [*geschieden*] from her husband, and Spielrein herself remarks upon the relation between *geschieden* and *Scheidewasser*. She then interprets the patient's enunciation as pertaining to her separation from sexual relations with her husband. For Spielrein, at this point in her trajectory, it is also a question of her own separation from her analyst and her analysis.

Just another …—No, let's wait a bit

We have read Spielrein's thesis, in part, as her indirect means of endeavouring to articulate something regarding her own analysis. While it is the account of a psychotic woman, it is also the account of a woman whose transference-love towards Dr. Jung turns into a wish for the transference to be realised in an erotic encounter. While for Jung, Sabina Spielrein was his "psychoanalytic training case", Spielrein's thesis was also a psychoanalytic training case, an original analysis of a case of psychosis. It was also an analysis conducted by and through her, in so far as she is able—now at the end of her own analysis—to lend herself to the words of her patient. One can hear the way in which she attends both to the patient's words as well as her own transference, whilst not locating herself as the object of the erotic transference. She takes up a position as one who is able to hear the words of the patient, but from an extraterritorial position, outside the psychiatric treating team. This is a novel position in the analysis and potential treatment of a psychotic patient through a transference that cannot be delimited to the one-to-one work as with neurosis. On the contrary, it indicates that a different approach is required with the psychotic patient. Such an approach entails the presence of others who are able to bear some of the psychotic transference—in this case for the patient via the transference to "Forel", "Dr. J.", and the treating doctor, as well as the nurses and other staff—in addition to Spielrein, who is then able to sustain the analytic work with the patient.

In 1923, when Spielrein left Switzerland to return to her native Russia, she carried with her many books. Amongst these was Rilke's *Duino Elegies*, as recounted by Renata Cromberg who describes this work as "the ten luminous poems on time and death" (Cromberg 2014, p. 42). It is from the end of the eight *Elegy* that we have taken the excerpt that follows, since it eloquently articulates this moment of separation for Sabina Spielrein, one in which there is a lingering last moment, a moment that becomes atemporal, fusing past, present, and future. This instant at the end of one's analysis, both terminable and interminable, is a point at which one is able to contemplate one's life, one's history, and one's symptom, and in which there is a possibility of taking a different path, to take leave from the singular way in which one's life has been knotted up to that point:

> Like he upon
> the last hill, from which his whole valley
> can once more be seen, turns, stops, tarries—,
> and so we live, always taking leave [Abschied].
> *(Rilke 1923)*

Rilke eloquently articulates this moment of separation for Sabina Spielrein, one in which there is a protracted last moment of leaving, a moment that becomes atemporal, fusing past, present, and future. This evokes what Spielrein had written in her diary in Vienna, when offended by Jung's curt letter, "'Just another …'— 'No, let's wait a bit,' just as it says in my poem", in which the moment of parting becomes a moment of hesitation, a moment deferred, despite her physical separation.

In the thesis, her patient insists upon the process of the dissolving of the male principle. In German, as we have seen, the word is *lösen*, literally to dissolve, to loosen, to free, or separate. In the religious delusions of Spielrein's patient, however, Jesus redeems [*erlösen*] through the pure air of his land. This air of Jesus, for the patient, is the spirit or psyche, in contrast to the earth—in other words, woman—which is physical. But this *erlösen* introduces a step back from the direction of the *lösen*: the redemption buys back—or redeems—the state of sin, or the looseness of souls. It therefore functions as a type of short-circuiting of a loss or loosening. That is, in redemption it is not a question of destruction or dissolution [*lösen*], but a turning back from such a confrontation. It is a reprieve from destruction, and therefore an inability to accede to becoming in Spielrein's formulation. We can hear through the speech of this psychotic patient how religion moves in the opposite direction to that of psychoanalysis. Rather than allowing the loss, it attempts to buy it back, to reprieve the subject from being a lost soul, in other words, to redeem the subject. Redemption is thus an attempted or imagined *re-lease*—or re-loosing—from the knots in which the subject is caught.

Spielrein, on the other hand, at the end of her analysis, is able to assume the loosing produced by her analysis. In English the verb *to loose*—with a scope not dissimilar to that of *lösen* in German—signifies *to part from, to release from one's bonds, to undo, to untie, to unfasten,* and *to dissolve,* etc. (SOED 2007). Thus Spielrein, in what she construes of her own analysis—and in what she teaches us about the position of the subject at the end of analysis—is able to loosen the bonds that knot her to her past, the bond that is the symptom itself, but not to release or redeem her from her symptoms, or her suffering. Rather, it allows the possibility of—through the loosing that has been produced—retying, or of splicing her symptom in a new way that allows a new becoming. In this way the symptom can be put to use, just as it is in her psychoanalytic writing.

We can hear the coextensiveness of the dissolving or loosening [*lösen*] that insists in Spielrein's remarks, in the same way that we hear its counterparts in the ancient Greek *lysis* or *ana-lysis* ["to dissolve" or "to loosen"], and in the signifiers of modern English, to loose or loosen, the German and the English both being etymologically derived from the Greek. In Homer's *Odyssey*, when Ulysses' vessel sailed past the sirens, he instructed his crewmen to plug their ears with wax and to tie him firmly to the mast, exposing himself alone to the lethal danger of the sirens' song. Here there is no redemption; Ulysses must expose himself to the full force of the sirens' lethal song. Once the danger was passed, the sailors then untied Ulysses, loosening his bonds. Pascal Quignard (1996, p. 183) recounts that in the version of the *Odyssey* that has been handed down to us, the word used for this untying was ἀνέλυσαν: analysis. This was the first record of the word "analysis" being written in the Ancient Greek language. From this—through Spielrein—we propose that psychoanalysis is not at all a redemption from a state of subjection, but rather the loosing of the knots by which the subject is bound so that there can be some movement. The knots of one's subjection to language, and to sex and death, however, remain intact but there is now some movement possible. In this way, through the writing of her thesis, Sabina Spielrein is able to loosen her own ties, giving her some room to move, and consequently to allow the possibility of loosing and retying the knot of her own symptom, and by extension to Carl Jung in the transference, in order to effect an ending to her analysis.

5

YOU MUST OVERCOME (DESTROY) YOURSELF

The chiefest reason why I made
The earth, I will confess with gladness:
Within my soul, like fiery madness,
A burning call to do so play'd.

Illness was the especial ground
Of my creative inclination;
I might recover by creation,
Creation made me once more sound.

Heinrich Heine, from Songs of Creation *(1823)*
(The last stanza cited by Freud 1914c, p. 85)

At the end of 1910, at the time she was sitting her final medical exams, Sabina Spielrein was already working on her second study that had as its provisional title, "On the Death Instinct". Even at that early stage, however, she sensed that Carl Jung wished to appropriate her work for himself: "I greatly fear that my friend, who planned to mention my idea in his article in July, saying that I have rights of priority, may simply borrow the whole development of the idea, because he now wants to refer to it as early as January" (Carotenuto 1980a, p. 35). There were thematic and theoretical similarities between Jung's work and the study that Spielrein was undertaking in so far as they both concerned the question of transformations, as well as the function of the libido. As it transpired, Jung's new work *"Wandlungen und Symbole der Libido"* (1911)—a revised form of which was published in English as *Symbols of Transformation* (1956)—appeared in the *Jahrbuch* alongside Spielrein's thesis, hence as feared, prior to "Destruction as Cause of Becoming". Jung's work was a watershed as it marked his revision of Freud's libido theory, and hence his theoretical divergence from Freud.

The question of plagiarism, though, was not just on Jung's side, since Spielrein's words of self-encouragement for her final exams were "Especially—plagiarize well!" (Carotenuto 1980a, p. 37). When Spielrein presented some of this work at the Vienna Psychoanalytic Society on 29 November 1911, furthermore, she did so from the third part of her paper that was concerned with mythology. This section, in the published form of the work, actually comes *after* the conclusion to the paper and literally reads as an afterthought. It is in fact completely omitted from the superior translation into English (1912c) without editorial comment. It contains no new theorisation but serves only to illustrate the theses that she had developed earlier in the paper with, as Spielrein herself states, "heterogeneous examples from mythology" (Spielrein 1912b, p. 184). This third section of her otherwise novel paper reads much like Jung's *Symbols of Transformation*. And as in that paper, what are referred to as "symbols" are linguistically nothing more than signs, or equivalences of one thing for another, for instance: "parturition = tooth extraction = castration" (p. 182). In other words, this section is devoid of the theory of language that emerges in her thesis and which continues to be elaborated in the first parts of "Destruction as Cause of Becoming".

Immediately following her presentation she was roundly criticised, including by Freud himself, for what was taken—for the most part correctly—as the introduction into psychoanalysis of Jung's loose use of mythology. Freud specifically stated on the evening that "the presentation itself provides the opportunity for a critique of Jung" (Nunberg & Federn 1974, p. 335). The discussion, focusing as it did on Jung's divergences, led Spielrein to express regret that, in not having put forward the fundamental chapter of her work "Destruction as Cause of Becoming", a conceptual confusion had impaired the discussion on the night. This conflation between Spielrein's work and Jung's was enacted the following day in Freud's quasi-slip of the pen in his letter to Jung: "Fräulein Spielrein read a chapter from her paper yesterday (I almost wrote the *ihrer* [her] with a capital "i"), and it was followed by an illuminating discussion. I have hit on a few objections to your [*Ihrer*] (this time I mean it) method of dealing with mythology, and I brought them up in the discussion with the little girl" (McGuire 1974, p. 469). So in his correspondence to Jung, Freud in his quasi-slip literally confuses Jung with Spielrein, and also diminishes Spielrein's contributions to those of a "little girl". On the other side, Jung also confuses Spielrein's work for his own. The German edition of Carotenuto contains letters by Jung to Sabina Spielrein— letters not present in the English edition—and in one of these we read the following, "I am glad that you represented me in Vienna" (1980c, p. 208, translated for this edition).

Still today Spielrein's work suffers the effect of her relationship with Jung and is overshadowed by his opus, explaining in part the paucity of translations and interest in her writings. Given all of the ways in which Spielrein and her productions had been identified with Carl Jung—including by herself—it remained extremely difficult for her to disentangle herself from their liaison. This separation or parting—her *Abschied*—was part of the effort that she needed to be able to successfully end her analysis and establish herself in her own right. This was also a separation from her family, and most particularly from her mother, which was being elaborated through her transference-love with Carl Jung. Spielrein's efforts to act upon her suffering through writing also evoke what the writer Margarite Duras said in a television interview in 1984 regarding her own experiences. She is often loosely cited as giving a generalised statement: "Only writing was stronger than the mother" (e.g. Lebrun 1988, p. 3, translated for this edition). What Duras actually says regarding her writing though is a particular statement that derives from her own singular experience: "It was stronger than my mother herself. It is what was stronger than her" (Léridon 1984, translated for this edition). A few years later in a paper entitled "My Mother had ...", Duras wrote, in regard to her family members, "I separated from them in life. One separates from people through writing" (Duras 1988, p. 205, translated for this edition). Writing was the methodology utilised by Spielrein in order to effect her own separation, a singular separation by virtue of the failure of her analysis, which then gave rise to a psychoanalytic writing.

At first glance, particularly given the use of some of Jung's terminology, Spielrein's work might appear derivative of Jung's elaborations of the time. Upon a closer reading, however, we can discern the manner in which Spielrein utilised both Jung and Freud's terms, as well as her own nomenclature, to produce a very original work that follows directly on from her thesis. Osvaldo Cariola states that with "Destruction as Cause of Becoming", as well as the more autobiographical "Contributions to the Knowledge of the Child's Soul", Spielrein produces a number of crucial innovations: 1) she produces a theory regarding her experiences; 2) she takes up the fantasm (not least of all Jung's) in which she was caught, and manages to write herself out of it; 3) she develops a theory of the transference by asking, "what really is this abominable thing called love?"; 4) she gathers all the reflections she had formulated—and written—in a desperate manner over the previous five to six years, and works them into a form that enables her to go beyond them (she does, then, what most analysands refrain from doing, and which is the condition of the analyst's coming into being: to formulate the schema that the analysis has produced); and, last but not least, 5) she sets out the questions with which she later came to occupy herself (Cariola 2014).

If Spielrein was caught in Jung's fantasm, it was only through writing that she was able to effect a destruction of it for her, which then permitted a new coming-into-being. These advances, and particularly the last two points that Cariola mentions, are truly new and original contributions to psychoanalytic knowledge and methodology. Out of necessity, Spielrein reformulated her analysis by giving an account of it through her writing. That is, by the very means that she used to put an ending to her analysis, she was also able to produce theoretical advances in psychoanalysis itself. Even though it is anachronistic to consider, like Yves Lugrin (2009), that Spielrein's procedure was a type of secret intuition regarding the *passe* that Lacan would invent many years later, there is nonetheless something of the same order that she effected. In any case, through these means, Sabina Spielrein was able to enact an ending to her analysis and accede to the place of analyst. The work that we examine here, far from being a dry theoretical proposition, is a work created out of the destruction of her analysis, through which she was able to come into being. From this proposition, she effectively produces a theorisation of her analysis and its ending. She had been developing the central questions of destruction and becoming for a number of years in her more personal writings, and in a letter to Freud in 1909 she reintroduces these questions, in reference to her relation to Jung, by citing a couplet from Goethe's Faust:

> Part of a power that would
> Alone work evil, but engenders good.
> *(cited in: Carotenuto 1980a, p. 107)*

It is the reworking of the forces of destruction that is able to engender her emergence from the analysis and her becoming a psychoanalyst. She continues on: "This demonic force, whose very essence is destruction (evil) and at the same time is the creative force, since out of the destruction (of two individuals) a new one arises" (pp. 107–108). Hence the destruction is literally the destruction—in the transference—of her relationship with Jung. The new knowledge that is produced from the ending of her analysis is precisely what is able to provoke the theoretical writing of "Destruction as Cause of Becoming".

Much has been made of Spielrein's articulation of the death instinct and how it did, or did not, influence Freud's elaboration of the death drive. But in this attribution Spielrein is only read in reference to Freud, which makes this discussion a sterile one. This somewhat hackneyed attribution, begun by Freud himself, ignores the particular way in which Spielrein's notion of the destruction drive is very different to Freud's death drive. For Sabina Spielrein, the death or destruction drive is part and parcel of the sexual drive, and not pitted against it as it is in Freud. This also marks her point of difference with Jung as we shall see.

A picture does not remain only a picture

Near the beginning of her paper, Spielrein gives a long citation from Jung, whose remarks, she states, "correspond for the most part with my own results" (Spielrein 1912c, p. 87). She quickly notes, however, that Jung, by way of contrast to her, brings the death presentations [*Todesvorstellungen*] not in agreement but in opposition to sexual presentations [*sexuelle Vorstellungen*]. Hence from the outset, she differentiates her position from that of Jung. The fundamental thesis of this paper is precisely that it is only through the destruction of a previously held position—principally in her case her transference-love to Jung—that a new coming-into-being can be caused.

Even though it is not articulated as such, Spielrein's paper can be read as an elaboration of her theory of language that emerged from her personal writings and then more explicitly put forward in the thesis, a language that differentiates the conscious from the unconscious. This is evident from the beginning of the paper in which she cites a phrase from Goethe's *Faust*, Part 2:

> In this sense "everything transitory" [*alles Vergängliche*] is only a saying that symbolizes some original event [*Urereignis*] unknown to us, which looks for analogs in the present, although we project the emotion into the present mental image [*Vorstellung*].
>
> *(p. 89)*

In this passage we must from the outset tease out three modes of experience that are imposed upon the subject in Spielrein's account. First, there is the original event that is unknown and even unknowable. Second, Spielrein posits that there is a mode of symbolisation of such an event, as a saying. Third, she puts forward that the saying that symbolises the event looks for analogues of it in the present. We can tie these three modes of experience to the concepts Freud introduced, first his notion of the unknowable Thing [*das Ding*], second the Thing-Presentation [*Dingvorstellung*] of the unconscious, and third the Word-Presentation [*Wortvorstellung*] of the preconscious. Unfortunately, the term *Vorstellung* that Spielrein employs, following Freud's usage, is mostly translated by the vague term of "mental image". As Spielrein's paper proceeds, she writes that language peculiar to the unconscious is articulated as presentations, elaborating that these are "affectless [presentations]" (p. 98), corresponding precisely to Freud's notion of the Word-Presentation. In this way Spielrein differentiates the thoughts, feelings, and images of the pre-conscious and consciousness which are imbued with affect, from the unconscious in which affect is not represented, as Freud also put forward. Here we will retain Spielrein's usage from the German and render *Vorstellung* as "presentation", as it is more precisely rendered into English (Laplanche & Pontalis 1973, pp. 447–449). We can also consider that these three modalities that we discern in Spielrein's paper roughly correspond to the registers elaborated by Jacques Lacan: the real, the symbolic, and the imaginary.

First there is the unknown original event that is thus outside our grasp. For Spielrein, this primordial event is also an original fusion with the "prime mother [*Urmutter*]" (p. 91), or an "original source [*Ursprung*]" (p. 102) to which one yearns to return. This event, designated as original by use of the prefix "*Ur-*", is repeated in a number of places in the paper, which can also be translated as "primal". This "original" notionally pertains to the origins of the subject, and also therefore to what is nominated by Freud as the primal scene [*Urszene*]. As we have elaborated elsewhere, the primal scene is a moment of exquisite enjoyment—or jouissance—of the creation of the subject, from which he or she is necessarily excluded (Plastow 2015, p. 138). It is in this same way that we read Spielrein's unknown original, or primal, event.

Second, there is the symbolisation of the original event into a saying, such as that derived from Faust. This symbolisation, with Spielrein, occurs into what she refers to as *Vorstellungen*, or presentations. These presentations are unable to reach or grasp the original event, and yet are the only means the subject possesses of endeavouring to approach them. According to Spielrein, "everything transitory" is the quality attributed to the *saying*, or enunciation, that symbolises the original event. In other words, nonetheless, the presentations of the unconscious are not entirely fixed but transient ones, which can then be utilised by the subject to create something new.

Third, the imaginary "analogs", which are sought in the present, are thus the analogues in consciousness to the presentations that are imbued with the timelessness of the unconscious. As Spielrein writes, "Every conscious thought- or [presentation]-content is accompanied by similar unconscious contents, by which the results of conscious thinking are translated into the language peculiar to the unconscious" (p. 90). These analogues betray a lingering reference to Jung as, according to him, consciousness and the unconscious both form symbols on the basis of analogy, which is the means of making things comprehensible (*cf.* Jung 1913, p. 240). Spielrein uses this notion in her own manner, however, to differentiate the symbolisation—or the language of the unconscious that is time-less—from the conscious which consists of analogues, or images, in the present.

Spielrein elaborates upon the timelessness of the unconscious, "which simul-taneously lives in the present, past, and future, and therefore outside of time; for which all places fuse together (at the original place [*Ursprungsort*]) and for which opposites mean the same thing" (1912c, p. 91). Besides taking up Freud's notion of the timelessness of the unconscious, she makes reference to his paper "The Antithetical Meanings of Primary Words" (1910e) in which he first articu-lates the structure of the unconscious from the point of view of linguistics. She stresses once again towards the end of the paper that "Freud shows that linguistics recognizes an 'opposite meaning of primal words [*Urworte*]'" (1912c, p. 116).

Spielrein demonstrates the functioning of the signifier in its polysemic capac-ity and therefore its undecidability: a final meaning cannot be decided upon. She refers to the patient of her thesis saying, "the earth was bored through [*durch-bohrt*]" instead of "I was impregnated" (p. 91). For Spielrein, the personal or differentiated presentation has been dissolved into an undifferentiated state, and the destruction implicit in the sexual drive becomes evident. Later she gives a citation from Stekel regarding a typical dream of young girls of being stabbed with a knife, which that author remarks is the death of virginity, but then the life of a woman. Spielrein criticizes this interpretation that she qualifies as moralistic, but again states that the woman is "bored through [*durchbohrt*]" (p. 103) in the sexual act. She goes on to give another example from Stekel that demonstrates the means by which language presentations of destruction are also simultane-ously presentations of becoming: "to bore and be born [*bohren und geboren sein*]" (p. 104). Finally, she cites Nietzsche who wrote, "Whoever must give birth [*gebären*]—is sick; however, whoever has given birth [*geboren hat*] is unclean" (p. 108). What Spielrein privileges is not the meaning that is put forward, but rather how that meaning is put into question, through her emphasis upon the signifier, in this case the play between the verbs *bohren* and *geboren sein*, as well as their various derivatives.

In reference to Nietzsche, she states that "The yearning for knowledge is hence for the poet nothing else but the yearning for the mother living in his depth". She goes on to cite Nietzsche with her own parenthesis: "Where is beauty? Where I must will with all my will; where I will to love and to perish, so that a picture does not remain only a picture" (cf. the earlier discussion: With activation a physical content—"picture" [*Bild*] is destroyed, or is activated through destruction) (p. 107). Here Spielrein posits that the beautiful picture [*Bild*] does not remain a picture as it is destroyed and simultaneously activated. We are reminded of her thesis, in which "Over a beautiful picture [*Bild*], one can become poetry" (Spielrein 1911, p. 333). Here she takes a further step, and it is specifically through the destruction of the picture or image [*Bild*], that one can accede to poetry. This destruction of the image is the destruction of the imaginary dimension of narcissism in the I, the narcissism articulated by Sabina Spielrein, which anticipates Freud's foundational paper on the topic, as indicated by Marcus Silva (pp. 137–138). Here we can propose, through Spielrein, that it is in the very destruction of the image, that the signifier—and the symbolic order through which the unconscious makes itself present—is formed.

We can read this at the beginning of her conclusion in which the conscious content "is adapted to the present and receives a specific, immediate color, which the character of the I-relation lends it" (Spielrein 1912c, p. 116). She then differentiates this personal content marked by the colour of the image, from what she literally calls the "symbolic form" [*symbolische Form*] of the unconscious. This she says is the assimilating or dissolving tendency [*Auflösungstendenz*], an expression in which we recognise the dissolution and dilution that springs from the study of the patient in her thesis. We can locate in this dissolving tendency of the symbolic order the very destructive quality of language itself. That is, the signifier comes into being through the destruction of the image, and is itself, at the same time, the instrument of this destruction. This is a completely different notion of the symbol to Jung's, and a theoretical advance on Freud's hitherto untheorised notion of language. It is a fundamental proposition of this paper that underwrites its other novel developments.

Expression, then, is born of the destruction of the personal, common, or imaginary meaning. The destruction of the image [*Bild*], furthermore, produces a saying, or a formation [*Bildung*]:

> the usual, tamed libido goes about with weak destruction-images as, e.g., with teasing, hurting, which has caused the formation [*Bildung*] of such proverbs as "those who love each other, tease each other".
>
> *(p. 115)*

It is striking that the love, rivalry, and aggressivity, which are the hallmarks of the imaginary order, are able to be dissolved to produce the symbolic form of an expression, a saying or proverb, or even a poem. We note that this is an active process of formation, no longer the stasis of an image.

The symbolisation serves to erode the private nature of thoughts: "Words are certainly symbols, which virtually serve to make the personal [*das Persönliche*] generally human and understandable, i.e., to rob [*berauben*] it of a personal character" (p. 100). There is a movement here in Spielrein's work away from the individual, or the ego, towards a function of underlining the Otherness of language. We might recognise here the theme by which we introduced this chapter, that of plagiarism, as well as the theme of robbery that runs through her personal writings. Plagiarism is to both rob someone of their writings, as well as to annihilate the name of the person who wrote the original. That is, to plagiarise here is to rob the original writing of its personal character. This concords with Spielrein's notion of the process of symbolisation—and its production or formation of a saying—that she is elaborating in this paper.

For Spielrein, it is precisely this symbolisation that may produce beneficial effects for the analysand. The destruction of the familiar image or meaning, nonetheless, produces a perturbing effect upon the subject. This is the point in her paper in which Sabina Spielrein, in accordance with Nietzsche, comes to the conclusion that "Language is there to bewilder itself and others". So the destruction of the familiar image, in the emergence of the language of the unconscious, produces bewilderment in the subject. Spielrein goes on to state the following: "And yet we feel a relief with expression, when we form a type-image at the expense of our I-image" (p. 100). The *type* here is associated with the baffling effect of language—of the joke, the dream, the blunder, and so on—just as the *I* had been imbued with the familiarity of the personal imagery. Here we must examine more closely this differentiation that Spielrein makes between the *I* and the *type*.

The I and the Other

Freud of course refers to I or *Ich*, which in English has the unfortunate Latinised, and thus less immediate translation, of *ego*. For Spielrein, the I partakes in both consciousness and the unconscious, just as it does for Freud. The *Ich* or I pertains to what we can call the *subject*, rather than just the ego or self (p. 93). That is, the I is an active proposition, not reducible to a purely passive, reflective, imaginary ego. She uses Jung's terminology of the *type*, with which we are familiar from such terms as the *archetype*. This distinction takes on a distinctly Jungian flavour in the third section of the paper which is entitled "Life and Death in Mythology", which was perhaps even written at Jung's suggestion, or certainly at least in deference to him and his emerging theorisation, in the same way that some sections of her thesis also seem to have been proposed by him. In that third section of the paper Spielrein refers to "hereditary [presentations]" [*ererbten Vorstellungen*] (Spielrein 1912b, p. 175) in accordance with Jung's notion of the collective unconscious, just as she talks elsewhere of "psychologically older contents" (Spielrein 1912c, p. 116). We must recall that Carl Jung supervised Spielrein on the writing of both of these works, as well as being the editor of the *Jahrbuch* in which they were published. Furthermore, Jung was also designated by Sigmund Freud himself as the Crown Prince of psychoanalysis, and hence responsible for its future. Thus, as Spielrein's doctor, "poet", analyst, supervisor, and editor, he could hardly be ignored.

In the main body of the paper, however, this distinction takes on a different tone, the *type-psyche* conveying a function of Otherness. The essential differentiation that she makes is between the *I-psyche* and the *type-psyche*. In discussing psychosis, she refers to the disintegration of the I, at the expense of an alien power. She again uses this expression in the Conclusion whilst discussing the place of love: "If love is lacking, then the [presentation] [*Vorstellung*] of a change of the psychic or bodily individual is under the influence of an alien power, as in the sexual act a destruction- or death [presentation]" (p. 117). Here the type-psyche takes on the character of an alien power: an otherness removed from the particular personal form that it otherwise takes. We find repeated references to the type-psyche or unconscious as "foreign intruder" (p. 88), "hostile beings" (p. 94), and so on. In the same vein she writes that in a "symbolic form, valid for type", the *I* is transformed into a *we*: "The dissolving and assimilating of a personal experience into the form of an art work, a dream, or pathological symbolism transforms this into a type-experience, and makes a 'we' from the 'I'" (p. 117). The return of the repressed, or a formation of the unconscious that might emerge through the course of psychoanalysis, emerges for Spielrein in the form of a *we*, that is, once again an alterity articulated as a *Oneness* [*Einheit*], removed the personal of the *I*.

Spielrein uses a number of terms and conceptualisations for the unconscious of which the type-psyche is but one. Another that we have discussed is the "symbolic", or "symbolic form". She also refers to the unconscious, and also in places, to the "complex", a term introduced by Jung that we see utilised in the passage below. But for Spielrein, as we can read here, the unconscious is always in the dynamic movement of transformation, and it is precisely in the very movement of formation that coming-into-being is effected:

> Every [presentation] reaches its maximum life when it waits most intensively for its transformation into reality; with such realization it is destroyed at once. That does not mean that with the realization of a powerful complex the whole psychic life stands still, for a complex is only a tiny vanishing little part which is differentiated out of the prime experience [*Urerlebnis*]. This actual event [*Ereignis*] produces ever new differentiation products, which are psychically transformed, now in the form of abreaction [*Abreagieren*], now as artwork.
>
> *(p. 101)*

There occurs an unknown and unknowable primal event—or primal scene—from which an "actual event" is the very moment of transformation. This presentation is transformed into speech (abreaction), or into an artwork, which might take the form of a written work such as a poem, or a work of visual art. The "differentiation products" also take the form of "abreaction" (another term adapted from Jung) in the form of the speech of the analysand. The event, however, produces something new, something Other than the personal and intentional speech of the analysand in a moment of the emergence of the unconscious.

Weltschmerz and separation

The differentiation and separation that Spielrein is effecting, both in regard to her relationship with Jung as well as to his theoretical position, is at the same time the differentiation she continues to make throughout this paper, between the conscious as image [*Bild*] and the unconscious as presentation [*Vorstellung*]. This is the same differentiation that she forges by her reference to the pre-Socratic thinker Anaxagoras, who, she states:

> sought the origin of world-weariness [*Welt-schmerz*] in the differentiation of beings [*Seienden*] from primary elements [*Urelemente*]. This pain consists precisely in the fact that each particle of our being longs for the back-transformation [*Rückverwandlung*] in its origins, from which then new becoming [*Werden*] comes forth.
>
> *(p. 92)*

Spielrein's psychiatry thesis is reiterated in this paper, in so far as it is through the yearning for the so-called primal event, or scene, that an actual event of the emergence of the unconscious is produced, by way of which a new becoming is possible. This event is an act of incest, incest once again in the sense of a disturbance of categories in so far as it brings together things that do not go together, in an encounter with a moment of bliss, or jouissance, in the approach to a togetherness that never existed, in an endeavour to erase the pain of separation.

In this schema, Anaxagoras becomes a primordial father who is able to articulate the principle of separation and differentiation. Spielrein is able to elaborate that the source of *Weltschmerz*—including her own—lies precisely in the pain of the differentiation of one's being from that of one's carers: in Spielrein's case her parents and family, and Jung in the transference. However, in accordance with her primary thesis in this paper, it is only through the pain of this destruction that a new becoming may spring forth.

By taking up the writings of the pre-Socratic thinkers, both directly with Anaxagoras, and indirectly through Nietzsche, Spielrein was able to access modes of thinking that had been lost to Western thought since Plato and Aristotle, perhaps even more so following the advent of nineteenth-century rationalism. One of the fundamental questions in psychoanalysis is that of the pleasure principle, which posits the restoration of a supposed harmony or equilibrium. This is the aim of most forms of psychotherapy, but at the loss of being able to address the joy and suffering, and their associated destruction and creativity. Spielrein finds a means to take these up in this paper, going beyond the theses of Freud, and most certainly Jung. In this way Spielrein articulates the impossibility of any stability, that is, a fundamental disharmony.

The writings of Anaxagoras are primarily concerned with the question of separation and coming together, of the universe as a whole, as well as the possibility of coming-into-being of any being. He writes, "Before there was any separation off, because all things were together, there was not any colour evident; for the mixture of all things prevented it" (Curd 2007, p. 19). This colour, to follow Spielrein's thought, is the colouring of the image of the personal, which is precisely the way Spielrein describes the content of consciousness: "This content is adapted to the present and receives a specific, immediate colour, which the character of the I-relation lends it". Spielrein refers to this as a "differentiation-tendency" (1912c, p. 116).

The word that Anaxagoras used in ancient Greek for *separating* was the verb *krinein* [κρίνειν], which means to separate, to distinguish, to judge or decide, or to choose (Curd 2007, pp. 9–10). This separation is the differentiation into the personal, whereas the longing for and movement towards the primordial oneness—the undifferentiated state that remains alien and unknowable to us—is what allows a new becoming. So, we can read Spielrein—with Anaxagoras—as articulating that the differentiation of beings from the primary elements involves the pain of the wish to return to the bliss of one's origins. The unknown origin can be denominated as the unconscious in Spielrein's schema, as the oneness of the *we*, as opposed to the individuality of the *I*. At the same time, through the procurement of a tiny portion of bliss, a new becoming is able to emerge. For Spielrein, this is never a definitive creation, but one that exists only in the very moment of the act of creating, of becoming.

The differentiated state of the *I*, on the other hand, is determined by pleasure and unpleasure, that is, it is regulated by the pleasure principle. The joy and pain of which Spielrein writes, which is the jouissance and suffering of becoming in the approach to the unconscious, is determined by forces that are more obscure and incomprehensible:

> Pleasure is only the affirmative reaction of the I to these demands sprung from the deep, and we can directly have pleasure in displeasure and pleasure in pain which, taken in itself, is really unpleasant, for pain certainly corresponds to a damage to the individual, against which the self-preservation instinct in us bristles [*sträubt*]. Therefore, there is something in our depth which, as paradoxical as it may sound, wants this self-damaging, for the I reacts to it with pleasure. The desire for self-damage, the joy in pain, is however completely incomprehensible, if we only consider the I-life, which wants to have nothing but pleasure.

(Spielrein 1912c, p. 94)

Here Spielrein, in this "joy in pain [*Freude am Schmerze*]", articulates, long before Freud, something that is not only outside the principle of self-preservation, but moreover beyond the pleasure principle. "Pleasure", she affirms, "is only the affirmative reaction of the I to these demands sprung from the deep" (p. 94). It is joy—enjoyment or jouissance—rather than pleasure, that articulates the unconscious as the mode of Oneness to which one's being strives.

For Spielrein, this new principle is foundational in regard to the subject. She notes, taking support from both Jung and Mach, that the I is "something entirely unessential, continually changing, only a certain momentary grouping of feelings" (p. 94) of eternally existing elements, but elements that have become separated from the primordial Oneness. From this she is able to conclude that "I had to reach the insight that the principal characteristic of the individual consists in the fact that it is a dividuum" (p. 94), or "dividual" (1912b, p. 160). The so-called individual is in effect divided by language, by the signifiers of the unconscious, and the signifieds—the meanings and images—of consciousness, or *I*. The dividual is the inevitable separated state of the subject, a subject that yearns for the primordial Oneness of individuality—in other words undividedness—in which there would be a merging with others, the loved ones in one's fantasm, in the impossible merger with the mother, and beyond that a joining with the primal scene.

Joy, terror, and becoming

For Spielrein, it is a question of a struggle between the two antagonistic streams of *type-psyche* and *I-psyche*. The I-psyche, however, "resists this dissolving [*Auflösung*]" (1912c, p. 97) into the type-psyche, in other words, the ego has an essentially defensive structure of resistance. Spielrein utilises *dissolving* rather than dissolution to emphasise the dynamic force of this movement. The function of the analysis would then be to allow the transformation, or evanescent production of new formations, from the type-psyche's overcoming of the I-psyche. What matters is the possible movement that might free up the resistance of the I-psyche in facilitating the openness to the unconscious and allowing an ongoing movement.

"Why the 'joy at recognizing the familiar?'" Spielrein (1912c, p. 98) cites, from Freud's book *Jokes and their Relation to the Unconscious* (1905c). For Spielrein, this joy pertains to the transformation-wish for dissolution into the type-presentation, explaining why infantile experiences are so pleasurable to us. Such experiences might then be expressed in an art work: the artist then "enjoys" (p. 100) his sublimation-products, that is to say, the production of his works of art. She puts forward that every presentation that we give to our fellow human beings, either directly or in the form of a work of art, is a differentiation product of the primary experience [*Urerlebnisse*] (p. 99). She gives the example of a sunny spring day "which has given joy many times to countless generations before us" (pp. 99–100). Whilst here, as in a number of places in this paper, she shows deference to Jung's notion of an archetype, we note that in *her* theorisation, it is in approaching the unknown primal experience that joy is procured.

It is precisely the resistance of the I-psyche that must be overcome in order to experience the joy that comes about in acceding to the presentations of the unconscious. Here Spielrein cites Nietzsche from *Thus Spake Zarathustra*: "'A human being is something that must be overcome,' teaches Zarathustra, 'so that the overman can come about'" (Spielrein 1912c, p. 110). She goes on to paraphrase Nietzsche: "You must understand that you must overcome (destroy) yourself. How could you otherwise create the higher, the child?" (p. 111). The human being that must be destroyed is the dividual, the I or ego, in order that the overman comes into being. And the overman, Nietzsche's *Übermensch*, is the child that is created from this overcoming. But from what Spielrein has said, the overman that is created is also the subject of the unconscious that arises momentarily from the act of becoming. In other words, in overcoming the resistance of the I-psyche, a coextensive creating and procreating takes place. The child that is created is not just a baby, but the subject as child, in the approach to the primal unknown event: the primal scene. So here again we discover the manner in which "the ecstatic feelings corresponding to becoming [*Werden*]" (p. 88) co-exist with the destruction inherent in the sexual drive.

We have already seen, from Spielrein's diaries, the place that she gives to Nietzsche's differentiation of the Apollonian from the Dionysian. From her reading of Nietzsche, the Oneness provoked by Dionysian celebrations is the Oneness of the jouissance of the Other, in which the individual becomes erased in favour of the unity of the dividual or dividedness. In Spielrein's notion of the unconscious, there is a coextensiveness between the division of the subject and the oneness of the experience of incest and the primal scene. In her conclusion Spielrein states, "Assimilation causes the unity [*Einheit*] regarded as 'we', to be formed from a unity regarded as 'I'" (p. 117).

Here we cite Nietzsche from his *Notes* in which he further elaborates upon this differentiation and separation:

> Fundamental psychological experiences: the name 'Apollonian' designates the enraptured lingering before a fabricated, dreamed-up world, before the world of *beautiful illusion* as a redemption from *becoming*. Dionysos, on the other hand, stands namesake for a becoming which is actively grasped, subjectively experienced, as a raging voluptuousness of the creative man who also knows the wrath of the destroyer.
>
> *(1885–1886, pp. 80–81, italics in the original)*

Nietzsche opposed the Apollonian world of the illusion of the imaginary order—the world of the I or ego—from the Dionysian experience of ecstasy. The Apollonian world is one that participates in the homoeostatic economy of the pleasure principle, maintaining order by reducing stimulation to within acceptable limits—the world of the individual or I. As in Spielrein's thesis, the redemption functions as a redemption from becoming: the loss and destruction necessary for the Dionysian state are averted. The Dionysian world, on the other hand, is one that lies beyond the pleasure principle, one in which the subject surrenders him or herself to the joy and terror of a fusion with others, with the Other, and to the destruction from which something new is born or created. This world is one that is "subjectively experienced": it is the evanescent experience of the subject of the unconscious. Here we again cite Nietzsche who articulates something akin to what Spielrein was elaborating:

> the orgiasm of the Dionysian spring festivals awakened almost at once and side by side: the destruction of individuation, the horror over the broken unity, the hope of a new creation of the world, in short, the sensation of a blissful shudder, in which the *knots* of joy and terror are tied together.
>
> *(1867–1873, p. 40, italics in the original)*

The "individuation" here is the separateness of the human or I, which for Spielrein is dissolved in approaching with simultaneous joy and terror the destruction of this illusory unity in the approach to the unconscious, which then allows the possibility of a new becoming, with both a division as well as a knotting of unity.

Spielrein also articulates for psychoanalysis Nietzsche's notion of eternal return that "the overman will always return, and the lowest … the smallest human will always return" (1912c, p. 114). Here Spielrein uses Nietzsche to articulate the Hegelian principle derived from the master-slave dialectic to state—again reiterating a theme of her thesis—"affirmation cannot come forth without negation; in the highest the lowest is also contained" (p. 114). Furthermore, this formulation once again expresses her dynamic principle that neither the human or *I*, nor the unconscious or the *we*, is a stable state: there is always movement possible—eternal return—between these positions. The eternal return is the eternal movement towards the primordial fusion, the eternal return to something that never was and never will be—an eternally elusive object—but which provides an asymptotic point towards which the subject is able to move in subjecting him or herself to language.

It is precisely in acceding to the destructive force of sexuality that a new becoming—an event or *Ereignis*—is achieved. Spielrein concludes her reference to Nietzsche by recounting how Zarathustra is overcome by the "gruesome component"—his sexuality—and lays motionless for 7 days. Then he struggles with a horrifying animal, "which is his own depth", before biting the head off the animal, "hence he kills his own sexuality, and in killing himself his abysmal thought attains the highest power of life [*Lebenskraft*] and with it arises the resurrected Nietzsche" (p. 114). Here it is clearly not a question of Nietzsche himself, but the manner in which the fictionalised Nietzsche, or Zarathustra, takes up the place of Spielrein or of any subject. Zarathustra must wrestle with his sexuality, and it is himself—or his self or ego—that is killed, or overcome, in order to bring forth his life power or *Lebenskraft*. This subject is not a human, since the overman that overcomes the self is no longer constrained by the illusions or *Bilde* of humanity. The new entity emerges from this experience, which we can read as a sort of *prototype*—rather than an archetype—of the subject. Spielrein's theorisation, starting out from the speech of her psychotic patient, is thus able to come to illuminate the place of each and every subject.

The instability of both the I and the unconscious is something that links Spielrein to Nietzsche's mode of thinking. Nietzsche stated: "It is a great disadvantage for a thinker to be tied to one individuality. When a man has succeeded in finding himself, he should try from time to time to lose himself again, and then to seek and find himself once more" (cited in Zweig 1925, p. 287). Stefan Zweig himself had, moreover, the following to say of Nietzsche: "He was ceaselessly undergoing transformation, ceaselessly losing himself and finding himself anew; that is to say, he underwent an everlasting process of becoming, was never rigid, never at rest" (p. 287). As we recall, the moment of becoming that Spielrein draws from Goethe is an *all transitory* [*alles Vergängliche*] one.

From analysis to analyst, from poet to poetry

> My project is coming to an end, and deep depression is taking hold of me. Who is this Prof. Freud to whom I am writing? Can he know what it means to a proud soul to be ridiculed in this way by her best friend?
>
> *(Carotenuto 1980a, p. 104)*

So writes Spielrein of the destruction of her ideal image of Carl Jung in one of her letters to Freud, letters in which she had already articulated the major thesis of this paper. In writing of Nietzsche's confrontation with his "gruesome component", she is articulating the confrontation in her analysis with her own horrifying animal, her sexuality and destruction, and the accession to her means of becoming through the very writing of this paper. By means of her own battle she comes to a conclusion that bears upon each analysand in psychoanalysis, something that carries a seal of truth. As Waldo Emerson notes, "To believe your own thought, to believe that what is true for you in your private heart is true for all men—that is genius" (cited in Sloterdijk 2000, p. 74).

Spielrein writes that one tends to overlook the destructive drive in the sexual drive, but that it does not take much to give preponderance to the destruction-presentations which predominate in neurosis, especially with children and emotional people. This destruction component that takes the form of "incest fantasies or more sublimated fantasy symptoms" (Spielrein 1912c, p. 115), she states, "expresses itself in all the symptoms of resistance against life and natural fate" (p. 116). Those symptoms of resistance are, in one sense, the unmediated fantasy or fantasm of the Other, whether it be that of each of her parents or that of Jung, in which she has become caught and constricted, and which serve to further restrict her possibilities.

It is only in allowing oneself to be subjected to the joy and terror of the transference that something else might be able to be done with one's symptom:

> With love the dissolution of the I in the beloved is at the same time the
> strongest self-affirmation, a new I-life in the person of the beloved. If love
> is lacking, then the [presentation] of a change of the psychic or bodily
> individual is under the influence of an alien power, as in the sexual act a
> destruction- or death-[presentation].
>
> *(p. 117)*

Through the dissolution—we could even say the dissoluteness—that comes
about through transference-love, the strongest self-affirmation may be produced.
The transference-love provides the means by which some of the joy and pain of
a formative event [*Ereignis*] may be procured from the Otherness of the primal
event. Without the device of transference-love in analysis, both the psyche and
the body remain firmly under the yoke of an alien power, of the Other. To submit oneself to the transference is to allow oneself to be mistaken, to allow one's
words to be otherwise spoken. Hence the transference is never reciprocal nor
reciprocated, as opposed to what occurs in a love affair. This is the position of
subjective disparity taken up by the subject in analysis, as Sabina Spielrein articulates from her own analysis.

As we have seen, the current, or actual event produces always new differentiation products, psychically transformed in the form of speech or a work of art.
One of Spielrein's major inventions in psychoanalysisis that one of these differentiation products is the formation [*Bildung*] of the analyst. In other words, the
analyst is literally one of the differentiation products of the destruction of the
image [*Bild*] of the I, which produces a formation [*Bildung*] that is the subject of
the unconscious. These formations are mediated by the signifier, which, as we
have seen, take the form of an expression, speech, artwork, or poetry.

In Spielrein's wake, it is beginning from the destruction of the image that
poetry comes into being. Poetry arises through plagiarism, which is at once to
"rob" something, but also to annihilate—or murder—the person who originally
wrote or spoke it. In other words, the other must be allowed to fall and the
signifier must be permitted to prevail. Plagiarism introduces an object which is
not an object of exchange, but rather the object of a theft which consequently
becomes received as a gift. This object is a product of the same order of the
"accursed share" that Bataille (1967) describes, an excess that is coextensive
with the jouissance of a violent consummation. In one moment this excess takes
the form of the letters that are a surplus from Jung and his writings, and then
through her own production the appropriated and reworked signifiers become
a new production, one that may be taken up by her own analysands—or ourselves—through reworking what Spielrein herself has created. What is produced
then in this creative movement is always something new, an eternal return akin
to a work of art or the words of a poem. From this theorisation that Spielrein has

created, it is possible to say that the transference exceeds any notion of translation, signification, or explanation of the symptom. Rather, the work of analysis is a forward-directed creative movement. Through this poietic mechanism of plagiarism, something original is able to be created.

Freud writes words to the same effect in relation to the separation of the son from the primordial father [*Urvater*] in "Group Psychology and the Analysis of the Ego". Here he speculates that a son, through the exigency of his longing, was moved to free himself from the group by taking over the father's part. "He who did this was the first epic poet", Freud writes. He continues, "Just as the father had been the boy's first ideal, so in the hero who aspires to the father's place the poet now created the first ego ideal [*Ichideal*]" (1921c, p. 136). In the analysis, the analyst embodies this function of I-ideal for the analysand. This I-ideal, however, is that of a poetic father-analyst who must be killed off to allow the emergence of the analysand as poet. It is not the person of the father who is literally killed here, but rather the son's *ideal*—image or *Bild*—of the father that has to be annihilated for the son to accede to the place of poet in his own name. The poet now takes this ideal of the father and from it produces epic poetry, a work that exceeds the person of the father.

But there is another step to be taken, which is that of the ending of the analysis. The subject in analysis, who is the analysand-becoming-analyst, is also the burgeoning analyst-poet whose words become poetry at the end of the analysis, such as the poetry of Spielrein's writing of this paper. In this way, the I or ego of the subject must disappear in order to privilege the "actual event" of the emergence of the unconscious. Even the name of the one who speaks and writes disappears, or is erased in plagiarism. Following Spielrein, we can propose that the position of the end of the analysis is one in which the new analyst, who is a differentiation product of the analysis, allows his or her own name to be destroyed or erased in order to privilege another's—or an Other—speech or writing. The analysand-becoming-analyst is the one who allows himself to be plagiarised, in allowing himself to separate from the analyst and the analysis. If the scene of the unconscious is an Other scene [*ein anderer Schauplatz*], then to become an analyst is to be able to allow this Other scene to exist.

We saw in the last chapter that for Spielrein, Jung's *letters*—his title *Dr.*, his writings, and his correspondence—were necessary to sustain her analysis, and to maintain Jung in the place of analyst, and not just friend, doctor, or poet. So too, at the end of Spielrein's analysis, is she able to allow herself to be reduced to letters. We already examined some of the ways that she allowed the letters of her own name to be borrowed so that from them something different might be produced. Whilst we have proposed with Spielrein that an image [*Bild*] has to be destroyed to permit the formation [*Bildung*] of the signifier, so too at the end of the analysis we can establish that the signifier or *Bildung* has to be destroyed to allow it to be reduced to its elemental letters. While it is impossible for the signifier to reach Anaxagoras' "primary elements [*Urelemente*]", in this movement, it can nonetheless be broken down into elements of the signifier: its letters. We can take this a step further to propose that the training [*Ausbildung*] of the analyst proceeds from the destruction of the formation [*Bildung*] of signifiers into letters. When the analysis is pursued to the point of the exhaustion—or destruction—of meaning, it must come to confront the primary elements of the signifier: its letters. It is from these letters that something new can be born, or come into being, including the writing of poetry.

In the paper that he submitted for the Australasian Medical Congress held in Sydney in 1911, Freud wrote that psychoanalysis made it possible to discover "the valuable attainments of the joke, myths, and poetry" (Freud 1912, p. 387). This discovery of the products of psychoanalysis is simultaneously the creation of these formations of the unconscious—including that of poetry—as a differentiation product of the analysis itself. We recall that Lacan writes, "I never spoke of analytical formation. I spoke of the formations of the unconscious" (Lacan 1975, p. 191, translated for this edition). In other words, in psychoanalysis it is not the production of the person of the psychoanalyst that is privileged, but rather the production of the letters of the unconscious.

One of the letters produced by Spielrein is the one derived from the element of cause in her title, "Destruction as Cause [*Ursache*] of Becoming", an element we have elaborated further elsewhere (Plastow 2017, p. 132). The destruction first produces a lack at the heart of being of the subject, effectively the fall of the object in the real. Coextensively, there is a corresponding destruction of the image [*Bild*], or meaning, in the imaginary register. Third, there is a corresponding destruction in the symbolic register, a crumbling of the signifier into its constituent letters, through the failure to be able to say all. This notion of *cause* is a positivised instance of the lack consequent upon the destruction of which Spielrein writes. Here we have an object of pure presence that is able to effect, or *cause*, a coming-into-being. In this sense it is not so far from Lacan's letter, or object *a*: the object cause of desire.

In Spielrein's case, after she acquires her *letters*, her speech becomes directed elsewhere, to Freud in the first instance in Vienna, and to others beyond him in her life after Zürich. Her art of writing takes the form of this paper and other writings that are imbued with poetry. In accordance with her work, each presentation reaches its maximum life when it waits most intensively for its transformation, and with such realisation it is destroyed at once. Through this means she is able to articulate another fundamental truth in psychoanalysis that any intervention produces effects in its immediacy. It is then up to the subject to make something more of it in its aftermath, that is, to do something with the letters with which one is left at the end of one's analysis. So too the analyst cannot be definitively formed; the analyst only appears at the moment of an "event".

We cannot ignore the place that Spielrein gives to the *belles-lettres*: poetry and literature, in this work. We have already mentioned Goethe and Nietzsche, but we must add Gogol, Shakespeare, Wagner, and the Swiss poet and novelist Carl Spitteler. Moreover, in the paper she refers to Nietzsche as "the poet", and through him—as an instance of formation—she elaborates something of her own poetry. Here Nietzsche serves as a stand-in for Spielrein, or for any subject. The poem, moreover, is itself a differentiation product of the poet: it is the poetry that remains from the destruction of the poet as person and as imaginary being, the destruction of the personal as image. As Spielrein states, "It is striking how passionate poets like to die in their works" (Spielrein 1912c, p. 114). The poet dies or is destroyed, but the poem remains.

Destroy, She Said

In a similar way to the manner in which Spielrein cites Nietzsche stating, "language is there to bewilder itself and others", the French author Pascal Quignard puts forward the following in reference to the German writer Heinrich von Kleist:

> In the interlocutor's speech, language fascinates itself, it speaks almost by itself, and in any case is barely heard or understood. This is Kleist's meditation called *Monolog*. It is also the Des Forêts' narrative entitled *Le Bavard* [*The Chatterbox*]. Speaking is an externalised irretrievable confusion. Language thinks the speaker and his thoughts.
>
> The listener hears [*ouït*].
>
> There is no profound listening without the destruction of the speaker.
> (*Quignard 1996, pp. 141–142, translated for this edition*)

The reference here to writing and literature allows us to move away from the commonly held notion that the speaker controls what he or she says. On the contrary, language not only thinks the speaker, but moreover it speaks the speaker, even fascinating and bewildering the speaker. This destruction of the speaker as an autonomous agency is one aspect of dissolution that Spielrein puts forward in her paper: the ego that must be overcome by the unconscious. The individual or self must be overcome, in order that the overman [*Übermensch*]—or the unconscious—come into being. It is through these means that there arises the possibility of a new becoming.

We have put forward that plagiarism is both to rob someone of their writings, as well as to annihilate the person who wrote the original through the obliteration of that person's name. Curiously, in the interview with Marguerite Duras that we cited earlier in this chapter, when asked if in her novels she took her characters from people in her life, she replied that her writing was fiction and elaborated that "I plagiarise myself in them" (Léridon 1984). Hence we must conclude that she robbed the stories and characters from her own accumulated experiences, but moreover destroyed or annihilated herself—or rather her *self*, her ego—in the process. But from this destruction of her self, Duras also came into being as the author of a work of literature. The accumulated experiences that one might plagiarise from oneself also arise from one's prior reading and writing. These experiences are not simply personal experiences since the subject of the experience—the subject of the writing that one has read for instance—has already become part of one's own experience: they no longer belong just to the writer. In any case, since no one owns language, each speaker and writer is necessarily a plagiarist, always borrowing from the words and phrases, the stories, myths and family romances, the papers and the books that have preceded him or her. This is what allows for the possibility of new writings to come into being.

In regard to her novel *Destroy, She Said* (1969a), when asked what she was referring to by destruction, Marguerite Duras responded that it is the end of the *moi*, or ego, and that the character in the novel by the name of Stein is a man who has lost his ego. In another way, she remarks that this novel is also about madness, precisely the madness of the abolishment of the ego. In another interview regarding this novel, Duras notes that "The madman is an individual who transgresses the essential prejudice—in other words the limits of the 'ego'—and who can no longer tolerate the lie of which we were speaking" (1969b, p. 1169, translated for this edition). That is, the ego—or we could even say the author—is a lie, a necessary lie perhaps, but which has to be transgressed in order to produce a writing, whether this is a piece of literature or a psychoanalytic writing. Duras also says of herself in relation to this novel: "I destroyed myself making it" (p. 1168).

Lacan, in his paper "Homage Given to Marguerite Duras", remarks that:

> The only advantage that the psychoanalyst has the right to draw from his position, were this then to be recognised as such, is to recall with Freud that in his work the artist always precedes him, and that he does not have to play the psychologist where the artist paves the way for him.
>
> *(Lacan 1965, p. 124)*

That is, the psychoanalyst draws inspiration, even borrows or plagiarises from the artist, as Freud also before him drew upon works of art and literature, but he or she has no right to "psychoanalyse" works of art.

Lacan also speaks of the ego "dissolving" (1961–1962, p. 276) in analysis, and this being precisely the point where anguish appears. For Lacan, the dissolution of the ego is an aim of an analysis, a type of asymptotic point towards which an analysis might move, but never arrive at. It is this same dissolution [*lösen*] or destruction of which Spielrein writes: the destruction of the ego and its identifications that is the basis upon which what Lacan calls the "sexual relation" is established. The destruction of the ego is the logical conclusion of the recognition that one does not control language; on the contrary, language bewilders not only the speaker, but even itself. In the destruction of the illusory sexual relation the poet can be annihilated to the advantage of the poem. For Spielrein, the destruction of the ego can allow a movement of invention through the plagiarism of writing.

6

WHAT WERE THE FANTASMS THAT OCCUPIED THE CHILD?

Trembling love. Fear of the prey.
I love your two striking instincts.
Tenacious fear. Trembling love.
Happily I know your style.
I am master in the night.
Tenacious love. Trembling love.
You alighted on the edge
Of the most miserable soul.
Like an eagle on a balcony!
Carefree traveller that I am
I had to beg for your beauty.
Tenacious love. Trembling love.
The hollow clock of death
I honour it in your beautiful eyes,
I recognise it by the injurious breasts.
Flowers we see only at night
Are what make us reflect.
But please watch our eyes.
When we suffer make us cry.
When we cry we are almost happy.
Tenacious love. Trembling love!

Léon-Paul Fargue, "Tremblant 7" (1895, p. 37, translated for this edition)

Here we will examine Spielrein's paper "Contributions to the Knowledge of the Child's Soul" (1913), which remains untranslated into English. This was one of the very first papers to theorise psychoanalysis of the child, following Freud's then recently published case of Little Hans (1909b). Following on from Freud's case history, it is one of the very first papers to address the question of child psychoanalysis as a specific area of practice. The paper, in part, is a response to Freud's call to his disciples to provide observations from the sexual life of children. This is specified right from Spielrein's first sentence of the paper: "The great doctrine of psychoanalysis requires much evidence that is easily comprehensible, especially from child psychology" (1913, p. 57, translated for this edition).

The paper consists of three cases, together with a conclusion and an appendix concerning the symbolic—or symbolism—of time. The first case is an account of Spielrein's own childhood and fantasy life, effectively an account of her childhood through a written reworking of her analysis. The second case in this paper is a narration of her analysis of a 13-year-old boy, in part through the poems that he writes, poems that evoke his relation to his mother, and the reality of death. In the third case it is no longer so much a question of the mother, as that of the place of the father, and even more specifically the place of the father's name.

Published in 1913, however, this paper is also an account of the end of her analysis, an ending that she continued to effect through her writing, including this paper. As we have already put forward, Spielrein's writing here—as an extension of her thesis and "Destruction as Cause of Becoming"—anticipates a theorisation of the end of a personal analysis which constitutes a contribution to psychoanalysis itself. Spielrein, in this paper, continues to theorise the mechanism of analysis, as well as that of its ending. This constitutes part of her endeavour to formulate the ending of her analysis, and the love affair that developed in the wake of the analysis with Carl Jung. She differentiates herself theoretically from Jung, utilising the Freudian method of free association by putting significant words and phrases into play, important signifiers regarding the manner in which she constitutes herself. Drawing upon both Freud's and Jung's work, she establishes a terminology and a theorisation of her own, also based upon the work that she has done in her thesis and the "Destruction as Cause of Becoming" paper.

This work is given short shrift by Spielrein's chroniclers and biographers, being limited by them to a mere paragraph, or at most a page. Kerr reduces this writing to the question of her relation with Jung and speculates that fearful sexual fantasies lay underneath the various fantasies that had occupied her as a small child. He proposes that such a conclusion would have been most unwelcome from Jung's point of view since Jung was arguing the exact opposite, thus sowing the seeds for his rupture with Freud. Kerr, however, does not discern any originality in Spielrein's paper, arguing that she "was assimilating herself to the local psychoanalytic idiom" (1993, p. 394), the idiom, that is, of Freud's Vienna. He concludes that she had simply adopted Freud's ideas, not recognising the manner in which, in this paper, she had pursued her own theses stemming from her previous writings. Launer—in contrast to Kerr—suggests that Spielrein's theoretical approach in this paper echoes that of Carl Jung, through her emphasis upon the similarity of the themes that emerge from children to mythical ideas. Launer suggests that such a comparison "would have appealed to Jung" (2015, p. 161). Spielrein's German biographer Sabine Richebächer makes

a more cogent assessment of this paper, emphasising the movement of separation that it effects, proposing that the paper can be read "as a swansong to Jung"
(2005b, p. 189). She pertinently comments that in the paper, "Spielrein elegantly
demonstrates that interest in scientific and intellectual work derives from sexual
curiosity" (p. 189). In this paper, while it is clear that there are themes that she
takes from both Jung and Freud, what stands out is the way in which Spielrein
is able to take elements from each in order to create an original theorisation of
her own.

This paper is a veritably psychoanalytic work in so far as Spielrein derived its
theorisation from her personal experiences and fantasies, some of which were
already committed to paper in her diaries and correspondence. She was able to
elaborate from what she had already developed from these in her own psychoanalysis, moreover, and utilise her theoretical advances in the analysis of the two
other cases. One of the salient themes is Spielrein's notion of the position of the
child, between the enjoyment of a blissful union with the parents and the pain of
separation from them. This is the place in which she locates the subject, caught
between the jouissance of the fantasm of fusion, and the desire that emerges
from the pain of parting. And it is the way in which the subject is able to take
up a new position in regard to the fantasm in which he finds himself that is able
to determine how he is able to put this to use in the creation of something new.
Sabina Spielrein also poses a question regarding the notion of *cause* that derives
from her personal writings and is further elaborated in the "Destruction as Cause
of Becoming", in which the cause [*Ursache*] that is produced from destruction is
precisely what causes a coming into being. She articulates this in the following
manner: "Where is the beginning of all beginnings and the end of all ends?"
(1913, p. 58), an unanswerable question in so far as the origin is structurally
homologous to the end as is implied in the question itself. The cause could
equally well be found at the end, as at the beginning, but is more precisely to be
found in neither place.

For Spielrein, the work of analysis is never done; the subject remains a dividual, suspended between the suffering and jouissance of destruction, and the
desire and creativity of becoming. The French author Henri Thomas, in his
introduction to the work of Léon-Paul Fargue—a poem of whose we have utilised to open this chapter—writes the following regarding Fargue, which might
be equally applied to Sabina Spielrein: "He is his own life, whose riches will
never be exhausted by his heart and his spirit—suffering and joy, solitude and
tenderness" (Thomas 1967, p. 9, translated for this edition). We read here the
way in which, as for Spielrein, the subject is forever divided, here between suffering and joy, solitude, and tenderness. Thomas cites Fargue himself who wrote,
"One is never cured of one's childhood" (pp. 9–10). This childhood is the temporal source of the riches of one's life, and the origin of one's pain. And, given
that there is no cure, what then? On this point Fargue is clear, hence his proposition: "So, it is better to be a poet, in other words, to act" (p. 11). Whilst speaking is the motor of psychoanalysis, writing is the means of leaving a mark that

is not so easily erased. And poetry is to be located somewhere between speech and writing, between re-citation and enigma, the font of a writing that retains its riddle. Thomas comments further upon this: "Living thought, like poetry, is first of all and always the refusal of appearance, of the picturesque, in the name of living substance. It is not the object that must be attained, but rather its very music, its secret cipher" (p. 11). This we can say is also Spielrein's project: to act through her writing and poetry in order to touch upon the elusive movement of life itself, to put paid to the beautiful picture and to endow this living substance with her own flesh and blood.

An unknown force wanted to snatch me away from my parents

Spielrein begins her own account with the letters derived from the destruction of her own name, that of purity, or *Rein-heit*: "My parents, and particularly my mother, were proud of their daughter's 'purity and naivety'" (1913, p. 57). Right from the beginning, she is able to articulate an aspect of the place that she occupied in her mother's fantasm. The sexual innocence in which she claims she was held, even until attending university, is belied by her elaborate infantile sexual theories. In any case, a university knowledge can only be a general knowledge, in contrast to the singular knowledge that she produces of herself from her fantasms in this paper. Her apprehension of her position in the Other's fantasm is augmented in this brief account, in which the striking observation is the manner in which Sabina Spielrein is able to articulate the ways in which she is subject to something beyond herself, the manner in which she is subject to the Other.

In continuing this thread, she states, "I felt that an unknown force wanted to snatch me away from my parents" (p. 58). This force to which she was subject thus had the quality of effecting a separation. And in relaying this in the account of her analysis, the force of which she speaks is none other than the force of the transference that carried her onwards and forwards, as opposed to the retrogressive movement of a retreat back to her childhood positions. She articulates this tension through the discovery in her personal writings and her analysis, which became the central thesis of her "Destruction as Cause of Becoming" paper: "Consciously or unconsciously, the woman surrenders herself to the new being that grows at the expense of the old. It is interesting that we react to these destruction-presentations, sometimes with pleasure, sometimes with anguish, or at least with displeasure" (p. 60).

She attributes this force to a paternal threat, one that was associated with a vision of two black kittens, and subsequent fantasies about little cats, stand-ins for children that she might receive from her father through her infantile sexual fantasies. "What were these 'fantasms'", she asks, "that occupied the child?" (p. 58). This question is the fundamental interrogation that occupies her, both in regard to herself, and consequently any analysis, particularly the analysis of a child who struggles to find his or her place in regard to the parental fantasm.

Her subjection to an unknown force, indeed an unknowable force, is marked by the anguish and fears that she describes in relation to certain infectious diseases, especially the plague—as a means of articulating the infectious disease of sexuality—as well as that of the great master: death. She experienced this subjection in her brother, who was "my faithful playmate [*Spielgenossen*], younger than me, who had to do everything I wanted. My immediate thought about the 'vision' was, 'Here is death' or 'the plague'" (p. 60). Here we find a fragment of Spielrein's name [*Spiel*] articulated in respect of jouissance [*genossen*]. Thus in a few words, she articulates what Freud called the two great enigmas of psychoanalysis—and the riddles for the subject: sexuality and death.

One of the forms that this took for Spielrein was a supernatural force of which she was in possession on one hand, and, on the other, it was a force that carried her away. She called this force the "[*Partunskraft*]" (p. 57), taking this from a French verb of her invention *parter*, this in turn being derived from the actual verbs *partir* (to leave) and *porter* (to carry). We might then render this as the *force of parting*. We are struck by her linguistic invention which in itself is able to carry her desire to leave and separate, but which was able to recognise the force, or fantasm, to which she was already subjected. We might also further recognise— as an anagram—in the letters of her new signifier, the Latin *pater*, or father, as a means of effecting her separation or *Abschied*. Moreover, this *Parter* is, at the same time, an allusion to *parturition* or childbirth, that is, an opening onto procreation—and the parting of a newborn from its mother—that took the form in her analysis of her desire for a child called Siegfried. In her account of her analysis, the destruction of the usual images—or meanings—of words is already in itself an act of creation, that of a new signifier.

Spielrein writes, "The animals and illnesses, which I saw as living beings, wanted to 'do me harm' [*Leid antun*] and lead me to an uncanny [*unheimlich*], dark death". The notion of being abducted from her parents insists in her writing. She remarks, "I felt a force that was trying to take me from my parents" (p. 60). Here she cites the first two lines of the following stanza from Goethe's "Erl King", a poem recounting the imagined seduction of a child in which the abductor, the Erl-King of the title, in part takes the form of the father:

> "I love thee, I am charmed by thy beauty, my boy!
> And if thou'rt unwilling, then force I'll employ."
> "My father, my father, he seizes me fast,
> Full sorely the Erl-King has hurt me [*Leids getan*] at last"
> *(Goethe 1782)*

Spielrein comments that Goethe would not have been able to describe the anguish of the young boy so well if he had not himself known this "anguished desire" of replacing the father figure with a new love object. This is the notion that she is elaborating in this paper: the anguished desire of the child to replace the desire for an incestuous object with one from outside the family. In other words, she endeavours to replace an endogamous object with an exogamous one. To do this the child must give up a quotient of jouissance that is invested in each of the parents and find a new position in the fantasm in which he is caught. She notes that her own Erl-King was, in the first instance, the figure of God, behind which her young uncle was hidden. In other words, the Erl-King is the sexual desire that draws the child beyond the immediate family and through which the child takes leave of his or her parents. Spielrein writes, "The fantasm of abduction by God (unconsciously by my uncle), was always very pleasurable for me, since from my earliest childhood I clearly entertained the unconscious desire for a replacement for the love I had from my parents. But only the paternal threat transformed the pleasure into anguish" (1913, p. 61).

This uncle, who was a chemist by profession, also showed Sabina and her siblings an experiment in which he plunged a stick of zinc into a solution of lead salts. She describes how from this a new form was crystallised, one that was "a 'real' tree". We recall what she had written in her thesis, from the words of her patient, that from the earthly mixture of water and dead bones a new animal is able to crystallise out: a psychotic theory of reproduction thrown out onto the world outside. In a similar, but neurotic theory of procreation, Spielrein declares that: "Chemistry is the power that creates miracles. And I became an 'alchemist'". She mixed food and drinks to create new colours and textures: "I cannot forget the mixture of joy and anguish that gripped me when a piece of material was transformed by some unknown force into paper" (p. 59). Her alchemy is able to effect a change of state—a transformation, she says—on the materials she works with in order to create something new. Alchemy is the production of gold and the elixir of life from base materials, that is, the effecting of a sublimation. This is a sublimation of writing that she is producing in order to produce a separation. Her alchemy here is to effect a transmutation in her being—once again from analysand and lover to analyst—by invoking and harnessing the unknown force.

Her production of a substance with a new colour or texture effected joy and anguish [*Freude und Angst*], two sides of jouissance and desire. She once again returns to this experience at the end of this autobiographical section of the paper saying, "So one can really create 'life' artificially!". It is from this alchemy that there commenced an enthusiasm for chemistry, which, as she writes, first begins in all primitive peoples as alchemy. She recounts how at university she developed a passion for organic chemistry: "It always seemed to me that I had known it all since long ago" (p. 61). Her analysis was a means of rediscovering and articulating what she had already known—her singular sexual knowledge of pro-creation—and which had determined her relation to others, and to the Other. In this way she is able to put a caveat upon the fantasm in which she finds herself.

She remarks that in fact, at least from the point of view of consciousness, it was not the case that she had this knowledge from long ago: "I explained this remarkable false memory to myself in the following way: that we inherit the wisdom of our fathers in the unconscious". Here, at the end of her account of her analysis, she refers to a Jungian notion of the unconscious—that of the hereditary unconscious. What is noteworthy, however, is the particular twist, or caveat, that she gives to this notion, adding that such "presentations or shadow-images" of the Jungian unconscious "must become saturated in blood [*Blut getränkt werden müssen*] (p. 61)" in order to enter consciousness. This very carnal expression articulates that for Spielrein, the unconscious must be realised in the flesh in order for the analysis to conclude, so that it does not remain the play of shadow-images in Plato's cave. The spilling of blood, then, is a type of initiation ceremony of her accession to adult life.

We recall that when Odysseus, in Homer's *Odyssey*, goes to Hades to consult the ghost of Tiresias, seer of Thebes, he set sail with his ship loaded with sheep and other animals to sacrifice to the dead. This he does, and lets their blood pour into a trench that already contained other libations. In Hades, Odysseus encounters the ghost of his mother who was not able to look him in the eye, nor speak to him. It is Tiresias himself who tells Odysseus how to make the ghosts speak, here in Pope's translation:

> Nor this (replies the seer) will I conceal.
> Know, to the spectres that thy beverage taste,
> The scenes of life recur, and actions past:
> They, seal'd with truth, return the sure reply;
> The rest, repell'd, a train oblivious fly.
>
> *(Homer)*

In this way the spirit that is soaked in blood—the beverage that Odysseus offers by sacrificing the animals he has brought—is able to permit the spectres to become flesh, which, as Spielrein also articulates, is necessary in an analysis. It is only then that the spirit is able to speak, and to speak the truth. We recall her words when she had cut Jung with a knife and literally drawn blood, "That's not my blood, that's his: I murdered him!" This very carnal moment was one that was necessary for her recognition and subsequent symbolic sacrifice of her Holofernes, in order to finish her analysis.

A number of years later, in a letter to Jung of 6 January 1918, she comes to utilise the same expression in regard to her analysis. In this letter she is still endeavouring to repair the rift in theory between Freud and Jung, but utilises her own analysis to exemplify her theses. She asserts that Jung and Freud utilise the same material—which she calls "subliminal"—and analyse it in opposite directions. Jung analyses the part of what she calls the "subconscious" that approaches consciousness, whilst Freud takes the same material and analyses the unconscious. Effectively she argues, *contra* Jung, that not all repression can be lifted, some is required for the individual to be able to function: "Depending on the personality of the patient and more especially that of the doctor, analysis of the 'unconscious' can rob [*berauben*] the analysed material of its energy, or 'saturate it with blood'" (Carotenuto 1980a, p. 70). If the doctor registers disapproval during the analysis, he increases the patient's resistance. On the other hand, if he displays too much pleasure, he encourages the patient's self-indulgent tendencies and thus the patient "saturates his desires with blood". These two extremes, she writes, are especially risky in analyses involving a doctor and a patient of different sex, thus referring to herself and Jung, which she does more specifically later in the letter.

She suggests that the neutral attitude of the Freudian method is better suited to the average patient, but clearly Spielrein is far from the average patient, particularly given that in her analysis the unconscious "must become saturated in blood". She notes an interaction with Freud regarding the analysis "of one of my Siegfried dreams" in which Freud had observed that "You could have the child, you know, if you wanted it, but what a waste of your talents, etc" (p. 71). This comment had a tremendous influence upon her, lending support to her conception that Freud's method supported the sublimation projects of his patients. On the other hand, she reproaches Jung for not having supported her to sublimate her libido in order to compose music as she was doing at the time of writing: "The suppressed need found expression in occasional outbursts and with such vehemence that you once told me I might lose my mind if I allowed myself to make music". But in German, Spielrein articulated this "if I allowed myself to make music" as *"wenn ich Musik treibe"*, in other words, if I allow myself to be moved, to be carried away with the *Trieb* or drive, or to drift away with the music. The effect, when she was finally able to permit herself to do this, was that "my teacher was deeply stirred by the freshness and intensity of my songs" (p. 72).

Once again Jung stands in for the implacable Apollo who wants to impose order and the logic of consciousness at a time when Spielrein experiences a need to sublimate her libido in music, to submit herself to the unconscious: the dithyramb, we must say, of the Dionysian song. For Jung, this impulse, directed towards creativity and becoming, would make her fly too close to the logic of the unconscious, and cause her to lose her mind—to lose, for a moment, the logic of consciousness that he privileged. As Spielrein says later in "Contributions to the Knowledge of the Child's Soul", the child—like the unconscious—"knows no contradiction" (1913, p. 68). Jung exhorts her to choose either the sublimation of her libido in music composition, or her mind. But she does not choose between Jung and Freud, between Apollo and Dionysus, or between music and psychoanalysis: for her, these are not mutually exclusive categories. Spielrein, through her opening onto the unconscious, privileges the disturbance of categories that constitutes incest, that is, the bringing together of what is not meant to be together. This incest is realised, not in an incestuous *relationship*, but rather in the approach to the unconscious as she construes it.

Spielrein asks herself why she did not compose earlier, and once again addressing Jung, replies to her own question: "Because I was afraid of life, afraid of thrusting myself forward, afraid of the 'demonstration' of my most intimate feelings, which I allowed myself to show only to you, and then in a very awkward manner, sometimes stiff, sometimes excessive". She notes that the same tendency was also transmitted to her sublimation tendencies, and that this derives from a fixation of the libido in an infantile attitude. This fixation, she asserts, results in a regression of the libido—the Jungian method—such that earlier wishes are "saturated with blood". The earlier the wishes, the more "the contents of the individual *conscious* become transformed into the collective conscious, individual problems appear as age-old problems" (Carotenuto 1980a, p. 72, italics in the original). Here Spielrein is writing against Jung's method, asserting to him that this is only an *appearance*, or a beautiful illusion. We recall the words of Henri Thomas: "Living thought, like poetry, is first of all and always the refusal of appearance". For Spielrein, the analysis has its effect specifically by the word being made flesh, by being saturated with blood, such that "individual problems and their solutions again crystallize" (p. 72). This is Spielrein the psychoanalyst taking Jung, her former analyst, to task.

In this way, Spielrein produces "life artificially": precisely through the working of her transference, creating something new from this through the artifice of language in the writing of this and other papers. This artificial life is also the life of the analyst, the life that is produced through the transference to her as analyst. She continues to establish her place as analyst through the writing of this paper, precisely in the two cases that follow. She produces a new life for herself through what we can call her plagiarism and reformulation of Jung's fantasm, a fantasm that includes his theorisation of the ancestral unconscious, and his notion of analogues. Freud himself noted the homology between theory and phantasy through the quasi-slip of the pen that he had made, from *theorising* to *phantasying* [*Phantasieren*] (Freud 1937c, p. 225). By putting a twist or a caveat in the fantasm in which she is caught—including that of Carl Jung—she breathes into it her own new life, her flesh and blood, through the artifice of her writing.

In psychic life, there are only products of our psyche

In the second case of which Spielrein writes, that of an intelligent 13-year-old boy named Otto, it is also a question of an anguished sexuality that takes the form of an abduction or seduction. Otto is caught between his fear of—and desire for—seduction on the one side, and on the other, a horrified flight back to his mother. As a child Otto was always afraid that he would be attacked by an old woman. This became crystallised in the form of an ugly old coalwoman, and their cook had taunted him that the coalwoman wanted to kiss him. Otto spoke of a series of dreams in which an "anatomical building" plays a recurrent role. Spielrein states that Otto's fantasm is not only preoccupied by the coalwoman, but also with anatomy, specifically with the anatomy of the woman, the anatomy of his mother. Spielrein states that Otto utilises the building to present the human body.

In the first dream, Otto is in front of some steps that lead up to this anatomical building; the ugly old woman wants to kiss him, and he wants to flee back to his beautiful mother. In the second dream, he wants to escape from the ugly woman into the anatomical building, but it is locked. The "building" is effectively a room, and Spielrein reminds us that the derogatory term *Frauenzimmer* (wench) equates the woman with a room [*Zimmer*], and remarks that "in each adult at every step one finds 'building' as a symbol for a woman" (1913, p. 63). Here Spielrein articulates a topographical reference of the unconscious. Otto's notion of "anatomy" is that of a science that deals with the presentation of the body by the unconscious.

The following day Otto recounts another dream, which Spielrein remarks derives from the same time as the others. A drawing of the anatomical building is included in Spielrein's paper (Figure 6.1). Otto enters a room with his back against the door [*Türe*] where his governess [*Gouvernante*] is seated. He goes to the window [*Fenster*], steals a piece of jewellery, and loses a bead from it. The word for "loses" is from the verb *verlösen*, variants of which figured prominently in Spielrein's thesis. The woman [*die Frau*] rushes in through the other door, and he wants to run away but the door is shut. The woman throws herself upon him, and she, in Otto's words, "gets me in a tangle". What was especially frightening for Otto was her wide-open mouth with big teeth. At this point in the analysis, Otto went and played "a melody that always haunted me" on the piano from Mozart's *Magic Flute*. Spielrein asks him what he remembered from this: "It's a chorus to Isis and Osiris. There are priests there with long flutes. One of the priests wanted to get married". Spielrein reproduces this chorus in which Tamino is to marry Pamina in Mozart's opera. She states that it is immaterial whether Otto's forbidden act occurs in reality or in the fantasm: "In psychic life there are nothing but products of our psyche". In other words, it is the fantasm that structures what we call reality. Otto's dream demonstrates the violence of realising his desire: "Otto robbed the forbidden jewels, just as Adam and Eve robbed the forbidden fruit". We have noted that for Spielrein the act of robbery—or plagiarism—is a forbidden endeavour to appropriate something for oneself, to make it one's own. To lose a bead is then Otto's means of making the forbidden jewels his own, to introduce a cut or difference in this object of desire. An act of plagiarism is also an act of violence towards

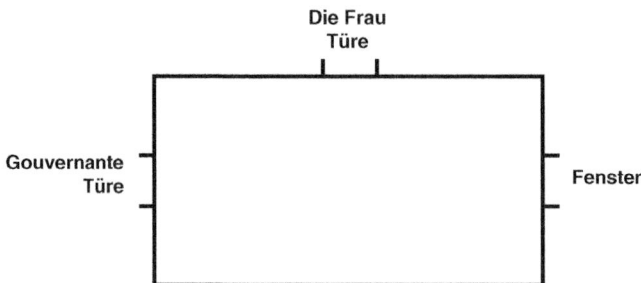

FIGURE 6.1

Figure reproduced from "Beiträge zur Kenntnis der kindlichen Seele" (Spielrein, 1913, p. 63).

the owner of the forbidden object, the mother in this case for Otto, from whom he robs the jewel of her sex. Her sex is also her forbidden fruit [*Frucht*], with all its associations to amniotic fluid, fertilisation, jouissance, and so on. Spielrein comments that in the dream Otto receives the punishment for his transgression by the mouth and teeth of the woman. By way of introducing his further associations to this part of the dream, she states that for him, "the woman is the devil that takes him" (p. 63). The woman, who is not the mother, occupies the place of desire for Otto.

Spielrein strikingly notes that "The dream demonstrates the opposite of self-consciousness" (p. 64). Tamino, who is bold, pure, and worthy, chooses God. Otto, on the other hand, acts in a way that is cowardly, filthy, and chooses the devil. For Spielrein, once again it is the self or the ego that must be overcome for the subject of the unconscious to be realised. Otto does not believe in God, for him Man consists of the trinity of a good man, a worm, and an evil man: "The division of Man into three parts is the aftermath of the domain of religious ideas that have been newly-rejected" (p. 64). After some thought, Otto clarified that the worm was really life, it moves like life itself, or desire, in a serpentine manner. Spielrein observes that "This is already a conscious reinterpretation of a fantasm that has emerged from the unconscious" and that the worm corresponds to "the enjoyment [*Genüße*] of the forbidden love-fruit" (p. 65). Here Spielrein emphasises not just the dialectic of desire, but also the dimension of enjoyment or jouissance. The difficulty here for Otto is how to appropriate some of this enjoyment for himself, a jouissance that would then be something different to an imagined blissful reunion with his mother in which the fruit of the tree of life that tempts him is her body, and her body alone. This love-fruit [*Liebesfrucht*] again evokes the *Fruchtwasser*, the fruit-water which is the term for amniotic fluid in German, and the *Befruchtung* or fertilisation or impregnation, which Spielrein recorded from the patient of her thesis. And it is to this fruit-water that Otto imagines he would like to return.

But the worm—or snake as Otto indicates—is *life*, specifically the devil that is able to eat the fruit from within; it is the element of decay and corruption through which Otto might be able to devour the fruit in his own right, in his own name. The worm eats the fruit by stealth, just as Otto steals the piece of jewellery. The worm eats some of the apple, and Otto loses a bead from the piece of jewellery: the fruit and the apple are no longer whole, but through the cut of this missing piece, Otto is able to appropriate the jewellery—which of course might also allow the possibility of possessing a woman other than his mother. The worm in the fruit is Otto's own mortality which he elaborates further on.

Following her sensitivity to the poetic, Sabina Spielrein reports on two poems that Otto wrote and which were dedicated to his mother. His mother believed that Otto had copied these poems from elsewhere, in other words that he had plagiarised them. No doubt he, like any poet, took words and ideas from writing and poetry that he had read elsewhere, in order to make them his own in the writing of this poem. The first of these is entitled "Life":

> Beginning is end
> End is song
> The beginning ends
> The end has won.
> *(p. 65)*

Otto explains that the best state is to have not yet lived; for him, the happiest time is that just prior to birth. For Otto, this is not an ongoing period of time, but rather a static moment on the very verge of birth. Spielrein adds that this is also the opinion of passionate poets, "who want to have the highest enjoyment [*Genuss*], and then death". Otto, like the Flying Dutchman to whom Spielrein refers in "Destruction as Cause of Becoming", longs for death as he wishes to return to his beloved mother, to the "anatomy building" of his dream. Birth and detachment [*Loslösung*] from his mother for him are death, and "The end, the Nothing, is the most beautiful state according to Otto" (p. 65). If things cannot be as beautiful as they once were, then it is better not to live. It is this transient moment prior to being born, prior to what might be called an *ending*, which is the Nothing in which there is a type of non-being. This formulation evokes the manner in which Sabina Spielrein articulated the transitoriness of the moment of becoming: "Every presentation reaches its maximum life when it waits most intensively for its transformation into reality; with such realization it is destroyed at once". Otto endeavours to wait at the point just prior to transformation, or becoming, since he cannot bear the destruction of the bliss that he imagines of the period prior to birth.

Spielrein then reproduces a poem in which, once again, the question of time is at the forefront, entitled "The Clock":

> At the table stands an old clock
> That our forebears had owned;
> To the clock it would seem proper
> to eke out the life of man.
> The only one who understood the oracle of the clock,
> Was the grandmother;
> And I had long been glad of the deadline,
> In which my age was indicated,
> Then one day I became ill;
> I was very glad of the right saying/judgement, [*Richtigspruch*]
> The old grandmother was no more.
> And I could not say to her,
> What I wanted so much to ask her.
> *(p. 66)*

What he wanted so much to ask her was driven, as alluded to in the poem, by the demand for an obsessional certainty about knowledge regarding the hour of his death. But of course this is an always-missing knowledge, an impossible knowledge that must be borne in order for one to live. Sabina Spielrein notes that Freud says that children and neurotics live outside of time because they live in their fantasms [*Phantasie*]. Spielrein also states that "The dreadful question as to when the blessed moment would come for him would not be solved [*gelöst*], since the grandmother (=clock) fell silent". That is, the grandmother could not tell him the moment of his death since in the meantime she herself had died. This equivalence between the grandmother and the clock also functioned in the other direction, and thus according to Otto's own words, "The clock is the grandmother of two coach-boys with whom he meets up", despite his mother's prohibition. Once again, Otto was eking out a separate existence for himself by stealth. Any certainty that might be gained from the Other's words would, in any case, be undermined by Otto's transgressions. The transgression would allow the production of a knowledge of his own, different to that of his mother, grandmother, or any other of his forebears. To effect this is to rupture the imagined similarity that Spielrein articulates in the following manner: "Each child wants to be the same age as the corresponding parent, to have the same rights and enjoyment [*Genüsse*]" (p. 66). The statement by Spielrein of the child's identification anticipates what Freud says in "Group Psychology and the Analysis of the Ego" in the chapter on identification, in which he states that the first true object relation of the child is to the father: "Identification is known to psycho-analysis as the earliest expression of an emotional tie with another person. It plays a part in the early history of the Oedipus complex. A little boy will exhibit a special interest in his father; he would like to grow like him and be like him, and take his place everywhere". It is only a little later that "the boy has begun to develop a true object-cathexis towards his mother" (Freud 1921c, p. 105).

There is no direct mention of the father in Spielrein's account, making it difficult for Otto to take up the age or position of the corresponding parent. This in itself emphasises his difficulty in taking leave of the mother, and yet the *worm*—in Otto's tripartite division of man—functions as a paternal principle, one that allows him to be able to produce a difference in the mother's fantasm of unity in which he participates. Otto fell ill—lovesick we might say—and "much enjoyed the great love of his mother at that time [*Er wurde krank, genoß wohl in dieser Zeit die große Liebe seiner Mutter*]" (Spielrein 1913, p. 66). Illness, for Otto, was a return to his mother, to a state akin to that prior to birth. The heaviness of the significance of a separation from his mother is that of death. Accordingly, at the time of his illness, he fell back into the enjoyment or jouissance of his mother, from which it was so difficult for him to free himself, just as this is a logical moment of separation for any subject.

We must not reject anything in the child's fantasms as nonsense

Spielrein's third case in this paper is the four-and-a-half-year-old Valli, who like the young Sabina Spielrein herself, has numerous fantasies regarding where babies come from. The first of these that he puts forward is "from Mama's blood". Spielrein notes that Valli takes this theory from a condensation of two fairy tales, that of Snow White who according to Valli "had red cheeks, like blood" (p. 66), and that of Sleeping Beauty who pricks her finger and dies. Valli's fantasies of birth and death are derived from the elements of what he knows—they are related to things seen and heard as Freud (Masson 1985, p. 240) wrote. Valli derives these in part from these well-known fairy tales. Spielrein notes that in the fairy tale, the curse of death that is first bestowed upon Sleeping Beauty is commuted to a 100-year sleep. She comments that the difference between death and sleep here is only one of degree.

This case gives us a useful idea of Spielrein's theorisation, technique, and interpretation in work with children. For this reason we will give prominence to the case here, particularly given that it is one of the very first accounts of the psychoanalysis of children. Spielrein states that she avoids suggestive questioning—alerting us to her technique in this new field of psychoanalysis of children. She writes that she does not enquire about the father's role, but rather she enquires where the father comes from. Valli's answer is "Also from Mama's blood". Hence Valli's theory of origins is literally "saturated in blood". This identical theory of origins of both son and father alerts Spielrein to the identification and rivalry with the father. She asks him, "Why do you call him Father then?", to which Valli gives what she calls a "nonsensical" answer, "Because he is an agronomist" (p. 67), citing his father's profession. However, even though it is a piece of nonsense, by these means Valli gives his father a name, even if it is the name of his profession, something that Valli lacks in his own right. Nonetheless Spielrein adds—in Jungian mythological terms—that this reference to Valli's father's profession pertains to the symbolism of human fertilisation, that is, the father's other profession as progenitor.

Valli's father is away on a voyage and his mother greatly misses him. Valli says to his mother, "Call me Father, then you will not long for him". His mother thinks he has expressed himself awkwardly, and that he had wanted to say, "Call me by my Father's name" (p. 67). Spielrein makes an acute observation here: she concedes that, due to Valli's rivalry with his father it is probable that he has articulated what he meant to say incorrectly, but that we should not arbitrarily correct the words of the analysand, but rather we must follow the "error". Curiously she remarks that here the "error" is also a "promise": a promise then of associations and "errors" to come. It is the promise of other signifiers that will be produced in a forward-directed analysis. To follow this promise is, for Spielrein, to find its justification in the unconscious presentations of the child.

In further following his various theories of origins, Valli puts forward that the father has made the mother, and the mother the father. Spielrein comments that this apparent contradiction should not lead us astray: "The dream, like primitive peoples, knows no contradiction, just like the child (Freud). For him, both theories have the same right to exist. He allows both to occur side by side, unconcerned by whether they exclude each other or not". Spielrein makes a footnote here that, as is well known, when a child is asked whether he likes Mummy *or* Daddy best, he often responds "Mummy *and* Daddy". The child demonstrates a knowledge of logic, but is not perturbed by a logical contradiction, the implication being that the child is closer to the logic of the unconscious than that of the ego of the adult. Spielrein refers to Freud's remark that in the unconscious—as well as in primal words [*Urworte*]—there is no contradiction: the different presentations co-exist side by side. The child demonstrates an opening onto the unconscious, the opposite of self-consciousness. And it is precisely this opening that, for Spielrein, is the creative force. She writes, "Like in folk creations [*Volksschöpfung*], we must not reject anything in the child's 'fantasising' ["*Phantasieren*"] as nonsense" (p. 68).

Spielrein reports that Valli tells his mother that he is not her son, but rather his father's, "If I were a girl I would be yours. I am Daddy's son because I am a man and I look like Daddy". Spielrein notes that this is a both mythological and childish conception, but it is also one that is contingent upon the primary identification with the father described by Freud. Spielrein further asks him what becomes of man when he dies, and after some resistance he replies, "Blood". Again for Valli—and Spielrein—life and love are literally "soaked in blood": without blood there is no life. Spielrein further pursues what happens to someone after death and Valli says, "You throw him in the pit". "And what does he do there?", asks Spielrein. "He swims in water" (p. 68), replies Valli. For Spielrein, this adds weight to her own hypothesis that "End of life = the beginning", the water being also the *Fruchtwasser*, the fruit-water, or amniotic fluid in which the child swims prior to birth.

The next day Valli reports that he dreamed of a "Hanswurst", literally Hans-sausage. The character Hans was a mediaeval German comic figure, a type of buffoon who is both stupid and cunning. Here, Valli produces a new name, a name of the father we can propose that contains the given name Hans, but also the *Wurst* or sausage that makes him into both a comic and also a phallic character. Valli's Hanswurst is a hoofed creature with little horns, in other words, the devil. Valli reported, "I dreamed that there were horses in front of the house, then Hanswurst came along. He was put in jail by the *Statthalter* (the governor or steward), because Hanswurst pushed everyone in the pit. He is the servant of the governor" (p. 69). Valli constantly sees the governor's servant, or watchman, since he lives next door to the governor. In his associations, he makes the watchman the equivalent of Hanswurst. This watchman also carries a gun that stabs as well as shoots, which Spielrein takes as being analogous to

Hanswurst's horns. Hanswurst brings not only death, but also birth and new life, his own life first of all: "He comes out of the chest, when we are drinking tea, he comes out of the tea-machine" (p. 68). Later, he makes an association with a farmhand, who, he says, produces a boy out of his mouth, and a girl comes from the mouth of this farmhand's wife, again articulating one of his theories of where babies come from. Spielrein shows us that the child's question pertains to the enquiry to which Freud gives voice, "where do babies come from?" This, at the same time, is a question concerning existence and death. The question of separation already anticipates that of death.

Spielrein states that "It is evident that Valli dreams of the devil, 'who kills people'. ... At the same time the devil is also the child that comes into being, now coming out of the chest, now out of the mouth, now out of the tea-machine". Hanswurst is also an effect of language, a "condensation of both personalities", that of the comic figure of Hanswurst as well as that of the actual person of the Watchman. Thus, he both kills and gives rise to new life, just like in his condensation of Snow White and Sleeping Beauty, who, following the deadly prick of her finger, also arises to a new life. Spielrein comments further, "The boy has not the slightest anguish regarding his destruction presentations" [*Destruktionsvorstellungen*]. She notes that the mother was surprised by the multitude of sexual presentations from the boy, whom she had believed to be asexual, and that like most mothers, "took them for meaningless fantasies" (p. 69).

In response to her question of "Where is the beginning of all beginnings, and the end of all ends?", Spielrein seems to find a response from her own analysis, and her analyses of her child subjects: The end is structurally coextensive with the beginning, and the beginning with the end. The question of both the beginning and the end is a question regarding origins and end, cast into a teleological schema. They both pertain to the question of *cause*, but cause only construed as temporal. There is no "beginning of all beginnings", however, nor an "end of all ends". The beginning and the end are both equally elusive. The subject pursues both, it is a motor that drives him or her on, towards an always elusive object. This cause then is a cause of desire, and this cause is exemplified both through the causation of the creativity that results from destruction, as well as the pro-creativity that results from the fusion of the two parents in the sexual act, and hence the destruction of the individuality of each.

Love overlooks the dangers of our self-destruction

In her conclusion, Spielrein underlines the fact that the children in all three of her case studies deal intensely with sexual problems, in particular the anguish or fear of being abducted from the parents. But this anguish of the child belies the desire to flee from the parents, and she underlines that even from very early on, children are already beginning to be unfaithful to their parents in their longing for something beyond them, in their love for other children and others beyond the immediate family circle. She notes that "The child's unconscious just knows this. The real objects can be replaced by those of fantasy" (p. 70). Thus, the child's desires take the form of wanderlust, wanting to leave home to become a God, a king or queen, or shaped by what the child has already been told by the parents and the upbringing that they give to the child through religion, fairy tales, and stories of heroes. The fantasms that the child inherits from his or her parents form the substance upon which the child wishes to leave his or her mark in an endeavour to appropriate the fantasm as their own.

Spielrein is also able to theorise the child's play, and then is able to intervene in this in her work with children, demonstrating her creativity in this new field. She notes that from the earliest ages, children play games that involve robbers, witches, and Robinson Crusoe games [*Spiele*], and that they are all pleasure-seeking. The time arises, however, in which pleasure turns to anguish. She notes that Freud himself put forward that all neurotic anguish comes from sexual wishes that have been repressed in the unconscious, and pleasure is thus transformed into anguish. In her case, she observes, her father told her that her pleasure of tormenting her brothers would turn to anguish, but that he did not tell her what she was going to fear. Like the prophecy of the oracle, her father's utterance remained enigmatic, and the object of her fear and desire continued to be elusive.

For Spielrein, there must be destruction of the old that then causes a new coming-into-being: "new life arises at the cost of the old". She notes that on first appearance it seems that we seek life and avoid transgression, but that deeper contemplation teaches us otherwise: "It is love that leads us to overlook the dangers of our self-destruction, indeed allows us to blissfully seek them out". She is able to come to such a conclusion by virtue of the analysis of her own experience, "My childish love for God was still too weak, so the father's threat was able to arouse the self-preservation instinct and the fear of transgression, which still seemed like a coming-into-being to me" (p. 71). She notes, as she does in "Destruction as Cause of Becoming", that destructive presentations prevail in the case of anxious or fearful people, and especially in young children. The question, then, is how to allow their symptoms to shift towards the side of becoming.

This paper also includes a short appendix on the symbolism of time. She notes that nothing is as entertaining to a child as a clock or watch that seems to move and talk of its own volition, and she connects to this the idea of children's toys that apparently speak or move independently. These toys are always destroyed by the child and then created anew, and a child soon has no joy in a toy that cannot be altered. The toy is like a symbol that is able to freely represent many of the child's desires, and the less determined it is, the more suitable it is. Spielrein again puts forward her understanding of the child's play, and what is required for the child to play. Again there is an implicit theory of language here in so far as what she refers to as a symbol is an element that does not have a determined meaning or signified: the "symbol" or signifier is polysemic. Here she distinguishes herself from Jung for whom a symbol, whilst not having a fixed meaning, is always "pointing to something not easily defined and therefore not fully known"

(Jung 1956, p. 124). Jung retains a belief in a mysterious referent, whilst we can discern that for Spielrein—like for Ferdinand de Saussure in the same era—the symbol or signifier is not reducible to any external reference point outside the circuit of "symbols", or rather, signifiers.

The paper concludes with the example of one of Spielrein's patients who suffers from anxiety and who believes that she will be struck down with a heart attack, and that she will be buried alive. This patient sees herself as a clock whose time is running out, and that the patient's verbatim associations are: "a trickle of sand or water from the clock. Grains of sand in the sea. Man is no more than a grain of sand". Spielrein indicates that the patient is trapped in this anguished situation: "The idea of becoming is impossible without that of transgression, and also vice versa" (1913, p. 72). Thus, the death fantasy is at the same time a birth fantasy. Hence she inverts the patient's associations to signify that the grains of sand are men, and that "the sea" is associated in the analysis with the amniotic fluid [*Fruchtwasser*]. This inversion, then, is the movement that Spielrein enacts, as analyst, in order to allow the production of a switch in the patient's fantasm, away from the emphasis on the destruction through *regression*, towards that of becoming via its necessary transgression. Spielrein asserts that the idea of becoming is impossible without that of *transgression*. Hence the task of the analytic act is to allow the necessary transgression to move towards the logical impossibility of becoming.

7

I VIOLENTLY RESISTED THE INTERPRETATION OF SIEGFRIED AS A REAL CHILD

Unknown and dirty child playing at my doorstep,
I don't ask you to bring me a message from the symbols.
I find you graceful for never before having seen you,
And naturally if you'd been clean you'd be another child,
Nor would you have come here.
Play in the dust, play!
I cherish your presence just with my eyes.
It's better to see something for the first time than to know it,
Because to know is never to have seen it for the first time,
And to have seen it for the first time is just to have heard about it.
The way in which this child is dirty is different to the way in which the
others are dirty.

Play! Picking up a stone that fits in your hand,
You know it fits in your hand.
Which is the philosophy that leads to a greater certainty?
None, and none can ever come to play at my doorstep.

Fernando Pessoa, untitled (1919, p. 782, translated for this edition)

During Sabina Spielrein's time in Zürich, in her ongoing transference-love towards Carl Jung, she dreamed and wrote in her diaries and letters of a hypothetical child named Siegfried. The first references to Siegfried appear in her diary in September 1910, at a point at which she states regarding Jung: "I wrote poems for him, composed songs about him" (Carotenuto 1980a, p. 12). In the same letter she writes the following, "At least (if I am so fond of him) I could give him a little boy, as we used to dream of?" We note that her proposition is predicated on a condition ("if I am so fond of him") and followed by a question mark, thus Spielrein herself twice puts this proposal into question. Regardless of what Jung's desires might have been, Sabina Spielrein appropriates her own by going on to write that "It is not easy to give up the thought of the baby boy, my longed-for Siegfried" (p. 13). We note here that Siegfried is presented as a *thought*—even as a thought to be given up—that is, it is a *presentation*—rather than an actual baby. In the very emergence of the thought of this baby boy, Spielrein proposes that it is a thought to be given up or lost.

In regard to the thought that Spielrein has concerning Siegfried of whom she dreams, we might well ask, *Who is the author of the thought?*, anticipating the title of Spielrein's later paper "Who is the Author of the Crime?" (1922). The thought is something that she describes as having a life of its own, a thought that happens to her and of which she dreams. It is something then that is effectively imposed upon her. This thought takes the form, in her dreams, of a formation of the unconscious. Spielrein herself puts into question whether this thought could go beyond mere fantasising: "What if I did not even get pregnant? Then our pure [*reine*] friendship would be destroyed by the intimate relationship" (Carotenuto 1980a, p. 13), indicating first that there was no intimate relationship—certainly not at that stage—but also that what she wished to sustain most of all was the purity that she envisaged in her ideal of Jung in the transference. But this wish is also a fear, a fear that betrays a desire to be free: "I dread the pain of parting [*Schmerzen der Trennung*]" (p. 13). Spielrein already anticipates that her ideal of the pure friendship has to be destroyed in order to create something new, and for her to be able to come into being, however painful that might be. We note here the signifier *rein* is one by which she constitutes herself through the destruction of her name into its component letters. In her transference to Jung, Siegfried appears as an imagined product of their love, but one whose existence as an actual child is simultaneously dismissed. But we can say from this that the power of Siegfried lies precisely in the fact that there is no sexual relation, neither in the common conception of that term, nor in the notion that Lacan gives to it. Siegfried appears where an actual baby is impossible: Siegfried's power is precisely in its loss or absence, thus designating a lack.

In October 1910 she writes the following: "Siegfried, my baby son! Someday you must express what your mother is feeling now. You must be able to find yourself a worthy father!" (p. 21). Siegfried has a life of its own: it must first be the *poem* that expresses what his mother Sabina Spielrein is feeling. Spielrein's longing for a baby Siegfried is a yearning for a poem—the expression of her feelings—but simultaneously a longing for a "worthy father" or *poet*. Siegfried comes into existence as a bastard child, one who secondarily has to go out in search of a worthy father.

Siegfried thus raises two separate questions: "What is a child?", and "What is a father?" In the transference, Siegfried also appears as her analyst Carl Jung: "at the same time my friend is my little son" (p. 30). Here Siegfried is manifested as a child, but as her analyst Carl Jung as a child, for whom Sabina Spielrein would be the mother. This substantiation of the child in the person of her analyst is clearly not an actual baby, but a baby in the transference, and one that refers to something beyond the transference. Furthermore, Siegfried raises the question of the father, specifically that of the worthy father, a worthy father who is the father of the words of the poem. Since the child must go out in search of the father, this conception of a father is one that is clearly not given a priori: not a father who engenders the child, but on the contrary, a father who is engendered by the Siegfried. This is a most interesting proposition of what a child and a father might be: the father is the one whom the child nominates—or even creates—in that position. The Siegfried is a child in search of a father, but also a child in search of a father's name, but this name is not Jung. Carl Jung, once again, occupies the place of this father in the transference for Sabina Spielrein. This father that is nominated as Siegfried ("at the same time my friend is my little son"), nonetheless, is not an actual being with whom the mother has a relationship. That is, Siegfried is not a substantial being, like a child who would be produced through a sexual relationship between the parents. Siegfried, however, is not at all predicated on a relation; rather it is predicated precisely upon a lack of relation. The lack of relation is, furthermore, reiterated through the disparity of positions between analysand and analyst.

Siegfried, then, is a two-sided entity, both child and father, but also both poem and poet. Siegfried, first and foremost, must be the expression of what his mother is feeling; he must be the poem that expresses his mother's feelings. But this poem then gives rise to the poet—it is the father who is found or created: the worthy father that Siegfried must find. Hence Siegfried is both the *creature*, the being that is created through the transference, but also the *creator* of the poem to which this creature gives birth. Again, as well as being both child and father, Siegfried is also both poem and poet.

The usual salacious interest in, and interpretation of, Spielrein's "poetry" as a sexual relationship with Jung functions to obscure the poetry of Spielrein's writing. A consequence of this is that one of the principal interests in Sabina Spielrein, in both clinical and non-clinical circles, has been in the imagined sexual relation between Spielrein and Jung. This supposedly delicious "secret symmetry" to cite Carotenuto's subtitle implies precisely such a sexual relation or correspondence. The other part of Carotenuto's title is "between Freud and Jung", since the sexual relation also serves to spice up the other emphasis that is placed upon a similar reciprocal rivalry that is attributed to Freud and Jung. If the insistence on the imagined sexual relationship between Spielrein and Jung serves to dismiss Spielrein's writings, the emphasis on the rivalry between Freud and Jung effectively functions to conceal the theoretical deviation that Jung was taking from Freudian psychoanalysis. Jung himself was under no illusion about this, nor the effect it would have on Freud, writing to Spielrein just prior to her presentation in Vienna: "I am rather worried about how Freud will take the corrections I am introducing into the theory of sexuality" (Covington & Wharton 2003b, p. 43). Jung's grandiose attribution of his theoretical divergence as "corrections" underlines his struggle as son with the figure of Freud that he took to be his "father", as he repetitively articulates in his correspondence to Freud.

Lothane insists that what came between Freud and Jung were the questions of "the Spielrein case, the case of Schreber, and a polemic about the libido theory" (2003, p. 214). This, however, is to give too much credence to the idea that the rupture between Jung and Freud was truly "about" a theoretical battle. No doubt Jung's rivalry with Freud came from the insecurity of the position of son in which he had placed himself, a son who had never undertaken his own analysis and, even if he analysed his own dreams, it was along the lines of his emerging preconceptions. In other words, he never subjected himself to his own speech, in order to perceive how he also was subjected to sexuality. Not having convinced himself, he then tried to make "corrections" in his "father's" doctrine of psychoanalysis, as part of his rivalrous battle to differentiate himself. Rather, here we emphasise the difference per se that Jung was deliberately effecting in taking his own path away from Freud, and secondarily from psychoanalysis.

Similarly, the tawdry debate concerning plagiarism is underwritten by the assumption that authorship is intentional and clear, in other words, it takes no account of the unconscious. Balsam's questioning over who owes what to whom descends into absurdity (*vide* Balsam 2015, p. 174). Whether Spielrein, Freud, or even Jung was the first to theorise a death drive, for instance, obscures the differences between each of their theoretical propositions. When Spielrein submitted her "Destruction as Cause of Becoming" paper to Jung, she wrote to him that this work "was done for Siegfried" and further told him to "indicate if I have slighted the work of any scholar" (Carotenuto 1980a, p. 48–49). As we have read, it was Jung himself who felt slighted, and insufficiently cited, by Spielrein. This is something he appears to have endeavoured to correct, as we have put forward, in his supervision and editorial influence upon this paper.

Pain rends all the world apart

As alluded to in the previous chapter, Freud differentiated between the *thought* Siegfried and a putative child Siegfried at the time when Spielrein showed him the analysis of one of her "Siegfried dreams". Freud's response, as we know, was: "You could have the child, you know, if you wanted it, but what a waste of your talents". Siegfried is thus "a waste", or an excess that overflows from her transferential desires. It is a surplus or a leftover that would remain even if she bore a child. In other words, it would be possible to have a child, but impossible to have a Siegfried as an actual baby: Siegfried would remain a waste, something that overcomes Spielrein herself.

In the same letter to Jung in which she recounts this, Spielrein writes, "I often wonder: what did my youthful Siegfried symbolism signify if it could not be taken literally?" (Carotenuto 1980a, p. 73). The "symbolism" existed long before her analysis, even if Siegfried was the name that it assumed in the transference to Carl Jung. This question of what Siegfried signifies beyond a child is in fact one that Spielrein actively takes up. She refers to a poem that she composed in her early youth:

Pastor, make the bells cease ringing,
let the village silent lie,
answer me the cruel question—
my child, it lived—but why, oh why?
Did it live that it might die?
And if it broke the mother's heart—
what good can life receive, please tell me,
when pain [Weltenschmerz] rends all the world apart?
But the bells just keep on ringing,
and the secret goes untold.
Can you explain, grey-haired wise man,
are we just born to turn to mould?

(p. 74)

These lines literally articulate Spielrein's *Weltschmerz* of apartness, a world-weariness that she bears, just as this pain could take the form of bearing a Siegfried. But her poem goes beyond this; it articulates the pain borne by any subject, a pain that pertains to the end point of life, in other words the death or lack that is at the heart of being. Bearing a child is presented as a means—no doubt an always failing means—to be able to bear a lack. As this early poem puts forward, the bells—like the clock of her young patient that ticks on towards death—continue to sound out the passage towards our demise, without regard for the wishes of any one of us, that is, for each and every subject. The bells also sound out a secret or enigma that cannot be told, in so far as it cannot be reduced to any one sense or meaning, such as that of an actual child.

Strikingly, Spielrein states that the reduction of Siegfried to an actual child was none other than Jung's interpretation: "My subconscious *thinking* and *feeling* were influenced by you to such a degree that I thought to find a solution [*Lösung*] to the Siegfried problem in the form of a real child" (p. 77, italics in the original). In other words, it was Jung who first made the Siegfried into a common signifier for the sexual relation and its product of an actual baby. However, since the time of discussing her Siegfried dreams with Freud, she states that she only dreamed of Siegfried one other time: "He appeared once more in a dream during my pregnancy, when I was in danger of losing my baby. And that is of course why my reborn daughter is called 'Renate'" (p. 77). This reappearance of Siegfried as *signifier* from the real only occurs when she is in danger of losing the child in reality. Siegfried is thus something entirely different to a child, denoting the very lack in being. And just as Freud articulated that the object could not be found—since it is always lacking—but only refound (Freud 1905d, p. 222), the baby for Spielrein is not born, but re-born: *Re-nate*.

Spielrein goes on to endeavour to explicate Jung's misapprehension of Siegfried, which she says is to be ascribed to *conscious* analysis. She has already made clear that Jung's approach is that of conscious analysis, rather than the analysis of the unconscious, which she writes is the approach of Freud. She affirms that *"in the beginning Siegfried was probably 'real' for my subconscious, which cleverly saw through your own subconscious attitude toward this problem"* (Carotenuto 1980a, p. 77, italics in the original). Spielrein, in the analysis, is able to discern Jung's *Gegenübertragung*, or against-transference. Nonetheless, Siegfried was not "real" for her conscious, it did not take the image or meaning of an actual child. For Spielrein, the "subconscious" can be encouraged to work through a problem in either a real or sublimated form. She goes on to assert to Jung:

> This is how you finally killed off the "real" Siegfried, as you explained it to me (proof that you, too, had a "real" one), i.e., sacrificed him in favour of the sublimated one. I, on the contrary, killed in my dreams the man who was supposed to become Siegfried's father, and then in reality found another man.
>
> *(p. 78)*

Here, towards the end of Spielrein's correspondence to Jung to be found in Carotenuto, she clarifies to her ex-analyst that the solution, and the end of the analysis, was not to be found—as he had imagined due to his misapprehension of Siegfried—in the fall of Siegfried, but rather in the fall of Jung from the place of analyst for her. The death of an imaginary and symbolic father in the analysis is a necessary event for Spielrein's coming into being. This then allows her to deploy her desires outside the analysis, and to take a man—*not* an analyst—as a father with whom to make an actual baby, *not* a Siegfried. Here Siegfried is not an object such as a child, but rather the entity that is the cause of becoming for Spielrein, via a corresponding destruction of her analysis.

Spielrein, in her next letter, continues to spell this out to Jung: "I violently resisted the interpretation of Siegfried as a real child, and *on the basis of my mystical tendencies* I would have simply thought that a great and heroic destiny awaited me, that I had to sacrifice myself for the creation of something great" (p. 80, italics in the original). Whilst Jung is not our immediate concern here, his erroneous interpretation of Siegfried was certainly not just mediated by both Jung's own narcissism and paranoia—well articulated in his correspondence with Freud—but also by his own desires in his *against-transference* towards Sabina Spielrein, something that he was not able to disentangle from her transference to him. This complicated situation made it exceedingly difficult for Spielrein to finish her analysis. Nonetheless the conclusion that she had to sacrifice—or *overcome*—her "self", in order to come into being, was precisely the ending that she had to arrive at in order to effect that termination.

A great destiny awaits you, my child

In a letter to Freud, Spielrein wrote the following verses that we have already examined, in honour of Siegfried:

Oh, once there was a dream so wondrous strange
One fine, cool night the Rhine sang long ago
It sang of a poet
Black eyes, golden hair...

(p. 108)

This "once there was", like "once upon a time", emphasises Siegfried as an atemporal or asynchronous entity, not a diachronic being of flesh and blood. We are struck by the fact that in these lines it is the song—or poem—that gives rise to the poet: the poet Siegfried is engendered by the singing of the Rhine, a *Spiel* of the *Rhein*. This purity [*Reinheit*] would of course be blighted if it were to be reduced to a sexual relationship. Spielrein continues, "Thus Siegfried came into being; he was supposed to become the greatest genius, because Dr. Jung's image as a descendant of the gods floated before me, and from childhood on I had a premonition that I was not destined for a mundane life. I felt flooded with energy, all nature spoke directly to me, one song after another took shape in me, one fairy tale after another" (p. 108). In these passages Spielrein's relationship is to song: she submits herself to the Dionysian dithyramb in the jouissance of her approach to the unconscious. As Nietzsche writes, "*Dionysian happiness reaches its peak in the annihilation of even the most beautiful illusion*" (Nietzsche 1885–1886, p. 82, italics in the original). To accede to the creativity of song, an image or illusion has to be destroyed. Sabina Spielrein's cup overflows with song, and with the poetry that is produced from it. In the transference, Jung, who had become her hero, provisionally embodied Spielrein's heroic destiny.

Even though Siegfried became the means by which her heroic destiny was nominated in the transference, Spielrein makes it clear that it did not have its origins in the analysis, or in some shared dream with Jung. It long precedes her encounter with Carl Jung and is the very means by which Sabina Spielrein comes to constitute herself. She refutes Jung's notion that Siegfried was a symbol of her heroic attitude: "My heroic attitude *toward the world* was never a secret to me, from earliest childhood on; I would have known it even without analysis. Without your instruction I would have believed, like all laymen, that I was dreaming of Siegfried, since I am always dwelling on heroic fantasies" (Carotenuto 1980a, p. 79, italics in the original). But Jung, in his letter of 21 January 1918, which he begins by telling her that she is "*typically*, misunderstanding the symbol" (Covington & Wharton 2003b, p. 54, italics in the original), effectively shrinks her Siegfried into a "symbol", or a "bridge to your individual development" in his insistence on "individuation". Sabina Spielrein, as we know, endeavours to overcome the individuation of the ego. She sacrifices her *self*, her own ego, in the promotion of the *dividuation* produced by the unconscious. She thus refutes Jung's interpretation of Siegfried as "symbolism" or a "bridge" to which he had endeavoured to reduce it, and to which in his letters he continues to endeavour to shrink it. After insisting on his well-worn interpretations, Jung finishes a letter to her with the question, "Do you understand that?" (p. 54). Rather than speaking from the position of psychoanalyst—which he had abandoned many years before—he instead takes up the position of the one who knows, the preacher, the one who is the bearer of a conscious knowledge.

In fact, Spielrein is *atypically* missing Jung's symbol, since what Spielrein is in search of is not the *typical*, that is, Jung's *type*. It is Jung who is afraid of losing his mind [*den Verstand verlieren*] (Carotenuto 1980a, p. 72), or of losing his senses through being carried away by the creativity of the atypical. Siegfried, though, is a singular entity, not one that can be reduced to a category in Jung's archetypes. Siegfried as a facet of Spielrein's creation has no type: it is atypical in its singularity. Moreover, while Siegfried is not reducible to any one thing, or any one meaning, neither is it to be found in any one place: not only is it marked by *atypia* but also by *atopia*. Siegfried, the name that Spielrein creates from the fragments of the analysis, is her cause of coming into being. It is thus constantly in movement, since, as we have read, every presentation reaches its maximum life when it waits most intensively for its transformation into reality; with such realisation it is destroyed at once. Siegfried is precisely what causes *becoming* to be in perpetual motion.

Jung's interpretation of Siegfried as "symbolism" is one that emerged at the time of the analysis, and he continues to insist upon it in his letters to Spielrein of 1917–1919. Jung's personification of the Siegfried effectively acts as a blockage to Sabina Spielrein's creativity, including her wish to compose. Jung impedes Spielrein's poetry and her music by his persistent interpretation of Siegfried—including in his correspondence to Freud—as a real child. This interpretation also makes it impossible for Spielrein to finish her analysis since Jung, in his *Gegenübertragung* or against-transference, counters her ability to make use of the Siegfried in her writing and in her work. Furthermore, this interpretation keeps Jung himself in the position of the hero, the one who is able to give the final answer regarding Spielrein and Siegfried. Here we also find his Apollonian position reinforced: Jung continues to want to impose the logic of consciousness, to shrink Spielrein's creativity into the inertia of a unitary meaning, indeed an inhibitory meaning.

We see more clearly the manner in which Siegfried was the entity that emerged in the analysis with Jung—in the transference to him—but an entity that had its roots in the thoughts and fantasies of her childhood. That is, Siegfried had strictly nothing to do with Jung per se, but only in so far as he occupied a place for Sabina Spielrein in the transference. This "complex" as she calls it, drawing from Jung's terminology, is the source of her poetry, of her song. She notes that when she first confessed this complex to Jung, he replied that "such wishes are not alien to him, but the world happens to be arranged in such a way, etc., etc." (p. 108). In other words, Jung from the beginning persistently interpreted Spielrein's Siegfried as an actual baby that would be produced by himself as the father. Whilst Spielrein, in her transference-love to Jung, participated in this fantasm, nonetheless, as we have read, there is no contradiction in the fact that she violently resisted Jung's interpretation.

Spielrein feared that she might be just one of the many for Jung, and that her "accomplishments might not surpass the ordinary". Furthermore, she dreaded that her "'higher calling' might be a ridiculous dream which I must now pay for" (p. 21). Siegfried is imbued with this question of a "higher calling" that Spielrein connects to her father, paying tribute to Jung's paper on "The Significance of the Father in the Destiny of the Individual" (1909). But Spielrein's reference is a very specific one that pertains not only to her father, but also to both her maternal grandfather and great-grandfather who were both rabbis, "and therefore—God's elect" (p. 21). Hence the idea or ideal of the Siegfried is from the beginning intimately tied up to her youthful notion of a heroic destiny that awaited her as presaged by her fore *fathers*. Such a heroic destiny is also part of her fantasm of the Other—whether of her great-grandfather, grandfather, father, Jung, etc.—in which she was held. That is, in regards to her future, the fantasm placed her in a position of compliance where she had no other choice than that of fulfilling this destiny.

For it is your will, and the will of my father Wotan

Sabina Spielrein goes on to say more about the ideal of a heroic destiny that awaited her: "How else could I interpret those dreams in which my father or grandfather blessed me and said, 'A great destiny awaits you, my child?'" (p. 80). This notion of a heroic destiny is something that emerges from her dreams— from her unconscious—something then to which she was subjected. This heroic destiny is composed of two elements: on the one hand she must create something great, and on the other hand she has to sacrifice herself in doing so. The two sides of her thesis in "Destruction as Cause of Becoming", having emerged from Spielrein's unconscious, are already in place: an image has to be destroyed in order for the new to come into being.

We hear this in Spielrein's diary from 1911, "I have something noble and great to create and am not made for everyday routine. This is the life-or-death struggle. If there is a God-Father, may he hear me now: no pain is unbearable to me, no sacrifice too great, if only I can fulfil my sacred calling!" She follows this with two phrases in inverted commas: "'He must be a hero'; for it is your will and 'the will of my father Wotan'" (p. 39). Although we cannot trace the source of what appears to be a citation, it is evocative of the voice of Brünhilde from Wagner's *Niebelungenlied*, his long poem that he published many years before he wrote the score for the operas that became known as the *Ring Cycle*. Spielrein speaks as Brünhilde, the daughter of Wotan who is the chief god, in regard to the hero Siegfried, who is also Wotan's son but to an earthly mother. In *Das Rheingold*, the first opera of the *Ring Cycle*, Siegfried is conceived in the ecstatic embrace of Siegmund and Sieglinde, twins who reencounter each other in an incestuous, impossible and deadly love. If, as we proposed above, there is a necessary death of the father, in Wagner's poem it is both Brünhilde's father Wotan, as well as Siegfried's father Siegmund, who must be destroyed. The inevitable counterpart of Siegfried's advent in Wagner's drama is the death and destruction of both his parents.

Spielrein's "heroic destiny", however, was destined not to remain as such. It also had to be destroyed in order for her to be able to become productive. And her creativity and productivity are something that came into being primarily through her writing. She writes that in working on her paper "Destruction as Cause of Becoming", there came "a passage directed against Siegfried, and after that I could organise my thoughts only very imperfectly" (p. 49). That is, her writing was the reworking of her destiny, but it involved the putting aside and destruction of any heroism. The passage from the operas that Spielrein cites in "Destruction as Cause of Becoming" is from the very last passage in *Götterdämmerung*, the final opera in the *Ring Cycle*, in which Brünhilde leads her horse into Siegfried's funeral pyre to be reunited with him in death:

> Grane, my steed,
> I salute thee!
> Dost thou know, friend,
> where I lead thee?
> In the glowing fire,
> There lies thy heart
> Siegfried, my blessed Hero.
>   *(Spielrein 1912b, p. 177)*

Spielrein comments that here death is a victorious song to love. Brünhilde merges into Siegfried who is now the incandescent fire of the sun. Brünhilde is dissolved [*aufgelöst*] into this primal procreator, becoming fire with Siegfried.

This victorious "song" is the poem that creates the poet: by putting words to this death she is able to create a new song. She remarks that "for Wagner, death is often nothing other than the destroying components of the instinct of coming into being" (p. 178). According to Spielrein's own heroic destiny, she had to sacrifice herself for the creation of something great. This destiny is fulfilled for her by the protagonists in Wagner's poem since she notes that Siegfried and Brünhilde sacrifice themselves to their love and die. But the coming into being also emerges in the writing: Wagner becomes the creator of his great work the *Ring Cycle*, and Spielrein becomes the author of her own writings. Siegfried is not at all an actual child, but very literally the writing that Spielrein produces from the residues of her psychoanalysis.

This is made more explicit when she writes of a fantasy of later being married, a fantasy very similar to that which we examined in her childhood journal. In this section of her intimate diaries from 1910, amongst her ideas she imagines the following interaction: "From time to time I may surprise my beloved husband with a little essay that I have written on my own, and he will receive it like a dear child. And this esteemed and beloved man will then become the father of my Siegfried" (Carotenuto 1980a, p. 32). Here, in her fantasm, Siegfried, the essay, is able to find a worthy father, who only then receives this poem she has written.

This becomes even clearer when she speaks of the publication of her thesis, of which she writes in a diary entry: "The idea I gave birth to should also appear under my name" (p. 35). This conception of Siegfried, the culmination but also the transmutation of her heroic destiny into a piece of writing, insists in a letter to Jung that accompanied her paper "Destruction as Cause of Becoming" that she was submitting to him: "Receive now the product of our love, the project which is your little son Siegfried. It caused me tremendous difficulty, but nothing was too hard if it was done for Siegfried. If you decide to print this, I shall feel I have fulfilled my duty toward you. Only then shall I be free" (p. 48). Siegfried here is stripped of its heroism and comes into being in the shape of a text, a poem. She lets fall the ideal of Jung as hero, and coextensively produces something to which she now gives birth. Siegfried is something that *causes* difficulty: it is a cause, a cause of becoming by virtue of the freedom afforded to her by having delivered her Siegfried.

In the next entry she continues, "It was … it was … a wonderful dream, and from it the words of the little song I composed came to me. Yes, and this dream was my Siegfried" (Carotenuto 1980c, p. 60). We translate this passage directly from the German here, as, amongst other things, the English translation omits the first-person possessive pronoun "my" by which Spielrein appropriates Siegfried as her own. Siegfried is not something that she intends, but something given to her through a dream. What is designated as Siegfried is on one side the song or poetry that is composed through the dream, but on the other it is the poet who expresses what its mother is feeling. Hence Spielrein's conception of father and child is not a biological one: her logic is a not *bio-logic*. Siegfried is not a baby of flesh and blood born of the union of a man and a woman. Hence there is no contradiction when Spielrein declares in her diary, "*I feel the unshakeable conviction: Siegfried lives, lives, lives!* No one can rob me of that certainty but my own death" (Carotenuto 1980a, p. 30, italics in the original). The Spielrein that lives through her writing is poetry, and the death of one's self is the necessary precondition to being creative.

The wish to create a great Aryan-Semitic hero

Siegfried appears in Spielrein's diaries as a symptomatic formation, in the articulation of the question of difference. At the same time that she states that her illness began with the death of her sister, she begins to recount various dyads, most of which are composed of one Jew and one Christian, beginning with her two school friends. The Jewish girl is now married to a Christian and the Christian chooses only Jewish men. Then there is the matter of her first two loves, the Christian history teacher and her (Jewish) uncle Adolf. She emphasises opposite characteristics, for instance in relation to herself and a female friend in Zürich, noting, "how two so different people find their way to each other. She—a person who blends in with the crowd, and I—a hermit" (p. 27), etc. The other pair she then speaks of is Jung and Freud. So self-evident is this pairing that Jung is described as the "Christian in it", and Freud, "a Jew, old [*cf.* young, or *Jung*] *pater familias*". She then compares herself to Anna Freud who "has the advantage of having a father who is widely known. I have no such advantage" (p. 30), emphasising this difference between them. It is precisely in this context that she declares that she feels the unshakeable conviction that Siegfried lives. Hence we can propose that in this moment, Siegfried has the function of endeavouring to resolve difference.

Among the differences that are outlined here are those between male and female, young and old, present and past, that between different stations in life, and that between Christendom and Jewry, but there are many others. The division in her own life of which she writes to Jung, as late as 1917, is that between her activity as a musician and a composer, and that of her "scientific" career, that is, in psychoanalysis. The dilemma is summed up by her music teacher: "Too much to choose—too much to lose" (p. 73). Jung also enters into this question of comparison and choice, proffering "Perhaps you are more a musician than a doctor". He even offers another difference, that between the world of dreams and the world of the real, which, as we know, is a differentiation to which Spielrein gives no credence. The solution that Jung suggests is that of being a type of traffic warden: "You have to stand between them and regulate the traffic in both worlds, just as Siegfried stands between the gods and men" (Covington & Wharton 2003b, p. 54). The main difference Sabina Spielrein is referring to, however, is effectively that of difference itself. Siegfried emerges here as the signifier of difference.

In her correspondence with both Freud and Jung, Sabina Spielrein explicitly endeavours to bring together not just the two men, but also their different bodies of work. Even as early as January 1913, Freud writes to her that "My personal relationship with your Germanic hero has definitely been shattered. His behaviour was too bad" (Carotenuto 1980a, p. 118). Despite this, Spielrein still professes the hope of leading Jung back into Freud's fold. She recounts a notion from her dreams that she could give a lecture as interesting as one by Freud or Jung. She recounts that "The same symbolism also revealed fulfilment of the wish to create a great Aryan-Semitic hero" (p. 60). Here we are struck by this condensed formulation of the reconciliation of difference by her use of the hyphen. This formulation is repeated a number of times, particularly in her letters to Jung.

But the hero takes the form of Siegfried, and she writes to Jung of Siegfried as "a child that resulted from the union of your and Freud's theories" (p. 86). Here we see Siegfried, once again, as her endeavour to resolve an irreconcilable difference. Of course, neither man is interested in such reconciliation, and both reject the Other that they discern in this hero Siegfried. Freud congratulates Spielrein on having had a baby girl: "It is far better that the child should be a 'she'. Now we can think again about the blond Siegfried and perhaps smash that idol before his time comes" (p. 121). Jung, on the other hand, criticises what he takes to be her Jewish predisposition to Siegfried the hero, as well as directly criticising Freud, strikingly characterising Freud as *the Jew*: "Do not forget that the Jew also had prophets … That is—'unfortunately'—the curse of the Jew: the aspect of his psychology which belongs to him most deeply he calls 'infantile wish-fulfilment', he is the murderer of his own prophets, even of his Messiah" (Covington & Wharton 2003b, p. 55). Siegfried's task of reconciling the difference between Freud and Jung, to bring them together in a blissful reunion, is clearly an impossible task in the common sense of the word. But there is also an encounter here with the logical impossibility of the reconciling of difference per se. Spielrein is confronted with what was later articulated by Lacan as: *there is no sexual relation.*

Freud recognises that the side of Siegfried as the hero must be "smashed", or destroyed, in order for Spielrein to accede to something else. Again, he recognises and emphasises that the actual child Renate is not the Siegfried. Jung, who had previously told Spielrein to let Siegfried fall, here fails to see that the function of the hero, whether it is the Siegfried or the Messiah, is that he must sacrifice his life to fulfil his destiny. Jesus becomes the true Messiah in the moment in which he lays down his life to save Mankind, as his father had sent him to do. In the same way, Siegfried must unknowingly sacrifice himself in order to fulfil the destiny that Wotan, father of the Gods, had wished for him to realise on his behalf. Spielrein must also sacrifice her *self* to realise a destiny that loses its heroism in the moment in which the idol is destroyed.

Spielrein, nonetheless, writes that, according to Freud, "The Siegfried fantasy is *merely* wish fulfilment. I have always objected to this *merely*" (Carotenuto 1980a, p. 80, italics in the original). As we have seen, Siegfried is also a piece of writing. We recall that in 1910 she wrote that she composed a poem with her friend after their first "poetry". Jung, in her fantasy, is the father of her Siegfried who rescues her from all the conflicts that assail her, and says to her, "for you I did battle with the raging waves", etc. In this fantasm of a sexual relation, Siegfried has found a worthy father, but it is only in the fantasy that the worthy father could be Jung. Rather, to take Spielrein literally, to take her to the letter, Siegfried is the poem itself that emanates from Spielrein's encounter with the Other in analysis, a writing that continues the search for the name of its father. The worthy father—the wordy father, or father of words—is quite literally the poetry she composes, not the imagined salacious "poetry" of a sexual relationship that various authors and filmmakers imagine between herself and Jung, whatever its characteristics.

We find that there are two sides to the Siegfried. The side we are underlining here emerges from the beginning of Spielrein's treatment through her poetry and other writing, and continues long after the fantasy of a personified Siegfried dissipates. This Siegfried, however, is quite the opposite to the imagined hero Siegfried as the reconciling of difference. Through her writing, there emerges from Spielrein a poetry that is utterly specific to her. It is the other side of the "poetry" that emerges from her encounter with Carl Jung: not the romance of a fantasised sexual relation, but a piece of writing that emerges from the inevitable lack of such a relation. This is the poetry that marks her singularity, the singularity of difference itself. It is her writing that marks her as singular, and thus totally distinct and different from others. Spielrein's conception of the unconscious is a unity of oneness, an *Einheit*. The difference, and notion of oneness that pertains to her writing, is one that denotes, not a unifying oneness on this occasion, but rather a distinctive oneness, a singularity or *Einzigkeit*.

Spielrein and Jung maintained a correspondence that appears to end in 1919. Nonetheless, in their letters there is a lack of correspondence, a failure of reciprocity. Additionally, at least in her early diaries, with Spielrein we encounter a writing that was addressed to Jung but which he was never destined to read. In other words, this was a writing in which there was no intention of correspondence, no reciprocity. Spielrein's writing, whether delivered to Jung or not, is a writing that bears the mark of the disparity of the transference, a transference that goes beyond the apparent recipient of her letters. Later in their exchange of letters they were of course at odds regarding Siegfried, but at odds in many other ways as well. And, quite literally, there was no correspondence since Sabina Spielrein on a number of occasions asked Carl Jung to return her letters to her. That is, this was not an *exchange* of letters since the ultimate addressee of Spielrein's letters was her writing itself. The last words that we have recorded from Spielrein to Jung are the following: "*Please be so kind as to return the letter to me, since it is one of the building blocks for my future development and I shall need it again*" (p. 90, italics in the original).

Human being is something that must be overcome

In her paper "Destruction as Cause of Becoming", it is remarkable that Spielrein references Nietzsche's work *Thus Spake Zarathustra* and its concept of the Overman or *Übermensch*. Nietzsche's work, on the whole, has been neglected by psychoanalysts, or considered too mystical. But when Nietzsche submitted this work to his editor, he wrote the following of it: "It is a 'poem,' or a fifth 'gospel' or something or other for which there is not yet a name" (cited in: Sloterdijk 2013, p. 29). Similarly, Spielrein's work, in the form of the writing that was her "poetry" and the poem that she calls Siegfried, was also sent out in search of a name, the name of a father. In Spielrein's gospel, Siegfried the Messiah, or hero, must be destroyed, as is indeed his function in the Christian faith. But Spielrein's writing, as a psychoanalytic work, has the transference as its mainspring, a transference that was once directed towards Carl Jung, and which became a transference to work, the work of writing.

The writing in which Siegfried becomes the signifier of pure difference, or *Einzigkeit*, is one which is driven by the transference. And what Spielrein discovers, not in an explicit theorised way, but rather articulated through her writing, is that transference has its power specifically by virtue of this singularity, by virtue of the fact that there is no sexual relation, no correspondence. In this way Siegfried is not an object, but rather an objection to the sexual relation. For Sabina Spielrein, the romantic relationship that occurred between herself and Carl Jung put into play the fantasy that Siegfried could be realised through such a dalliance. This relationship, though, could only be a failed interlude, or a dead end of the analysis. Through writing, however, Spielrein was able to redirect the transference from this cul-de-sac into a means of production. Given that the analysis came to such a premature end, Spielrein's task was literally to write herself—and *right* herself—out of the analysis. The relationship was a beautiful illusion, a *Bild*, that had to be destroyed for the analysis to be redirected into work, a work that was her means of coming into being. To return to the words of the subject of her thesis aptly recorded by Sabina Spielrein, "over a beautiful picture, one can become poetry".

Hence we can say that for Spielrein, destruction is a statement of an impossibility, the impossibility of the sexual relation. With Jung, the impossibility was that of imagining that she could realise her fantasm with her analyst, rather than taking stock of the impossibility of realising the fantasm itself. The destruction of this illusion is in no way an act of aggression or nihilism. On the contrary, it is a necessary response to a logical impossibility. To be able to respond to this impossibility is quite literally to take responsibility for it, in order to act in accordance with it. To not remain trapped in trying to enact the impossible enabled Sabina Spielrein to put her fantasm to work in a way that was creative. Sabina Spielrein's writing, then, was both the means, as well as the product, of this creativity.

In the first part of *Thus Spake Zarathustra*, Zarathustra speaks the following words to the townspeople: "*I teach you the Overman* [*Übermensch*]. Human being is something that must be overcome. What have you done to overcome him?" (1883, p. 5, italics in the original). For Nietzsche, it is specifically the human, the ego, or the self that must be overcome to accede to the *Übermensch*, or the unconscious in Spielrein's terms. Spielrein paraphrases this in "Destruction as Cause of Becoming" in the following way: "You must understand that you must overcome (destroy) yourself. How could you otherwise create the higher, the child?" (Spielrein 1912c, p. 111). We can see that Spielrein's *destruction* is coextensive with the Nietzschean *overcoming*. And when she says, "I had to sacrifice myself for the creation of something great", this is something strictly of the same order: she has to sacrifice or destroy her *self*, her *human being* in order to come into being differently through a creative act. That is to say, a psychoanalytic act for Spielrein is completely different to a human or humanistic act. On the contrary, what we take as the being of the human, in other words the ego or illusion of one's self, is yet another beautiful illusion that needs to be destroyed, or overcome, in order to be able to submit to the productions of the unconscious. It is only in this manner that one might accede to the creativity of becoming.

We find something similar from the writer Pascal Quignard who comments on what he discerns to be the misplaced humanism of the French philosopher Emmanuel Levinas:

> At the end of the 1960s, Emmanuel Levinas, stripping back every image, wanted to see a human countenance everywhere, adding a type of halo to each and every face, thus nourishing the illusion of restoring humanity to

the confidence that it had had in itself before its destruction by the German Third Reich.

(Quignard 2005, p. 41, translated for this edition)

Similarly, the contemporary German philosopher Peter Sloterdijk, in his lecture on Nietzsche, asserts that the term "humanism", such as ethicists use it today, "suggests the return to a carefully considered sort of self-affirmation that is only barely distinguishable from medium-level depression" (2013, p. 26). This reinforces the view that such humanism, that is, the affirmation of the *self* or ego, is precisely what is in itself symptomatic.

But in Nietzsche's view the redeeming feature of man is precisely his capacity to overcome himself. Again we hear this echoed in Spielrein's paraphrasing of Nietzsche, "You must understand that you must overcome (destroy) yourself". The redeeming feature of the symptom is that it exceeds the dimension of the human being, of the ego. For Freud the symptom is both "a sign of, and a substitute for, a [drive] satisfaction which has remained in abeyance" (1926d, p. 91). That is, the symptom is not only the substitute satisfaction of the drive, but also a sign of something that exceeds it. For Nietzsche, this dimension is language itself: one must make oneself worthy of language, to submit oneself to language rather than to imagine that one might be able to control language, to use it as a tool, even a tool of communication. This of course is an impossible task since it is the speaking-being that remains irreconcilable: there is always a leftover that cannot be resolved, dissolved, or *gelöst*. It is this excess that Spielrein, through her analysis—and her writing which prolonged it, and enabled her to finish it—designated in language as *Siegfried*.

Lacan designated the symptom as that which does not cease from being written. Whilst this is a logical formulation that denotes the Necessary, we can also take it literally in Spielrein's case as her incessant and necessary effort to write what could not be said in her truncated analysis. Where the speaking-being was impeded, she interposed as a solution the *writing-being*. In Spielrein's singular case, it was specifically the writing-being that was imbued with the capacity to overcome itself. The Necessary is in itself inadequate; rather it is the necessary condition to face the Impossible, that of not ceasing to write what cannot be written. This Impossible is also the impossibility of saying or writing everything that needs to be said or written. This is the impossible conveyed by Siegfried: the designation of difference per se, a difference that stands in opposition to an imaginary wholeness, that for instance of an Aryan-Semitic hero. In the face of the impossible, confronted with the analysis of her own long history of suffering, Spielrein was able to overcome her *self* and produce a singular linguistic creation, a poem of just one word: Siegfried.

Spielrein's project is also that of the destruction of such beautiful illusions as those of humanism—illusions that detain and inhibit us in fruitless endeavours that are the lot of our suffering—in order to be able to put the symptom to use in a creative act. But to overcome one's self is also to recognise the way that one is already overcome by the jouissance of one's suffering. Nietzsche also articulates this in the following way through the words of Zarathustra: "The overman is in my heart, *that* is my first and my only concern—and *not* human beings" (1883, p. 233, italics in the original). The overman is thus what exceeds the being of the human, what is in excess already within one's own heart, within one's own unconscious. The excess is the child Siegfried that would be a waste of Spielrein's talents. Siegfried then, is something beyond the idea or illusion of any child. It is also "a waste", it is what is in excess of the illusion of a sexual relation. It is this other Siegfried that is left over and which exceeds the possibility of an actual child that can profitably be put to work.

8

I SAT THERE WITH SIEGFRIED AND WORKED

Lovers and madmen have such seething brains,
Such shaping fantasies, that apprehend
More than cool reason ever comprehends.
The lunatic, the lover, and the poet
Are of imagination all compact:
One sees more devils than vast hell can hold;
That is the madman: the lover, all as frantic,
Sees Helen's beauty in a brow of Egypt:
The poet's eye, in a fine frenzy rolling,
Doth glance from heaven to earth, from earth to heaven;
And as imagination bodies forth
The forms of things unknown, the poet's pen
Turns them to shapes, and gives to airy nothing
A local habitation and a name.

Shakespeare, A Midsummer Night's Dream *(1595–1596)*

Spielrein follows the progression of which Shakespeare writes, first being presented by her family to the Burghölzli as a madwoman, one who was not able to be handled outside the asylum due to her erratic behaviour. She has also been treated as a madwoman by some recent authors. Through her treatment with Jung she becomes the lover, one who assumes her place in this schema by virtue of her transference-love towards Jung, and "Sees Helen's beauty in a brow of Egypt" as Shakespeare puts it. Jung, through his own unanalysed fantasies, incorporates her in his own desire for a Jewish woman, also calling her "the Egyptian", involving both an idealisation and a denigration of this figure of his imagination. But it is through the third position described by Shakespeare, that of the poet, that Spielrein is able to invent a name that permits her to overcome both Jung's fantasm, and then to locate her own. Through the act of writing Spielrein is able to accede to a place where she is able to be useful, and to work.

In the last chapter we stressed Spielrein's invention of Siegfried as *poetry*. Nonetheless, we recall that the title of Goethe's autobiography is *Aus meinem Leben: Dichtung und Wahrheit* or *Truth and Fiction Relating to My Life*. As we have noted, in this title the *Dichtung* could be translated either as Poetry—as Lacan renders it in his paper "The Neurotic's Individual Myth" (1953a)—or as Fiction. Here we can also emphasise the dimension of the *fiction* of Siegfried, that Siegfried is a fiction created by Spielrein. That is, through her writing, Spielrein produces a fiction whose name is Siegfried, rather than reproducing by making an actual child. Siegfried is an uncommon signifier, one that has to be written in order for Sabina Spielrein to finish her analysis. We are proposing that it is precisely through the production of the Siegfried, a signifier that is at the heart of her writing, that Spielrein is able to transmit something fundamental regarding her analysis and its termination. It is a fiction that is born of love: it is born of Spielrein's transference-love, later diverted into a transference to work, necessitated by Jung's abandonment of the place of analyst. As Spielrein wrote, "I killed in my dreams the man who was supposed to become Siegfried's father". Spielrein allowed her analyst to fall and directed her transference to writing: to producing a fiction.

Here we must follow Spielrein's intuition through our own transference to her work. That is, we take up our own transference-love to her writings, enabling us to produce a new work, a new reading of what she was able to write by allowing her analyst Carl Jung to be killed through her writings. In doing so, we also have to kill off whatever we might imagine about Spielrein's story. In other words, we have to allow all of the stories and our imaginings about them to fall, in order to address her writings in their own right. In this way we no longer try to follow the inevitable temptation—itself a type of sexual relation—of imagining we can elaborate and explain Spielrein's history by reference to her writings. This of course does not mean that Sabina Spielrein was not marked by her own particular trajectory. Rather, from the destruction of an apparently consistent picture, a beautiful illusion that is produced from whatever story we might have regarding Spielrein, something entirely new can be produced. Taking inspiration from Spielrein's own work, this implies for each one of us that in the destruction of the story of origins that we have about ourselves, a new account can be created in which we are no longer held hostage to our own history. The implication that flows from this is that Spielrein's work is the enactment of a *de novo* theory of creativity.

While the biographers seek to find the cause of Spielrein's suffering through the productions of her analysis, Spielrein herself seeks, in the remains of her analysis, a cause that drives her forward and allows her to work. Unlike her biographers, through her analysis Spielrein does not seek to find cause or fault with her parents or others. Rather, she discovers in the Siegfried—something that as she herself notes had its antecedents in her history—a means by which she is able to locate and repair a fault, and which henceforth is able to serve as a means of allowing herself to work. Otherwise Siegfried would remain but a lost dream of something that she might have had with Carl Jung, something that she encountered but let slip between her fingers. On the contrary, and despite the encouragement from both Jung and Freud to abandon Siegfried, she grasps it and makes use of it in order to make something of her life through her work. We recall that when Spielrein was admitted to the Burghölzli, there was no record of her having written for some 2 years prior to this. Siegfried, however, became the means and the purpose of her emancipation. For Lacan, in an analysis there is a necessary double looping of first locating in one's fantasm what needs to be loosed [*gelöst*] or cut, and then of reknotting or splicing this in a new way that allows the possibility of some movement. Such a movement again evokes Freud's adage that "The finding of an object is in fact a refinding of it" (1905d, p. 222). It is this endeavour to refind an object that drives Spielrein forward, in the momentum of a never-ending search for an object, for the font of her creativity. For Spielrein, this ending of her analysis on the first occasion involves encountering and even constructing the Siegfried in her analysis, and on the second occasion writing both of, and through, Siegfried.

Freud, despite his extensive references to poetry, had already articulated that the story given by the subject regarding his or her origins was a narrative account. This, as we have noted, is the whole thrust of his paper "Family Romances" (1909c), more literally translated as the "Family Novel of the Neurotic". The novel is a work of fiction that each one of us produces in a narrative form in order to try to explain who and what we are by reference to an assumed temporal and relational mode of causality. Erik Porge noted that Freud's method, especially as articulated in his case histories, was that of constructing an *account* [*récit*] of his patients by making these into a series of *case histories* for the benefit of the public that he addressed. Porge cites Roudinesco and Plon who, in reference to Freud and Breuer's *Studies on Hysteria*, assert that "these patients' histories, transcribed in a novelistic style, contribute to giving life to feminine figures resembling those described by Gustave Flaubert (1821–1880) or Honoré de Balzac (1799–1850)" (In: Porge 2005, p. 16).

Porge puts forward, though, that if Freud's major reference was that of the novel and thus of *prose*, for Lacan it was that of *poetry*—without it being necessary to consider either of these terms as pre-established literary genres. For Porge, the reference to poetry is, rather, that of a transgression of genres whose object is language itself (p. 45). Without being able to expound upon the whole development of this theme given by Porge in his work, we can cite, amongst other indications, the poem written by Lacan in 1922 and published in 1929 under the title, *Hiatus Irrationalis*, the numerous sequences of alexandrines—a classic French verse—discerned in his *Écrits*, and his elaboration upon the theory of the signifier through the poetic devices of metonymy and metaphor. Furthermore, Lacan made numerous references to psychoanalytic theory by reference to poetry, some of which we will address in this chapter.

Here we might return to the differentiation that we took from Roland Barthes in our Introduction, between the structural analysis that might be applied to the narrative model of the *account*, and the textual analysis that is applicable to a text, such as Spielrein's writings. We recall that Barthes made a categorical distinction between the two, stating that "writing arrives just exactly at the moment when speaking ceases", in other words, for Spielrein, the writing was precisely what was necessary for her to be able to finish her psychoanalysis, when the speaking with Carl Jung was no longer possible or productive. Writing for Spielrein then was her means of being able to go beyond what could be said by means of the narrative, in order to put her words to work.

Whilst in "The Neurotic's Individual Myth" Lacan translated Goethe's *Dichtung* as poetry, he was no less receptive to its translation as *fiction*, since for Lacan truth itself has a structure of fiction: "There is so little opposition between this *Dichtung* and *Wahrheit* in its nakedness that the fact of the poetic operation must make us notice, instead, the following feature which we forget in every truth: truth shows itself [*s'avère*] in a fictional structure" (1966a, p. 625). Lacan here, in his paper on the writings of André Gide, is referring both to poetry and to psychoanalysis: he finds in literature the operations of language that function equally in analysis. Spielrein demonstrated, in both the poetry *and* fiction of Siegfried, that the truth which was at play was not a pre-established one, but rather a truth that could be created through the productions of her unconscious, by means of her poetry.

I don't want to write, or rather I do but that it would be written by itself

Spielrein's theorisation of this is succinctly encapsulated in the thesis of her paper "Destruction as Cause of Becoming", in other words, that something—in particular the image or *Bild*—must be destroyed in order to create something new. The something new is produced by means of the enunciation [*aussprechen*], that is to say, through the poietic force of the signifier. Hence the style of her writing is the very enactment of a production that cannot be pinned down to a single meaning, or a series of meanings. On the contrary, it serves as a means of dis/solving, ungluing, or loosening [*lösen*] common, or a priori meanings. This is not a speech or writing by virtue of which the author insists upon her intentions, but rather a production or effect that allows the unconscious to speak. Spielrein's style of writing is not something that we would call a personal style. Rather her style is the means by which she allows herself to be marked by the productions of the unconscious.

We have commented upon this question of Spielrein's style right from the beginning of this work and mentioned that this is something often commented upon by other authors. However, many commentators refer to her style in a negative way since Spielrein's message remains elusive. We have to assert, against this, that it is not just the contents, or presentations, that are important in her writing, but also the mode of writing: the *mode of presentation*. It is specifically her style, moreover, that is the means by which she was able to transmit the *method* of psychoanalysis, rather than a set of givens.

Spielrein's method is also evident in her adaptation of Nietzsche's notion of the eternal return: that of returning *destructively* each time to dissolve what has become fixed, in order to produce, not a repetition, but a creation that is always new. Unlike Freud's work, and even more so the works of the post-Freudians, Spielrein's writings have resisted being set into a fixed doctrine since they are the very means of the dissolution of a set of teachings. This, we can say, is the precursor of the method later employed by Lacan when things became stuck in the *Freudian School of Paris*. His solution was to dissolve the school: "This problem is demonstrated in such a way as to have a solution: it is the *dis*—the dissolution" (1980, p. 318, translated for this edition). The dissolution was effected, in Lacan's terms, in order to address the deviations and the compromises made in that school. Lacan did not want his school to go the way of the International Psychoanalytic Association—which he referred to as the "Church" due to its fixed doctrine—a phenomenon that occurred when psychoanalysis "veered towards meaning [*sens*]" (p. 318).

Spielrein thus places her trust in style, the style by which her writing is marked, rather than the conveying of any information that is set in advance. This is what makes her work both properly psychoanalytic, and at the same time poetic. Poetic practice is always a practice of invention, whose tool is the letter. Her best writing, as we have put forward—and in this we include her letters to Freud and "Destruction as Cause of Becoming"—draws upon Freud's psychoanalytic method: that of free association. Lacan, in his "Overture" to his *Écrits*, adapted Buffon's formula, "style is the man himself" to include the fundamental notion of transference: "style is the man … the man one addresses" (1966a, p. 9). That is, in writing, style is not an affectation, it is the very purpose and means of writing since it is both the transference itself in its address to another, and to a public beyond. It is also the manner in which a psychoanalytic knowledge is to be transmitted to others through the style itself. With Spielrein we have affirmed that poetry is the creation of a mode of address that carries no fixed meaning, and, furthermore, it is directed to no addressee specified in advance. The addressee may be any reader who is able to take up Spielrein's poetry and to do something with her writings. We recall her wish in recovering from her illness to become a "useful combination". This utility is something she put forward later on as something that could be done by the analysand with his or her symptom: "It is only the collaboration of subconscious thought with conscious thought that can engender a creative work in this world: conscious thought must grasp what it is that the subconscious thought offers up to us, and utilise it" (Spielrein 1923, p. 309). Here the function of consciousness is to *use* what is offered up by the unconscious, in order not to *lose* this.

For Lacan, this was specifically what was in question in 1966 when he was assembling his writings—his *Écrits*—for a public beyond that of his seminar.

Lacan here also puts trust in his style as the means by which he is able to address his letter to the reader, in order for this reader to produce something from it for him or herself. Lacan elaborates upon this by reference to his first paper in the collection based upon Edgar Allen Poe's *The Purloined Letter*: "Poe's message, deciphered and coming back from him, the reader, in so far as he reads it, is said to be [he tells himself that he is] no more feigned than truth when it inhabits fiction" (1966b, p. 10, translated for this edition). Here I translate this passage myself so as to retain the ambiguity and richness of Lacan's assertion which concerns the fictional nature of both the subject matter or *it*, as well as that of the truth of the subject or *he*. This is a complexity and richness that is lost in the published translation. We have emphasised this double movement from our reading of Spielrein's work, that between the analysand and the analyst, and that between the poet and the poem. In Chapter 3 we referred to Lacan's citing, once again from the "Overture" to his *Écrits*, of Pope's poem *The Rape of the Lock*. Lacan utilises the resources of the French translation of "lock" as *boucle*—as this word also signifies a "loop"—in order to propose that, "Our task returns to us this charming lock [*boucle*] in the topological sense of the term: a knot whose trajectory closes upon itself from its inverted redoubling—namely, such as we have recently put it forward as supporting the structure of the subject" (1966b, p. 10). We can hear in this the manner in which Lacan's notion of the end of analysis, "when one has twice turned around in circles" (1977–1978, p. 33), is coextensive with his notion of the structure of the psychoanalytic subject, one that is supported by this double looping which is also the trajectory that the analysand must describe within the analysis. This second loop is inverted since the message is returned to the subject in an inverted form from the Other, in this case the reader. But since it is ourselves as readers of Spielrein who receive her writings in a first loop, in a second moment we return these to psychoanalysis as a new reading or deciphering of Spielrein. This is what we can designate as our return to Spielrein.

What remains from this analysis then is some litter, some letters that can be utilised to produce a creative work. The reading that each subject makes is a singular one: it is a reading that, if it be successful, creates a new truth regarding both what it is one is reading, as well as the subject of the unconscious itself. It is also in this way—following Spielrein and again anticipating Lacan—that we can say that the subject is a dividual: the subject remains divided between knowledge and truth. On the one hand this is a knowledge that concerns the subject matter, and on the other a truth by which the psychoanalytic subject is marked: this is the very division that we have elaborated through Spielrein between the poem and the poet. It is how we might define Spielrein's use of the term "poetry" in inverted commas: this poetry is the double looping of the poet or psychoanalyst who writes, privileging the letters or poem that he or she leaves behind, thus rendering the poet or psychoanalyst an insubstantial being. We recall once again Lacan's words, "I am not a poet but a poem".

In concluding the "Overture" or opening of the *Écrits*, Lacan emphasises this in the following way: "From the journey of which these writings are the milestones, and from the style which their address commands, we want to take the reader to a consequence where he must put in something of himself [*mettre du sien*]" (In: Plastow 1997, p. 22). Here I take my own translation from a paper that I wrote some 20 years ago regarding *style*, given that it is much more literal than the later published translation, and thus follows what Lacan wrote to the letter, rather than to an attributed meaning. In that paper I put forward that style is "a symbolic function which marks the relation of the subject to the signifier" (p. 21). This formulation primarily concerns the *speech* of the subject through the transference. However, given what we have been elaborating through Spielrein's *writings*, this formulation must also be dissolved in order to produce something new. Hence we could propose, in regard to Spielrein's style, that *style is the means by which, through the analysis, the destruction of sense or meaning is able to be effected by reducing the signifier to its component letters, permitting the poiesis from this of ever new productions.* Style is therefore something by which the subject is marked, and by virtue of which this subject is enabled to produce something from the symptom. The subject of style, even if it is an insubstantial being, is nonetheless not an inconsequential one.

We can refer, as does Erik Porge, to Roland Barthes' work *Writing Degree Zero*. In the chapter on poetic writing, Barthes differentiates modern poetry from classical poetry. For Barthes, the latter is an embellishment and a mode of expression that fundamentally pertains to prose and does not yet define a separate field from it. He makes the point, moreover, that classical language, whether prose or poetry, is relational: every word is the sign of a thing, or the path to a relationship. Here we can emphasise that the numerous biographies and histories regarding Sabina Spielrein pertain to narrative prose in so far as they concern a mode of relationship. On the other hand, modern poetry that Barthes dates from Rimbaud is no longer an art of the expression of relationships, but rather a field of invention. Poets henceforth establish their writings as a separate field that at once addresses both the function and structure of language itself. Modern poetry, he asserts, "*destroys* the spontaneously functional nature of language, and leaves standing only its lexical basis" (1953, p. 39, my italics). The relations of language are not eliminated here, but rather they are emptied out, allowing "the density of the Word to rise out of a magic vacuum" (p. 39). Although Barthes' formulation arises from a different era and discipline, in both his and Spielrein's theorisation there is a coextensiveness in which a linguistic act of destruction permits a passage beyond the fascination with images and relations. This leads on towards something more fundamental that pertains to the letter, which then secondarily permits an invention, or creativity. Barthes maintains that poetry "is in fact a certain linguistic ethos", in such a manner that writing soaks up style. For Barthes, the poetic act itself is productive of a style: "when the poetic language radically questions Nature … there is no mode of writing left, there are only styles" (p. 43). It is also in this sense that we can speak of Spielrein's poietic mode of writing as *style*.

Spielrein's style—her writing—is the very means of its transmission and its non-reduction to a pre-established message. In addressing her writing, however, the reader must put in something of his or her own in order to produce something from these writings. Sabina Spielrein took up writing as a necessary step to put a term to her analysis, in order to produce an ending.

Towards the end of the novel *The Narrow Road to the Deep North* by the contemporary Australian author Richard Flanagan—the title of his book unashamedly plagiarised from a work by the Japanese poet Bashō—the principal protagonist, on his deathbed and delirious, recalls some fragments of a poem. This poem is not named but is evidently Tennyson's *Ulysses*, a now aged Ulysses who also embarks upon the ultimate adventure of death. Flanagan's protagonist states that "it were as if this poem had been written for him, his life was now a poem, so totally the poem was him" (Flanagan 2013 p. 462). This character finds himself at the point of an ending, subject to the crumbling of language, which confronts him with a failure of the notion of the individual: no longer any "I am". The poetic act of writing is here a de-identification: the poet—the "I am"—disappears in favour of the creation of the poem. His life is a poem that is written, and which is to be read, however unreadable or impenetrable. The poem is also on the border of the spoken and the written: it is to be re-cited, whether by the poet himself or by the reader. This is how we consider our return to Spielrein's writings: not as a personal story that might allow us to imagine relationships, but rather as a poem to be read through our own transference, and whose effects are to be elaborated by the reader, by ourselves.

I wrote a poem to you

Sabina Spielrein had to write to effect a cut, in order to no longer remain entangled in sexual relations with no way out. As we have seen, she formulated that in the analysis, through the transference the analysand is subjected to an event [*Ereignis*], by virtue of which always new differentiation products are able to be produced, and these can be psychically transformed into speech, or a work of art. It is not fortuitous that Spielrein referred to her accession to moments of intimacy between her and Jung as "poetry". This poetry, as we have seen, was not just a code, or metaphor, for a sexual relationship. Rather, we can propose that Spielrein's poetry is metaphor, in so far as a metaphor is literally a poetic device of language. Spielrein wrote poetry in order to psychically transform the experiences that occurred through her transference-love into writing. It was specifically writing that transformed the event into an abreaction or a work of art. From her own account, she literally wrote poems and songs to produce her own reading of events.

Some 50 years after Spielrein formulated this, Lacan also conceived of psychoanalysis as a work of poetry. In particular on two occasions, in his seminars in 1971 and again in 1977, Lacan makes reference to, and elaborates upon, a short poem of only four lines by Léon-Paul Fargue entitled *Air du Poète* (1866–1933, p. 41), or [*Song of the Poet*]. The poem is one of five from the series of playful poems entitled *Ludions*, later set to music by Eric Satie. There is no published translation of this poem, and translations accessible on the Internet completely miss the thrust of the poem that is given in its title, by turning it into no more than a love story in an exotic location. We are not surprised at this, since it is the very manner in which Spielrein's encounter with psychoanalysis has been interpreted in the limited way that insists upon the sexual relation, and is not able to move beyond this. We could consider that this poem is strictly speaking untranslatable since it functions through the decomposition of words into their constituent letters, producing something entirely new. It operates in this way, both through its thematics, and also in its very style or mode of operation, it spells out the poietic nature of the poem in reference to the poet. We will thus restrict ourselves here merely to explicating it:

From the first line, literally "In the land of Papua [*Au pays de Papousie*]", the poet carries the second part of *Papouasie* into the second line as *Pouasie*: "I caressed the *Pouasie*" [*J'ai caressé la Pouasie …*], *Pouasie* is in one sense a nonsense word elevated to the status of a proper noun by the use of an initial capital letter. We can hear this as an approach to an ineffable and unknowable object designated as *Pouasie*, one made all the rarer by being located in a foreign land. However, as suggested by the title, the neologism *Pouasie* is assonant with *poésie* or poetry. Hence the line, "I caressed the *Pouasie*" also proposes Fargue's approach to poetry itself. In this encounter the poet finds a means to brush up against the very nature of poetry. The last two lines read concretely as "The grace—or charm—that I wish upon you, is to not be (a) Papuan [*La grâce que je vous souhaite C'est de n'être pas Papouète*]". However, given the reference to poetry, and breaking down *Papouète* into its homophone *Pas pouète*, we can separate out *pouète* as "poet" from the negation *pas*. Now we can read these last two lines as "The grace that I wish upon you, is to not not be a poet". In other words, by the use of the double negation we encounter by splitting the signifier *Papouète* into its constituent letters, the author articulates what a grace—or charm—it is to *be* a poet.

This is made explicit in the brief reference that Lacan makes to the poem in 1971 where he picks up on the spelling of Fargue's *Pouasie* to speak of the poet as "*le Pouate, le poète de Pouasie comme disait le cher Léon-Paul Fargue*" (the Poat, the poet of Poatry, as dear *Léon-Paul Fargue* used to say) (1971–1972, p. 108). Here Lacan takes up the letter "a" that he finds in Fargue's Pouasie and applies it to the poet, making him or her a *Pouate*. Lacan's object a is the object *cause* of desire. This of course is a completely different notion of cause to that of conventional logic in which it is an antecedent that is followed by various effects. Lacan's notion of cause, though, is not an antecedent, but rather a cause—or a lack at the heart of the subject—that drives this subject forward in an always failing endeavour to be realised or satisfied by an object. We have elaborated Spielrein's notion of cause from her paper "Destruction as Cause of Becoming" as a positivised instance of the lack, but one that requires a necessary prior destruction. It is this that Spielrein introduces into psychoanalysis, this conception that there must be a logically prior act of destruction in order to produce a lack from the demands of the subject, and thus cause desire to come into being. What is also important in Spielrein's contribution is her emphasis upon the creative or poietic effect of this cause that is consequent upon the psychoanalytic act of destruction. This function of cause in Spielrein's paper has previously been entirely overlooked, despite it having a central place in the title of her paper.

Lacan returns to the question of poetry and of Fargue's *Song of the Poet* in his seminar of 1976–1977. Here he reiterates that sense or meaning acts as a plug, in so far as it obturates any movement in the analysis, but that "with the help of what is called poetic writing, you can have the dimension of what might be analytic interpretation" (p. 119). Lacan notes that analysts may be inspired by something of the order of poetry in their interventions. He then puts forward the following proposition: "It is in so far as a right interpretation extinguishes a symptom, that truth is specified as being poetic" (p. 119). He goes on to say that "It is only poetry … that allows interpretation". This, Lacan suggests, puts a limit upon interpretation. It is here that he says, à la Fargue, "I am not enough of a *poat*, I am not *poat*-enough [*pouâteassez*]!" (p. 130). Here once again we encounter the a, the object little a that Lacan discerns in the poetry.

In his seminar of 1977–1978, *The Moment to Conclude*, Lacan asserts that: "The analysand speaks. He makes poetry. He makes poetry when he is successful— that is infrequent—but he is *art* [*il est* art]. I am cutting because I don't want to say he/it is late [*il est tard*]" (p. 25). Here Lacan utilises a homophone to emphasise that in the timely accession to poetry, the subject—the psychoanalytic subject—*is* art: an artwork or poetry as Spielrein articulated. Lacan goes on to articulate that the cut of the analyst's intervention is a participation in the practice of writing. But this writing is not the writing of a story, but a writing of letters, "through the grace of spelling, in a different way to writing, it sounds out something other than what is said" (p. 25). And it is because of this, Lacan says, that the analysand says more than he intends. He goes on to put forward that the practice of psychoanalysis is a practice of poetry: "Why did someone called Freud succeed in his own poetry, I mean to introduce a psychoanalytic art?" (p. 30). What Lacan proposed and formulated in this way from Freud's writings, which he specifically here calls his *poetry*, was also elaborated by Spielrein through her necessity to terminate her analysis through writing.

For Lacan the question of the end of analysis—that of when one has twice turned around in circles—is something that can be illuminated by the device that he invented and named the *passe*. In *The Moment to Conclude*, Lacan proposes that the *passe* "could perhaps be done by writing" (1977–1978, p. 35). The *passe* was a mechanism proposed and introduced by Lacan into the *Freudian School of Paris* to be able to speak of the end of analysis. We can retrospectively consider, however—through the effects of *Nachträglichkeit* or *après-coup*—that what Spielrein effected through her writings was something of the same order. We have already proposed that these were a means of writing her way out of her analysis, that is, as a means of being able put a stop to the endless sliding of meaning and significations, which kept her tied to certain relationships, in the transference with Carl Jung. Since this was done in an effort to terminate her analysis, it thus constituted something akin to the *passe*. This passe was her endeavour to extricate herself from the impasse in which she was caught with Carl Jung. Our present work is also an endeavour to hear and to read, through our deciphering of Spielrein's early writings, what she endeavoured to produce through these. What we are writing is an effort to elaborate upon what Spielrein was working, to produce a different account to the stories that have now begun to proliferate about Spielrein and her relationship with Jung, with Freud, and others. Here, we endeavour to read her writing as a type of *passe* through which she was able to transmit a work that is worthy of interest for psychoanalysts and psychoanalysis: for the poets and the poem of psychoanalysis.

Objects solitary and terrible

Through her own psychoanalysis, her psychoanalytic work, and her reading of Nietzsche and the pre-Socratics, Spielrein was able to produce a theorisation of what lies beyond the pleasure principle, in a way that Freud was not, at least at the time of Spielrein's early writings. Freud in fact refused Nietzsche, writing to Fliess in 1900, "I have just acquired Nietzsche, in whom I hope to find words for much that remains mute in me, but have not opened him yet. Too lazy for the time being" (Masson 1985, p. 398). Later on in his 1914 paper "On the History of the Psycho-Analytic Movement", laziness is no longer the reason that Freud cites for his reluctance to read Nietzsche: "I have denied myself the very great pleasure of reading the works of Nietzsche, with the deliberate object of not being hampered in working out the impressions received in psycho-analysis by any sort of anticipatory ideas" (1914d, pp. 15–16). This refusal of Nietzsche is a curious exception to the anticipatory ideas that Freud eagerly sought from other thinkers and philosophers, writers and poets. There is in this something more specific for Freud, which is surely connected to the Dionysian, to the particular sensation of "eternity" which is of something limitless and unbounded, that he designates elsewhere as something "oceanic": "I cannot discover this 'oceanic' feeling in myself" (1930a, p. 65), he states. We can propose that here Freud articulates something of the limits of his own neurosis.

Spielrein, on the other hand, has no such compunction that restrains her from drawing upon Nietzsche, whose work she has clearly read and absorbed. The style of Spielrein's work, which lends itself to a polysemy, moves in quite another direction to most of her commentators who endeavour to find in them a condensation into a single meaning. Furthermore, through her reading of Freud's "The Antithetical Meanings of Primary Words", as well his enunciation that there is no contradiction in the unconscious, Spielrein is able to discern the polyphony of the signifier which, in her hands, is no longer limited to the dialectic of two opposite meanings but opens up onto associations that can lead in multiple directions or senses. Spielrein's method is in fact the destruction of the immediate image or meaning that is attributed to a particular word, in order to cause the creation of ever new productions.

In other words, the direction of Spielrein's work is a movement from monosemy to polysemy. Through Spielrein's notion of destruction as a cause of becoming, moreover, the signifier is broken down into its component letters, as we indeed find in poetry. If we consider the doctrine of a single sexual meaning that biographers attribute to Spielrein's transference to Jung, we might consider this reduction to a univocal meaning as a type of monotheism. Through Spielrein, however, and particularly her use of Nietzsche and the pre-Socratics, there is a return to a type of polytheism, or even a pantheism in so far as it is no longer a question of an Otherness embodied in a particular entity or doctrine. Rather, it is now a question of the destruction of the word into its component letters, which leads towards an encounter with the object. Modern poetry, as Barthes defines it, empties out the relations of language through an autonomous violence, and is thus able to interrupt Nature. This singular notion of Nature—which from psychoanalysis we can designate as the real—reveals the object in fragments, or piecemeal [*par blocs*] as Barthes writes. In this way it elevates the place of the *object* in discourse: "Nature becomes a fragmented space, made of objects solitary and terrible" (1953, p. 42). In reference to Spielrein's schema, destruction is necessary in order to confront us with the impossible encounter with the object, an object that remains both solitary and terrible.

But for Barthes, each poetic word, being devoid of a pre-established relation to a meaning, is reduced to a zero degree of language, pregnant with all past and future specifications. This is what he refers to as the "Hunger of the Word" (p. 40), which makes poetic speech terrible and inhuman. Following this line of reasoning, Roland Barthes goes on to say that there is no poetic humanism of modernity: "This erect discourse is full of terror, that is to say, it relates man not to other men, but with the most inhuman images in Nature; heaven, hell, holiness, childhood, madness, pure matter, etc" (p. 42). Poetry here short-circuits relationships—or the sexual relation—confronting the subject with the object. This encounter with the object by means of destruction as cause is something that Spielrein articulates—no doubt from her own experience—as joy in pain: "there is something in our depth which, as paradoxical as it may sound, wants this self-damaging, for the I reacts to it with pleasure. The desire for self-damage, the joy in pain, is however completely incomprehensible, if we only consider the I-*life*, which wants to have nothing but pleasure" (Spielrein 1912a, p. 94). Here Spielrein encounters something that she articulates as beyond the pleasure principle.

For Nietzsche, pleasure, or lack of pleasure, is only a question of degree, that is, of a quantitative difference. For him this is the dissoluble [*auflösbare*] part of feeling that language—or concepts—has anything to do with and can be exemplified for Nietzsche by a beautiful painting: "this defines the limit of '*poetry*' as far as its ability to express feeling is concerned" (1870, p. 134). According to

Nietzsche, however, there is always an indissoluble residue [*ein unauflösbarer Rest*] that is susceptible only to the language of gesture and musical tone.

Once again we encounter an indissoluble object, here as sound stripped of any meaning or sense, an object that has been isolated from the subject, no longer caught in a dialectical relation. This object is created de novo along the lines of what we have cited from Nietzsche, through "a raging voluptuousness of the creative man who also knows the wrath of the destroyer". It is here that we can appreciate the scope of Spielrein's notion of "destruction": the destruction is that of the dialectic which is the illusory foundation of the sexual relation. What is destroyed then—by the analysand in analysis—is specifically the dialectical relation that the subject maintains with the object, mediated by the fantasm. It is here that Spielrein is inspired by Nietzsche who, in the words of Gilles Deleuze, railed against "the mystifying character of so-called dialectical transformations" (1962, p. 153), which for him is exemplified in the Nietzschean overman pitted against the dialectic. This dialectical relation, inherited from Hegel in the form of the master-slave dialectic, is what underpins any relation between subject and object, and is at the heart of what Lacan referred to as the sexual relation. And for Lacan this dialectic "has no other outcome—Hegel's very elaborate ideas teach us this—than the destruction of the other. There is no type of resolution of this tension" (1953–1954, p. 304). I have translated this myself here, since the abridged published translation of this seminar removes Lacan's reference to resolution. As we have already developed with Spielrein, there is no possible reconciliation of this dialectical relation of the subject to the other, no Aryan-Semitic hero. As Lacan stresses, "man's ... relation to the object and the libidinal object ... falls short of synthesis" (p. 299). Of course the dialectic, the sexual relation, or the fantasm cannot be fully and permanently destroyed, but what Spielrein allows us to put forward is that they can be momentarily suspended through a properly psychoanalytic intervention. For this to occur, Spielrein grasped that the destruction of the image of the other was necessary to strip the subject of the dialectical relation mediated by the fantasm, thereby, in the instant of the event, precipitating the object in its naked form.

It is this indissoluble residue or remainder that we can designate as the object, one that can be disarticulated from the subject by the analytical act of destruction. The analysand must come to destroy the dialectic in order to take stock of the failure of the fantasm. As a consequence, the subject may be able to put the transference to work in the production of speech or writing, a poem, or a work of art. It is specifically in endeavouring to utilise this excess or residue that the beautiful picture of the dialectical or sexual relation can be overcome. This overcoming is none other than what Lacan called many years later the "traversal of the fantasm". Hence it was also necessary for Spielrein to overcome the beautiful picture of her affinity with Carl Jung in her transference-love, in order to be able to come into being in her own right.

This is where Nietzsche marks a differentiation between epic poetry and lyric poetry. The former, he proposes, leads to the plastic arts—such as the *beautiful picture*—and the latter to music, specifically the Dionysian dithyramb. With Spielrein's advances, we have proposed that it is precisely through the destruction of the picture or image [*Bild*] that one can accede to poetry, that is, poetry here defined as lyric. Epic poetry—which we might also call classical poetry according to Barthes' definition—operates in the realm of the pleasure principle, whereas what Nietzsche refers to as lyric poetry touches upon the beyond of this principle. He states the following, "In the Dionysian dithyramb the Dionysian enthusiast is stimulated to the utmost intensity of all his symbolic powers; something never felt before demands to be expressed: the annihilation of *individuatio*" (Nietzsche 1870, p. 138, italics in the original). It is the sexual relation, nonetheless, that is the premise of any individuation, and this is what is able to be annihilated in the moment of a psychoanalytic act.

For Nietzsche the two realms are able, nonetheless, to be tied together through poetry: "Shared between both worlds, poetry, too, attains to a new sphere where there is, at one and the same time, sensuousness of imagery, as in epic poetry, and the emotional intoxication of sound, as in lyric" (p. 138). In the apprehension of the language of lyric poetry as its constituent sounds, there is also an encounter with the voice, an *object* of language. Here again we find a first looping in the dissociation between epic poetry and lyric poetry, and then a second loop that allows these to be reknotted or spliced in a novel manner. For Spielrein, the individual or *individuation* pertains to the self or ego, whereas what is approached in the unconscious is a primordial unity, or *Einheit*. The psychoanalytic subject's encounter with the letter of the unconscious, moreover, is able to be marked by a distinctive oneness, an *Einzigkeit*. Spielrein thus is able to draw upon the analysis of her own suffering in an original manner to produce a new psychoanalytic theorisation.

Much is made of Spielrein's destruction instinct, or drive, but always through a comparison with the Freudian death drive. Freud himself contributed to this tendency in a footnote in his paper "Beyond the Pleasure Principle", differentiating his position from that of Spielrein's. There he writes that: "A considerable portion of the speculations have been anticipated by Sabina Spielrein … in an instructive and interesting paper which, however, is unfortunately not entirely clear to me. She there describes the sadistic components of the sexual instinct as 'destructive'" (Freud 1920g, p. 55). Spielrein had presented part of her paper "Destruction as Cause of Becoming" to the Vienna Psychoanalytic Society on 29 November 1911 where, as we have discussed, she was met with great criticism, in part because she was associated with the so-called Swiss group, and Jung in particular. In a footnote to the title of her paper in the *Minutes* for that particular meeting, the editors strikingly felt the need to write the following: "She was strongly influenced by Jung; during her studies she suffered a psychotic episode" (Nunberg & Federn 1974, p. 329). Here in the very introduction of her presentation the editors find cause to discredit her on two levels. No doubt she was inexorably influenced by Jung, but the editors' insistence is upon their promotion of her supposed *strong influence*—what, in other words, we are referring to as the promotion of the sexual relation.

What the editors fail to appreciate is that Spielrein's writing itself is the very means by which she is able to take her leave of him, and they are therefore unable to hear and read what it is that is singular in her work. As for a psychotic episode during her studies, this is an invention of pure fantasy, but one that goes along the lines of Jung regarding his revision of his diagnosis of Spielrein, for the purposes of his presentation in Amsterdam, from that at the Burghölzli of hysteria to that of "psychotic hysteria" (1908, p. 20). The diagnosis of psychosis has since been propagated in a repetitive fashion, evolving into a diagnosis of psychosis and schizophrenia in the hands of Carotenuto (1980a p. 159), and of schizophrenia for Bruno Bettelheim (In: Carotenuto 1980b p. xvi).

It is curious that the editors of the *Minutes*, who generally limited their footnotes to clarifying references and contexts, found the need to criticise Spielrein's presentation and to differentiate her notion of the destruction instinct from Freud's death drive. Another editors' footnote endeavours to enlighten us regarding the following: "At first glance it might seem that, under Jung's influence, Dr. Spielrein had formulated, many years before Freud, the hypothesis that instinct life (see: "Beyond the Pleasure Principle") consists of two opposing drives—the life instinct and the death instinct. Closer scrutiny, however, discloses that she does not express this theory at all, but rather believes that the sexual instinct—that is, the life instinct, the creative instinct itself—contains a destructive component" (Nunberg & Federn 1974, p. 330). It would appear that the editors do protest too much, once again insisting that this new theorisation of Spielrein's actually pertains to Jung, which is in fact not the case, even if she draws upon some of Jung's work as a springboard to her own. Nonetheless, even though this footnote again is an effort to discredit Spielrein's work, its differentiation of Spielrein's notion of the destruction instinct from Freud's theory of the death drive is essentially correct. As we have seen, Spielrein isolates the function of the ego in regard to drives of self-preservation, effectively in order to dismiss these in her discussion of the sexual drive and the destruction drive. From this point she is able to describe something more fundamental in the nature of the drive, in other words its necessary character of destruction that is the cause of becoming, a becoming which is in marked difference to any ego tendencies towards self-preservation.

Hence we can discern the movement in Spielrein's elaboration of the instinct of destruction, something quite different to the duality that Freud produced between the libido and the death drive. She begins her paper "Destruction as Cause of Becoming" with the clinical insight of the coextensiveness of the reproductive drive and the destructive instinct, but in effect as two sides of one drive, not a duality of drives as Freud later construed it, nor opposed to any supposed drive of self-preservation. Spielrein anticipates Lacan's notion of the drive as singular, encapsulated in his statement that: "The distinction between the life drive and the death drive is true in as much as it manifests two aspects of the drive" (1964, p. 257).

For Spielrein, *life* is not to be found in the stasis of self-preservation, but rather the life force, or *Lebenskraft*, which is manifested in a moment of creativity. For this life force to become manifest, it is only the logically a priori act of destruction of pre-existing presentations that can effect such a movement. It is here that we can grasp Spielrein's notion of cause, as a cause of becoming. We can use Spielrein's methodology of necessary destruction, moreover, on this central word itself in the title of her paper. The German word used by Spielrein for cause, *Ursache*, is etymologically, and to the letter, the *Ur-sache*, the primal thing, or object, akin to the Freudian *das Ding*, the unassimilable object. Through the destruction of the word for cause into its component parts, the joy or jouissance of an encounter with the thing itself can be produced.

I fear my singing'd come to harm

In "Destruction as Cause of Becoming", Sabina Spielrein remarks that Nietzsche had come to the conclusion that "language is there to bewilder itself and others" (1912c, p. 100). It is precisely the nonsensical aspect of language that Spielrein discovers in which one can no longer sustain the belief that one is in control of language, but rather we are subjected to it and bewildered by it. Language, moreover, bewilders itself, it is not a consistent and knowing agency—like a God—language is itself bewildered, confused, and incomplete. But this side of language that bewilders and is bewildered is also the side that Freud described: it is the dream, the parapraxis, and the joke, which, as he pointed out, are always reported by the patient through language. It is through her work with psychotic patients that Spielrein is able to encounter the destruction of common sense and meaning that are both the mainstay and the main hindrance of the neurotic. Through this work, Spielrein discovered that her psychotic patients were themselves the playthings of language. Of course the neurotic is no less so, but he or she is supported by the illusion of meaning, whist the psychotic, in which it is the delusion that prevails, is stripped of this illusion. And it is via the psychotic that Spielrein is able to develop her theory of language that we have discerned first in her thesis, and then elaborated in "Destruction as Cause of Becoming". If in her analysis with Jung there was an over-insistence upon meaning, she was able to go beyond this in the extension of her analysis through her writings, by subjecting herself to the signifier. Sabina Spielrein made her discoveries regarding the laws of language by submitting herself both to the bewilderment of her own language, as well as to the speech of her psychotic patients in her work at the Burghölzli, where she herself had not long before been a bewildered patient.

And through the analysis of her own suffering, Spielrein is able to isolate the position of the subject in relation to the Other, what she refers to in her own terms as the relation of the *I-psyche* to the *type-psyche*. This isolating is what we can also refer to as *separation*, a separation referred to by Spielrein in her own analysis through the term she invented for herself as a child, *"Partunskraft"*, akin to the Nietzschean *Lebenskraft*. This force of parting, derived from the overcoming of the dialectical relation subtended by the fantasm, is something she was able to reencounter in her analysis. It was this *Partunskraft* that allowed her *to part* from her analysis through her writing, thus separating herself off from Jung. And, at the moment of her graduation from University, having trained as a doctor and specialised as a psychiatrist, it was by virtue of the writing of her thesis—which she had published to be disseminated to a wider public beyond Bleuler and Jung—that she was recognised as an analyst by the Psychoanalytical Circle of Vienna. Her separation also enabled her to not return to Russia as her parents had wished, but to remain in the West, and to no longer practice the Jewish faith of her parents. As we have emphasised, her transference parted ways from Jung to be able to be directed towards her work.

Sabina Spielrein is no doubt the first person to have become a psychoanalyst through having had her own psychoanalysis. This has since come to be considered a necessary requisite for any psychoanalytic training or formation, even having become obsessionalised into a statutory requirement in many psychoanalytic associations. But in Spielrein's case it was driven by her singular suffering, and then the transference that was established when she was admitted by Dr. Carl Jung to the Burghölzli asylum. This transference was the necessity that drove her forward and permitted her symptom to be put to use in her studies in medicine, psychiatry, and psychoanalysis. This was her invention, and even if it was an unintended one, it was nonetheless an original invention: to make the individual psychoanalysis the mainspring of any formation of a psychoanalyst. This emphasises what we have elaborated through Spielrein's work, as the poet giving rise to the poem in the psychoanalytic poetry.

Spielrein's psychoanalytic formation was a very particular one that was established both on the basis of her own psychoanalysis, but also through her clinical experience with psychosis. Jung also came to psychoanalysis via psychosis, although not through his own analysis. Jung, moreover, was not able to submit himself to his own speech, nor to the speech of the psychotic as Spielrein allowed herself to do. Jung was too caught up in his neurotic insistence upon meaning, and the manner in which he conducted his further researches in mythologies led him even further down this path. In not separating out the subject from the object in an anti-dialectical movement as we have asserted that Spielrein was able to effect, there is no destruction of the dialectic, confining Jung to the impasses of the sexual relation. Spielrein's psychoanalytic formation with the psychotic gave her an openness to language itself, which anticipated that of Lacan some 20 or so years later. We have taken very literally Spielrein's reference to what transpired through her transference-love as "poetry", that is, as a very singular form of language. Similarly, Lacan put forward the following in regard to the training of psychoanalysts: "The least we can ask might be for psychoanalysts to notice that they are poets" (1967, p. 44). Spielrein had in fact noticed that she was a poet and wrote accordingly.

Both Spielrein and Lacan left us with work that we can consider to be poems, enigmatic poems to be read and deciphered, and to be declaimed and re-cited. This poetry is the creation of a form of address that carries no fixed meaning.

It transcends the common meanings of the words that are the material with which it has to work, in order to produce something that has effects, including upon the body. Spielrein was not insensitive to such effects. We recall how she wrote of how she allowed herself to be played by her name, and also in her "Contributions to the Knowledge of the Child's Soul" paper, the question of what to do with remainders of the body that were transposed onto foodstuffs: with the excess from the family meals, which she would create new forms, colours, and textures. The poetry becomes written in the attempt to harness the excess that transcends the affinity of the sexual relation. Writing, moreover, has a physical presence, and betrays the presence of the body. It is not for nothing that we refer to an author's writings as a body of work.

In his *Letters to a Young Poet*, Rainer Maria Rilke has the following to say: "Spiritual creativity originates from the physical. They are the same essence— only spiritual creativity is a gentler, more blissful, and more enduring repetition of physical desire and satisfaction" (Rilke 1929, p. 37). Spielrein, as a reader of Rilke, was also imbued with the creativity that arises from the jouissance, the *Freude*, of the body, including its pains, or *Schmerzen*. In this regard we might consider what Rilke wrote regarding Auguste Rodin: "His work was invincible because it came into the world mature; not in a state of development, seeking its justification, but as a triumphant, existing reality which must be reckoned with" (1903, p. 10). Spielrein's work comes into being in an instant of destruction and creation: it is not a developmental emergence, but rather a creation that can be produced in any fecund moment. This is Spielrein's contribution to psychoanalytic listening and interpretation: in a fertile instant the meaning, the signifier, and the dialectical relation can be destroyed or cut in order to confront the subject with the polysemy of the word, the letters of the signifier, and the terror of the object.

Spielrein's Siegfried was at once the signifier of the impossible union, but also that of the destruction or at least suspension of such a dialectical relation: the imaginary union that has to be constantly destroyed in order to permit new creations to come into being. Siegfried is Spielrein's invention from her analysis, a necessary fiction that is at the same time her poetry. This is what enabled Sabina Spielrein to compose, and to write. Siegfried allowed Spielrein to establish a distance between destruction and becoming. Or, drawing from Lacan, we can say that through the resources of the transference, Spielrein maintains the distance between the identification through the sexual relation, and the object that comes into being through the analysis. We can hear this expounded in the folk song, which Spielrein says is her favourite, cited in a letter to Jung that Carotenuto dates from the beginning of 1911:

> Wand'ring is my greatest pleasure,
> Off I start when e'er I can.
> Should you try to cause me sorrow,
> Off I'll shake it like a man.

Lovely ancient songs I'll sing you,
Standing in the cold, unfed,
Plucking strings to serenade you,
Know not where I'll rest my head.

Many a beauty looks with favor,
Says she might give me her heart,
If I only weren't unworthy,
If I played a finer part.

May the Lord grant you a husband,
Well equipped with house and farm,
If we two should come together,
I fear my singing'd come to harm. […]
(Carotenuto 1980a, p. 47)

Spielrein at the end of her analysis—as the subject of the song—eschews material comfort, as well as the comfort of the relationship. She abstains from the illusory, well-endowed husband in the song, in other words, from the imagined unbarred Other who has it all, of whom one might imagine availing oneself. This abstention is equivalent to Nietzsche's aphorism *God is dead*: one can no longer sustain the illusion of the omnipotence and omniscience of otherness. Jung can no longer occupy the place in which she had located him in her fantasm.

Spielrein plays a part, but not the "finer part": the destruction of the togetherness of the sexual relation involved in the choice that concludes the song punctures the deceptions and misapprehensions of a comfortable existence. We could say, moreover, that she plays a-part, not *a part of* a larger whole, but a part that is *apart from* the well-endowed Other. It is in finishing her analysis that she is able to procure this separateness for herself in *parting from* the Other by virtue of her *Partunskraft*. It is this separateness, or apartness, that is able to produce an object cause of desire. This object that she thus creates is not an object that is part of a larger whole that might sustain the illusion that it might complete an otherness, but rather *an object apart*, or *an a-part object*.

The two to be kept apart then are perhaps not what we might imagine, Spielrein and Jung, or Spielrein and Freud, or any other imaginary pairing. Here what Spielrein privileges above all is the singing, the poetry, regardless of what pairings or relationships may or may not take place. Her life was dedicated to her work, but her writings have become forgotten by the constant emphasis on her relationships that are not allowed to be destroyed, preventing her poetry to come to the fore. What it is that Spielrein endeavours to keep apart are the destruction and becoming, a separation in which cause is able to emerge.

REFERENCES

Al Hariri of Basra. (1054–1122). *Makamat or Rhetorical Anecdotes of Al Hariri.* (Trans. Theodore Preston). Accessible at: https://archive.org/stream/makamatorrhetori00 hariiala/makamatorrhetori00hariiala_djvu.txt

Ariès, P. (1960). *L'Enfant et la Vie Familial sous L'Ancien Regime.* Paris: Seuil, 1973.

Balsam, R. (2015). Sabina Spielrein in Vienna, 1911–1912: Muse and Nemesis. In: Covington, C. & Wharton, B. (Eds.). *Sabina Spielrein: Forgotten Pioneer of Psycho-analysis.* 2nd Edition (pp. 172–184). Hove & New York: Routledge, 2015.

Barthes, R. (1953). Writing Degree Zero. In: *Writing Degree Zero & Elements of Semiology.* (Trans. A. Lavers & C. Smith). London: Jonathan Cape, 1984.

Barthes, R. (1972). The Grain of the Voice. In: *Image, Music, Text.* (Trans. S. Heath) (pp. 179–189). London: Fontana, 1977.

Barthes, R. (1973). Textual Analysis of a Tale by Edgar Poe. *Poe Studies, 10;* 1977: 1–12.

Bataille, G. (1967). *The Accursed Share: An Essay on General Economy.* New York: Zone, 1993.

Cariola, O. (2014). Hvad mon det er for Noget, denne Skrækkelige ting man Kalder Kærlighed? *Freuds Agorás Seminarer 2014–2015.* (Non-commercial publication) (pp. 11–18). Copenhagen, Freuds Agorá.

Carotenuto, A. (Ed.). (1980a). *A Secret Symmetry. Sabina Spielrein between Jung and Freud.* New York: Pantheon, 1982.

Carotenuto, A. (Ed.). (1980b). *A Secret Symmetry. Sabina Spielrein between Jung and Freud.* (Commentary by Bruno Bettelheim). New York: Pantheon, 1984.

Carotenuto, A. (Ed.). (1980c). *Tagebuch einer heimlichen Symmetrie: Sabina Spielrein zwischen Jung und Freud.* Kore: Freiburg i. Br., 1986.

des Cars, J. (1975). *Louis II de Bavière ou Le Roi Foudroyé.* Paris: France Loisirs.

Cifali, M. (1988). Sabina Spielrein, A Woman Psychoanalyst: Another Picture. *Journal of Analytical Psychology, 46;* 2001: 129–138.

Comment, B. (2015). L'Énergie du Vivant. In: *Le Monde Hors-Série: Roland Barthes, L'Inattendu* (pp. 6–19). Paris: Le Monde, 2015.

Covington, C. & Wharton, B. (Eds.). (2003a). Burgholzli Hospital Records of Sabina Spielrein. In: *Sabina Spielrein: Forgotten Pioneer of Psychoanalysis* (pp. 79–109). Hove & New York: Routledge, 2003.

Covington, C. & Wharton, B. (Eds.). (2003b). The Letters of C.G. Jung to Sabina Spielrein. B. Wharton (Trans.). In: *Sabina Spielrein: Forgotten Pioneer of Psychoanalysis* (pp. 33–62). Hove & New York: Routledge, 2003.

Cromberg, R.U. (Ed.). (2014). *Sabina Spielrein: uma Pioneira da Psicanálise*. São Paulo: Livros da Matriz.

Cronenberg, D. (Director). (2011). *A Dangerous Method*. Sony Pictures Classics.

Curd, P. (Ed.). (2007). *Anaxagoras of Clazomenae: Fragments and Testimonia*. Toronto: University of Toronto.

Deleuze, G. (1962). *Nietzsche and Philosophy*. London: Bloomsbury, 2013.

Douglas, R.B. Alexander Pushkin: Three Poems on Imprisonment and Freedom. *FIDELIO Magazine, VIII*; 1999. Accessible at: https://schillerinstitute.com/fidelio_archive/1999/fidv08n02-1999Su/fidv08n02-1999Su_066-alexander_pushkin_three_poems_on.pdf

Duras, M. (1969a). *Détruire, Dit-Elle*. Paris: Éditions de Minuit.

Duras, M. (Ed. G. Philippe). (1969b). Extrait d'un entretien avec Yvonne Baby. In: *Œuvres Complètes II* (pp. 1168–1170). Paris: Gallimard, Bibliothèque de la Pléiade, 2011.

Duras, M. (1988). Ma Mère Avait. In: *Le Monde Extérieur: Outside 2* (pp. 198–206). Paris: Paul Otchakovsky-Laurens, 1993.

Faenza, R. (Director). (2002). *Prendimi l'Anima (The Soul Keeper)*. Medusa Film.

Fargue, L.-P. (1866–1933) Ludions. In: *Poésies: Tancrède. Ludions. Poëmes. Pour la Musique.* (Préface d'Henri Thomas) (pp. 39–54). Paris: Gallimard, 1967.

Fargue, L.-P. (1895). Tancrède. In: *Poésies: Tancrède. Ludions. Poëmes. Pour la Musique.* (Préface d'Henri Thomas) (pp. 15–38). Paris: Gallimard, 1967.

Flanagan, R. (2013). *The Narrow Road to the Deep North*. Sydney: Vintage.

Forel, A. (1899). *Hypnotism, or Suggestion and Psychotherapy*. H.W. Armit (Trans.). New York: Rebman, 1907.

Freud, S. (1905c). Jokes and their Relation to the Unconscious. *S.E., 8*. Hogarth: London.

Freud, S. (1905d). Three Essays on the Theory of Sexuality. *S.E., 7*. London: Hogarth.

Freud, S. (1909b). Analysis of a Phobia in a Five-year-old Boy. *S.E., 10*. London: Hogarth.

Freud, S. (1909c). Family Romances. *S.E., 9*. London: Hogarth.

Freud, S. (1910e). The Antithetical Meaning of Primal Words. *S.E., 11*. London: Hogarth.

Freud, S. (1911c) Psycho-Analytic Notes on an Autobiographical Account of a Case of Paranoia (Dementia Paranoides). *S.E., 12*. London: Hogarth.

Freud, S. (1911e). The Handling of Dream-Interpretation in Psycho-Analysis. *S.E., 12*. London: Hogarth.

Freud, S. (1912). On Psycho-Analysis. *The Australasian Medical Gazette, 31*; 1912: 385–387

Freud, S. (1914c). On Narcissism: An Introduction. *S.E., 14*. London: Hogarth.

Freud, S. (1914d). On the History of the Psycho-Analytic Movement. *S.E., 14*. London: Hogarth.

Freud, S. (1915a). Observations on Transference-Love (Further Recommendations on the Technique of Psycho-Analysis, III). *S.E., 12*: 157–171.

Freud, S. (1920g). Beyond the Pleasure Principle. *S.E., 18*. London: Hogarth.

Freud, S. (1921c). Group Psychology and the Analysis of the Ego. *S.E., 18*. London: Hogarth.

Freud, S. (1926d). Inhibitions, Symptoms and Anxiety. *S.E., 20*. London: Hogarth.

Freud, S. (1930a). Civilization and its Discontents. *S.E., 21.* London: Hogarth.

Freud, S. (1937c). Analysis Terminable and Interminable. *S.E., 23.* London: Hogarth.

Fried, M. (1984). Foreword to the John Hopkins Edition. In: Lessing, G.E. (1766). *Laocoön: An Essay on the Limits of Painting and Poetry.* (Trans. and Ed. E.A. McCormick) (pp. vii–viii). Baltimore, MD & London: Johns Hopkins.

Goethe, J.W. (1782). The Erl-King. Accessible at: http://www.gutenberg.org/files/1287/1287.txt

Goethe, J.W. (1795). Who'll Buy Gods of Love? Accessible at: http://www.online-literature.com/goethe/2631/

Goethe, J.W. (1808). *Faust Part I.* Accessible at: http://www.iowagrandmaster.org/Books%20in%20pdf/Faust.pdf

Goethe, J.W. (1833). *Autobiography: Truth and Fiction Relating to My Life.* Accessible at: http://www.gutenberg.org/ebooks/5733

Guibal, M. & Nobécourt, J. (Eds.). (2004). *Entre Freud et Jung.* (Dossier découvert par Aldo Carotenuto et Carlo Trombetta). Paris: Aubier., 1981.

Hampton, C. (2002). *The Talking Cure.* London: Faber & Faber.

Heine, H. (1823). Songs of Creation. In: *The Poems of Heine Complete.* (Translated into The Original Metres with a Sketch of His Life. Trans. Edgar Alfred Bowring). London: George Bell and Sons, 1908. Accessible at: https://www.gutenberg.org/files/52882/52882-0.txt

Homer. *The Odyssey.* (Trans. A. Pope). Accessible at: http://www.gutenberg.org/cache/epub/3160/pg3160-images.html

Jung, C. (1908). The Freudian Theory of Hysteria. *In: Freud and Psychoanalysis: Volume 4 of the Collected Works of C.G. Jung* (pp. 10–24). New York: Bollingen, 1961.

Jung, C. (1909). The Significance of the Father in the Destiny of the Individual. *In: Freud and Psychoanalysis: Volume 4 of the Collected Works of C.G. Jung* (pp. 301–323*).* New York: Bollingen, 1961.

Jung, C. (1911). Wandlungen und Symbole der Libido. *Jahrbuch für psychoanalytische und psychopathologische Forschungen, III*; 1911 *Hälfte*: 120–227.

Jung, C. (1913). General Aspects of Psychoanalysis. *In: Freud and Psychoanalysis: Volume 4 of the Collected Works of C.G. Jung* (pp. 229–242). New York: Bollingen, 1961.

Jung, C. (1956). *Symbols of Transformation: Volume 5 of the Collected Works of C.J. Jung.* 2nd Edition. Princeton, NJ: Princeton University Press, 1967.

Kafka, F. (1931). The Silence of the Sirens. In: *The Great Wall of China and Other Short Stories.* London: Penguin, 1991.

Kerr, J. (1993). *A Most Dangerous Method: The Story of Jung, Freud & Sabina Spielrein.* New York: Vintage, 1994.

Lacan, J. (1932). *De la Psychose Paranoïaque dans ses Rapports avec la Personnalité.* Paris: Seuil, 1975.

Lacan, J. (1953a). The Neurotic's Individual Myth. *Psychoanalytic Quarterly,* 48, 1979, 405–425.

Lacan J. (1953b). Le Mythe Individuel du Névrosé ou Poésie et Vérité dans la Névrose. (Transcribed by J.-A. Miller). *Ornicar? 17–18:* 290–307. Paris: Seuil. Also accessible at: http://aejcpp.free.fr/lacan/1953-00-00.htm

Lacan, J. (1953–1954). *Les Écrits Techniques de Freud.* Paris: Association Lacanienne Internationale (Non-commercial publication), 2016.

Lacan, J. (1954–1955). *The Ego in Freud's Theory and in the Technique of Psychoanalysis.* (Ed. Miller, J.-A.). (Trans. S. Tomaselli). New York: Norton, 1988.

Lacan, J. (1961–1962). *L'Identification.* Paris: Association Freudienne Internationale (Non-commercial publication), 1996.

Lacan, J. (1964). *The Four Fundamental Concepts of Psychoanalysis*. (Ed. J.-A. Miller) New York, Norton, 1978.

Lacan, J. (1965). Hommage fait à Marguerite Duras. In: *Marguerite Duras by Marguerite Duras* (pp. 122–129). San Francisco, CA: City Lights, 1987.

Lacan, J. (1966a). *Écrits*. (Trans. B. Fink). New York & London: Norton, 2006.

Lacan, J. (1966b). *Écrits*. Paris: Seuil.

Lacan, J. (1967). *My Teaching*. London: Verso, 2008.

Lacan, J. (1969–1970). (Ed. J.-A. Miller). *The Other Side of Psychoanalysis*. (Trans. Grigg, R.). New York: Norton, 2007.

Lacan, J. (1971–1972). *The Knowledge of the Psychoanalyst/Le Savoir du Psychanalyste*. Paris: Association Lacanienne Internationale (Non-commercial publication), 2013.

Lacan, J. (1975). Intervention dans la Séance de Travail "Sur la Passe". *Lettres de l'École freudienne, 15*; 1975: 185–193.

Lacan, J. (1976–1977). *L'Insu que Sait de l'Une-Bévue S'Aile à Mourre*. Paris: Association Lacanienne Internationale (Non-Commercial Publication), 2005.

Lacan, J. (1977–1978). *Le Moment de Conclure*. Paris: Association Freudienne Internationale (Non-commercial publication), 1996.

Lacan, J. (1980). Lettre de Dissolution. In: *Autres Écrits* (pp. 317–319). Paris: Seuil, 2001.

Laplanche, J., Pontalis, J.-B. (1973). *The Language of Psychoanalysis*. London: Hogarth, 1985.

Launer, J. (2015). *Sex vs. Survival: The Life and Ideas of Sabina Spielrein*. New York & London: Overlook Duckworth.

Lebrun, J.-P. (1988). Écrire Comme Symptôme. *Bulletin de l'Association Freudienne Internationale*, 77; 1988: 3–6.

Léridon, J.L. (Director). (1984). *Apostrophes: Marguerite Duras/Bernard Pivot Vous Présente*. Paris: Vision Seuil. Also accessible as: *Apostrophes—Marguerite Duras* (1984) on: www.vimeo.com

Lessing, G.E. (1766). *Laocoön: An Essay on the Limits of Painting and Poetry*. E.A. McCormick (trans. and Ed.). Baltimore, MD: Johns Hopkins, 1984.

Lévi-Strauss, C. (1947). *The Elementary Structures of Kin*ship. Boston, MA: Beacon, 1969.

Lévi-Strauss, C. (1955). The Structural Study of Myth. *The Journal of American Folklore, 68*; 1955: 428–444.

Lothane, Z. (2003). Tender Love and Transference: Unpublished Letters of C.G. Jung and Sabina Spielrein (with an addendum/discussion). In: Covington, C. & Wharton, W. (Eds.). *Sabina Spielrein: Forgotten Pioneer of Psychoanalysis*. Hove: Routledge.

Lugrin, Y. (2009). Sabina Spielrein et la Transmission de la Psychanalyse. *Le Coq-Héron, 197*; 2009: 93–104.

Masson, J.M. (Ed. & Trans.) (1985). *The Complete Letters of Sigmund Freud to Wilhelm Fliess: 1887–1904*. Cambridge, MA: Belknap.

Márton, E. (Director). (2002). *Ich hiess Sabina Spielrein (My Name Was Sabina Spielrein)*. IDE Film.

McGuire, W. (Ed.) (1974). *The Freud/Jung Letters*. (Trans. R. Manheim & R.F.C. Hull). Princeton: Princeton University Press (Fourth printing, with corrections and additions (in the notes)), 1994.

McGuire, W. & Sauerländer, W. (Eds.) (1974). *Sigmund Freud/C.G. Jung Briefwechsel*. (Abridged by McGlashan, A.). Frankfurt am Main: Fisher, 1984.

de Mijolla, A. (2014). *Sabina, "la Juive" de Carl Jung*. Paris: Pierre Guillaume de Roux.

Minder, B. (2003). A Document. Jung to Freud 1905: A Report on Sabina Spielrein. Trans. Wharton, B. In: Covington, C. & Wharton, B. (Eds.). *Sabina Spielrein: Forgotten Pioneer of Psychoanalysis* (pp. 137–142). Hove & New York: Routledge, 2003.

Nansen, P. (1893). Julie's Diary. In: *Love's Trilogy. Julie's Diary, Maris, God's Peace.* Boston, MA: John W. Luce, 1908.

Nietzsche, F. (1867–1873) (Eds. R. Geuss & A. Nehamas). *Writings from the Early Notebooks.* Cambridge: Cambridge University Press, 2009.

Nietzsche, F. (1870). (Eds. R. Geuss, & R. Speirs). The Dionysiac World View. In: *The Birth of Tragedy and Other Writings* (pp. 117–138). Cambridge: Cambridge University Press, 1999.

Nietzsche, F. (1882). *Die Fröhliche Wissenschaft* [*The Gay Science*]. Accessible at: http://www.nietzschesource.org/#eKGWB/FW

Nietzsche, F. (1883). (Eds. N. Del Caro, & R. Pippen). *Thus Spoke Zarathustra.* Cambridge: Cambridge University Press, 2006.

Nietzsche, F. (1885–1886). (Ed. R. Bittner). *Writings from the Late Notebooks.* Cambridge: Cambridge University Press, 2003.

Nietzsche, F. (1887). (Ed. K. Ansell-Pearson). *On the Genealogy of Morality.* Cambridge: Cambridge University Press, 2007.

Nunberg, H., & Federn, E. (Eds.) (1974). *Minutes of the Vienna Psychoanalytic Society, Volume III: 1910–1911.* New York: International Universities Press.

Pessoa, F. (n. d.). Là-bas, Je ne Sais où … In: *Obra Poética e em Prosa, (Vol. I): Poesia* (pp. 1040–1041). Porto: Lello & Irmão, 1986.

Pessoa, F. (1919). Untitled. In: *Obra Poética e em Prosa, (Vol. I): Poesia* (p. 782). Porto: Lello & Irmão, 1986.

Plastow, M. (1997). On the Subject of Style. *Papers of the Freudian School of Melbourne, 18*; 1997: 17–30.

Plastow, M.G. (2015). *What Is a Child? Childhood, Psychoanalysis and Discourse.* London: Karnac.

Plastow, M.G. (2017). The Watershed of the Symptom: from Rhine to Rhône with Piaget and Spielrein. In: Owens, C. & Farrelly Quinn, S. (Eds.). *Lacanian Psychoanalysis with Babies, Children, and Adolescents: Further Notes on the Child* (pp. 123–137). London: Karnac, 2017.

Poe, E.A. (1845). The Facts in the Case of M. Valdemar. In: *The Collected Works of Edgar Allen Poe* (pp. 266–272). Ware, Hertfordshire: Wordsworth, 2009.

Porge, E. (2005). *Transmettre la Clinique Psychanalytique: Freud, Lacan, Aujourd'hui.* Ramonville Saint-Agne, France: Érès.

Quignard, P. (1996). *La Haine de la Musique.* Paris: Calmann-Lévy.

Quignard, P. (2005). *Les Paradisiaques.* Paris: Gallimard.

Rey, A. (2013). *Le Grand Robert.* (Dictionnaire Électronique). Paris: Le Robert.

Richebächer, S. (2005a). *Sabina Spielrein: de Jung a Freud.* Martinschen, D. (Trans.). Rio de Janeiro: Civilização Brasileira, 2012.

Richebacher, S. (2005b). *Sabina Spielrein: Eine fast grausame Liebe zur Wissenschaft.* Munich: btb Verlag.

Rilke, R.M. (1903). *Auguste Rodin.* Mineola, NY: Dover, 2006.

Rilke, R.M. (1923). Die Achte Elegie. *Duineser Elegien.* Accessible at: http://gutenberg.spiegel.de/buch/duineser-elegien-829/8

Rilke, R.M. (1929). *Letters to a Young Poet.* (Trans. Burnham, J.M.). Novato, CA: New World Library, 2000.

Roudinesco, É. (2005). Préface á l'Édition Française: Voyager avec Freud. In: Freud. S. (2002). *"Notre Cœur Tend Vers le Sud". Correspondance de Voyage, 1895–1923.* Capèle, J.-C. (Trans.). Paris: Fayard.

de Saussure, F. (1916). *Course in General Linguistics.* Accessible at: https://archive.org/stream/courseingenerall00saus/courseingenerall00saus_djvu.txt

Schreber, D.P. (1903). (Eds. and trans. I. MacAlpine & R.A. Hunter). *Memoirs of My Nervous Illness*. New York: The New York Review of Books, 2000.

Shorter Oxford English Dictionary. Oxford: Oxford University Press, 2007.

Shakespeare, W. (1595–1596). *A Midsummer Night's Dream*. Accessible at: http://archive.org/stream/amidsummernights01514gut/2ws1710.txt

Silva, M. (2015). *A Construção da Pulsaão da Morte Freudiana: Um Estudo Histórico da Formação do Conceito a Partir de suas Fontes*. Montes Claros, Brazil: Unimontes.

Sloterdijk, P. (2000). *Nietzsche Apostle*. Los Angeles, CA: Semiotext(e), 2013.

Spielrein, S. (1911). Über den psychologischen Inhalt eines Falles von Schizophrenie (Dementia Praecox). *Jahrbuch für psychoanalytische und psychopathologische Forschung, III*: 329–400.

Spielrein, S. (1912a). Die Destruktion als Ursache des Werdens. *Jahrbuch für psychoanalytische und psychopathologische Forschungen, IV*; 1912: 465–503.

Spielrein, S. (1912b). Destruction as the Cause of Coming into Being. *Journal of Analytical Psychology, 39*; 1994: 155–186.

Spielrein, S. (1912c). Destruction as Cause of Becoming. *Psychoanalysis and Contemporary Thought, 18*; 1995: 85–118.

Spielrein, S. (1913). Beiträge zur Kenntnis der kindlichen Seele (Contributions to the Knowledge of the Child's Soul). *Zentralblatt für Psychoanalyse und Psychotherapie, II*; 1913: 57–72.

Spielrein, S. (1922). Qui est L'Auteur du Crime? In Spielrein, S. *Sämtliche Schriften* (pp. 229–235). Geißen: Psychosozial-Verlag, 2002.

Spielrein, S. (1923). Quelques Analogies entre la Pensée de L'Enfant, celle de L'Aphasique et la Pensée Subconsciente. In Spielrein, S. *Sämtliche Schriften* (pp. 281–310). Geißen: Psychosozial-Verlag, 2002.

Spielrein, S. (1983). (J. Moll, P. Bennett, B. Wharton, Eds.). Unedited extracts from a diary: with a prologue by Jeanne Moll. In: *Sabina Spielrein: Forgotten Pioneer of Psychoanalysis*. Hove: Routledge, 2003.

Spielrein, S. (2006). (T. Hensch, Ed.) *Sabina Spielrein: Nimm meine Seele. Tagebücher und Schriften*. Freiburg: Freitag.

Thomas, H. (1967). Préface: Léon-Paul Fargue. In: Fargue, L.-P. *Poésies: Tancrède. Ludions. Poëmes. Pour la Musique* (9–14) (Préface d'Henri Thomas). Paris: Gallimard.

Van Waning, (1992). The Works of Pioneering Psychoanalyst Sabina Spielrein— 'Destruction as a Cause of Coming Into Being'. *The International Review of Psycho-Analysis, 19*; 1992: 399–414.

Zentner, O. (2012). Freud, Jung, Spielrein and the Death Drive. *Australasian Journal of Psychotherapy, 30*; 2012: 74–84.

Zweig, S. (1925). *The Struggle with the Daemon*. London: Pushkin, 2012.